SILENCE BROKEN

Korean Comfort Women

SILENCE BROKEN

Korean Comfort Women

Dai Sil Kim-Gibson

Mid-Prairie Books
Parkersburg, Iowa
1999

Printed in the United States of America

Published by: Mid-Prairie Books
P.O. Box 680
Parkersburg, Iowa 50665

ISBN 0-931209-88-9

*Dedicated to those who suffered the insufferable
and endured the unendurable*

AUTHOR'S NOTES

Koreans and Japanese place their family name first, followed by given names. In this book, I do the same, though many adopted the western style of using their given names first. Some Koreans hyphenate their given names like Chong-Ok and others don't like mine, Dai Sil. Those remain unchanged. In short, I use whatever English rendering people give to their names. For all others, I did my own transliteration as closely as they sound without following the most common practice of using the McCune-Reischauer system.

In the stories, I include my comments, feelings and questions. Those are indented, and in italics.

The five poems used for the stories are all by Yun Dong Ju and I translated them. His brief biography is included.

TABLE OF CONTENTS

INTRODUCTION

In November 1992, I was asked by a group of Korean Americans in the Washington D.C area to translate for one of the surviving comfort women, Hwang Keum Ju. For over an hour, I sat beside this 70 year old Korean woman and translated her story for television cameras. As she talked, I felt the tremors going through her body, the pain from her past, so remote and so close.

Then, the tremors stopped and her voice, tainted with a regional Korean accent, shook, drawing my attention. She said, "This Japanese officer took his thing out and wanted me to lick it like a dog." I yelled, "I would rather die than do that, you son of a dog!" "When they were on top of us, shamelessly exploding like animals, we were simply imprisoned sex machines but to use one's mouth actively . . ." Her breath became rough, her body literally shaking. "He took away the last shred of human dignity from me." Forgetting the camera, she turned to me and said, "They had no idea that for us, Korean women, chastity was more precious than life itself." She was kicked and beaten until she passed out. When she woke up, her friends told her that she had been unconscious for three days and nights. She was not happy to regain consciousness.

I was no longer just putting her story into English words. I was drawn into her past, which became tragic beyond telling by the horrific crimes committed by the Imperial Army of Japan. Tears rolled inside of me for Korean women, for women everywhere, and for humanity. That's how I was introduced to the lives of these women, often referred to as "comfort women."

The term *Jungun Wianbu* in Korean, *Jugun Ianfu* in Japanese, means "military comfort women," and is a euphemism for women forced to serve as sexual slaves for Japanese soldiers. Many advocates replacing the term "comfort women" with military sex slaves (MSS). I choose to keep "comfort women," because "comfort" more accurately depicts the sexual servitude committed in a chilling casualness as well as a dehumanizing brutality.

I am a Korean American woman who came to the United States as a graduate student in 1962. I was born in northern Korea while Japan ruled our country. They made us change our names to Japanese, speak their language, and worship their Emperor. In the spring of 1945, as an enthusiastic first grader, I played *gong ki*, a popular game with five small stones, much like dice, throwing them into the air and placing them in sets. The animated chatter and laughter of girls, as I recall, spread through the school yard like a symphony of spring.

A Japanese teacher suddenly grabbed my arm and jerked me to my feet. "You are speaking Korean!" "Of course!" I said, fearful but with pride. She took me to a huge teacher's room where each teacher had his/her own table. I was ordered to stand by a window where everybody could see me, to stretch my arms upward like a surrendering soldier and repent! One by one, the teachers left, and when the evening settled in the sky, I was told to go home. On the way, I was met by my mother who ran toward me from a great distance. Only at the touch of her hand and the sound of her gentle voice asking me what had happened, did I begin to cry.

Living in America, my adopted country for over a quarter century, like many others, I had decided to let my past with Japan be just that, the past. Burying the war and the colonial experience in Asia, in 1988 I shared the excitement of many Americans witnessing the 100th Congress of the United States pass Public Law 100-383 to "acknowledge the fundamental injustice of the evacuation, relocation, and internment of United States citizens and permanent resident aliens of Japanese ancestry during World War II."

I was moved that the Congress made an historic apology "on behalf of the people of the United States" and "on behalf of the Nation" for this fundamental violation of basic civil liberties and the constitutional rights of these individuals of Japanese ancestry. The $20,000 restitution to those individuals did not make up for the grave injustices they had suffered. However, it addressed not only the wronged past but also the future as one of the purposes of the Act was, "to discourage the occurrence of similar injustices and violations of civil liberties in the future."

Then came my encounter with Grandma Hwang and the history I had tried to push out of my ken. The past was pushing its way back into my consciousness with startling force. Soon my desk was covered with unpublished papers and newspaper articles— what little there was about them. My journey into the lives of these women had begun.

The journey was complicated in 1995 by a series of events commemorating the 50th anniversary of the end of the Second World War. Dropping the bomb on Hiroshima and Nagasaki was brought to the fore and was heatedly debated, especially surrounding the Smithsonian Institution's Enola Gay Exhibition which in the eyes of some critics, cast Japan as the victim. I do not defend the use of the atomic bomb, especially on civilians, the majority of whom had already suffered in a brutal war. Further, had I encountered Japanese viewing themselves as victims, not victimizers, in the immediate aftermath of the War, I would have understood why. An overwhelming sense of defeat in conjunction with the tragic sight of the war-torn country would be enough to make anyone feel as a victim. Not surprisingly, many Germans saw themselves as victims in 1945.

However, half a century later, looking back, was Japan a victim of the Second World War? Not in the face of the total picture and with enough time to put the conflict in proper perspective. After all, they were brutal aggressors who committed unspeakable atrocities. What was happening? What Japan did to its Asian neighbors had become a non-issue, a mirage in the face of the dispute between Japan and the United States. Clearly, what we were seeing was one sided history, with a large part of the past buried and ignored.

Gavan Daws writes in his book, *Prisoners of the Japanese*, "The war in Asia and the Pacific was a clash of armies, a clash of cultures — and most brutally — a clash of races." "In the eyes of the Japanese," he writes, "white men who allowed themselves to be captured in war were despicable. They deserved to die."[1] John W. Dower speaks of it as a race war in his book, *War Without Mercy*. Japan set out to carry out its holy task of emancipating Asia and its people from the European and American powers. In this conflict, the yellow and white soldiers fought like bloodhound dogs. Dower writes, "Race hate fed atrocities, and atrocities in turn fanned the fires of the race hate. The dehumanization of the Other contributed immeasurably to the psychological distancing that facilitates killing, not only on the battlefield but also in the plans adopted by strategists far removed from the actual scene of combat."[2]

True, but the Pacific War was not just a war between the American/European powers and the Japanese; it was not a war just between yellow and white. It was also yellow against yellow. It was about what Japan did to fellow Asians and others under the pretext of emancipating the Asian race from the West. This history has been largely repressed in Japan and ignored elsewhere.

If Americans and Japanese choose to be selective about history, and avoid facing the past in all its complexity, they are not alone. China, for instance, treads carefully when it denounces the Japanese slaughter of countless innocents, fearful that with the word "massacre" in Beijing, people might think of Tianamen in 1989 instead of Nanjing in 1937 and more fearful that it might damage relations with an important trading partner.

In August 1995, I went to the NGO Forum on Women held in conjunction with the Fourth World Conference on Women in Beijing to help place the issue of Japanese military sexual slavery during World War II before the eyes of the world community. While there, I was able to contact former comfort women living in Wuhan. Fortunately, I obtained the help of a taxi driver, one Mr. Li, who arranged to bring Ha Kun Ja, a former comfort woman and a friend of his deceased mother, to the Wuhan airport to meet me. On my way to Wuhan, looking down a long stretch of the Yangtze river from the plane, I felt overwhelmed by what I could only call "an historical sense of sorrow," soon to be shared by me as a Korean American and a Korean living in China, unable to return home.

In sneakers, with a brown knapsack on my back, I walked among people greeting those who came on the flight with me, and then spotted a grandma in a navy blue dress, her face brown and lined but with a smile so full of compassion that it could have come only from absorbing human suffering as has the Yangtze river. Before I opened my mouth, she grabbed my hand and asked in halting Korean, "You are a Chosun person, aren't you?" She still called Korea "Chosun," the land of morning calm, the much cherished name of her motherland when she was taken by the Japanese at the age of seventeen. "Yes! You must be Grandma Ha, Ha Gun Ja. She nodded, wiping her eyes with a handkerchief. Her small hand, enclosed in mine, was chapped, but it sent such a soft warmth through my body that I was mystified. Standing in almost tropical heat, I shivered with the connection I felt with this stranger.

Mr. Li, the taxi driver, was introduced. We bowed with smiles. "If only his mother were alive to see how well he is doing. You know, she suffered with me under the Japanese. You should have seen the hardships she endured. Now he lives in a house with all kinds of nice furniture and he even has a phone." In the small, red taxi, squeezing my hand, Grandma Ha talked non-stop as if she had met a long lost daughter, about her life, which has been one long struggle, about her deceased Chinese husband, and about her step daughters.

In Hankou, the taxi turned into a sidestreet that was barely wide enough to pass through and stopped, with many eyes gazing at us. The houses were dirty and run down, virtually a slum. Soon a tiny woman appeared, about four feet tall, all skin and bones with hardly any flesh. She was dressed in a neatly pressed white blouse and dark gray pants. She looked as light as a feather, but I saw a fearless woman with eyes full of childlike mischief, Grandma Hong Kang Lim. Her Korean was minimal, hardly any complete sentences, just a few words thrown around. Grandma Ha was embarrassed but I felt pure delight for those words.

Accompanied by Grandma Hong's unemployed son and Mr. Li, we went to a restaurant. As we ate, Grandma Hong sang many Korean songs in a soft voice, encouraging me to sing along. "I forgot Korean but I still remember these. I sing when I think of my kid brother." Her eyes were far away. "What brother?" "My kid brother. He's in Korea. I not see him for long. He very small when I left. Some Koreans found him for me." "Couldn't he come see you?" "He too poor. Sick, very sick. I want to help. I want to go but can't. Nothing but these." She unfolded her fists. "See, nothing. These all I have. Empty hands. Can't help. Can't go." The Korean verses of her songs were amazingly clear.

The next morning, Mr. Li, the taxi driver, took me to another back street, full of dirty, gray concrete buildings. We entered one and climbed up the narrow stairs, blackened by coal ashes and fumes. On the third floor, Grandma

4

Ha opened the door and revealed a clean room with two single beds and a couch. Grandma Hong was also waiting for me there. My instinct was to start the interview but Grandma Ha argued that we go to a police station to obtain permits first, especially if I wanted to video tape them at the actual sites where they had worked.

We went to the station. The officials interrogated me: where was I from; what was I doing in China; when had I arrived in Beijing; when and why had I come to Wuhan; how had I found these women? On and on the questioning continued. After a while, they ordered lunch for me and escorted the two grandmas to a maroon colored station wagon. As they left, Grandma Ha yelled in Korean, "This is it. They are not going to let us see you again. Take care of yourself. This is good-bye." She wiped her eyes as the car took off. My head spun, realizing that I had to think fast. Nothing seemed right.

When I was ordered to go back to my hotel, I asked the police chief to take me to grandma Ha's house. "I simply want to say good-bye to them," I pleaded. However, I was repeatedly told "no." In desperation, I told him that I had left some things at her house. "We can arrange for your luggage to be brought back to the hotel." I stood up with my lunch untouched and left the room.

On the street, I stopped the first taxi in sight and gave the driver the piece of paper with Grandma Ha's address. I simply had to see them one more time. I can't remember how many times the driver had to stop to ask for directions. Miraculously, he found the dirty gray building. I paid him double the fare on the meter and climbed the stairs. I was politely greeted by a young Chinese woman. No grandmas. I was terrified. In about fifteen minutes, the door opened and the women rushed in with the cold eyed police chief, the interpreter and a young man, obviously the driver. Grandma Ha told me quickly that they had met the interpreter outside and had been asked about the luggage. She recognized that she had given the "wrong" answer.

"You must go," the chief ordered me out, his voice full of killing rage. Grandma Ha, with her arms stretched toward me and her eyes gleaming with tears, said, "Now you know our reality here. This is our reality. We are a sorrowful people. There is no escape for us. They watch over us all the time. You see, we are not Chinese." I took both of her hands into mine. Grandma Ha begged me to write to them through Mr. Li. "Get his address before you leave. Now you must go." "Come back at night," ordered Grandma Hong, unshaken, "Must see you again." Ignoring her, Grandma Ha said that the fellow "Chosun" persons such as I are their only ties to the motherland. "Please don't forget us. Write to us. I will get people to read your letters to us."

I was pushed out the door and into the street, the two grandmas following. As we got into the car, Grandma Ha wiped her tears and Grandma Hong grabbed my hand and said, "If you go now, when will you return?" The grip of her bony hand was strong and firm. The car drove off, leaving them behind in the crowded backstreet. "If you go now, when will you return?" I repeated Grandma Hong's question and a sharp pain passed through my chest.

Had it not been for the NGO badge I was wearing and the bad publicity China had received in conjunction with the World Conference on Women, I believe they would have thrown me into jail. For years, the Chinese government has maintained strict control of individuals taking stands against Japan, fearful that China might upset its important trading partner. The authorities, for example, prohibited individual survivors of the Nanjing Massacre from seeking reparations. I had known this but I guess I didn't quite believe it.

Back at the NGO Forum in Beijing, on the 4th of September, I sat in a booth and translated the heart wrenching testimony of a former comfort woman from South Korea, Chung Seo Woon. "Half a century has passed since the time when every day was a dreadful nightmare for me but Japan still tells lies and avoids responsibility. How can they do that in the presence of myself and many others like me, victims who are alive and kicking. The seed the Japanese planted, the evil seed, they must harvest no matter how dreadful if they wish to be part of the human race. Don't you believe so?" Loud applause. "Then they say, 'for all those poor Asians, we will raise private funds and help.' I have a message for you. I might be poor, but not that poor. I demand the compensation that is rightly due to me, even if I would burn the money after it's in my hand. It is not a matter of money but of principle. The Japanese defiled my body but not my spirit. My spirit is strong, rich and proud." Thunderous applause, a standing ovation.

I spent the rest of the day listening to an equally tragic story of a former comfort woman from the Philippines, and endless discussions about military sexual slavery, and the continuing rape and violence against women around the world. The elaborate discussions and eloquent debates passed through my ears like distant thunder. I only saw the faces of those grandmas in Wuhan, gentle faces hardened and aged by long suffering and toil, being swept up in the flow of speeches and polemical outbursts.

China is not alone, though, in wanting to put aside Japan's brutal past because of Japan's economic dominance. "I think the Second World War was very harsh. But I really like Japanese electronic products because of their quality," says a 21 year old Vietnamese accountant, Duong Huy Hoang.[3] If that is understandable coming from a generation that does not know the War, listen to the Prime Minister of Malaya, Datuk Seri Mahathir Mohamad, "We prefer to look towards the future rather than harp on actions in the past. I cannot understand why the Japanese government keeps apologizing for things that happened 50 years ago."[4]

Then, there are the Koreans. The infamous 1965 Treaty between Japan and the Republic of Korea was a clear expression of the government's priorities.

6

Economic interests outweighed human rights, especially women's rights. Boasting economic progress, many of them do not want to recall the painful and what they sometimes call "shameful" experience of their colonial past, not to mention the fear of upsetting the current economic relationship between the two countries.

Many would be happy to forget the Japanese atrocities, victims and victimizers alike, often for the splendid reasons of "looking toward the future," instead of digging up the uncomfortable past. However, the past can repeat, if it is not faced. The brutal tragedy of the comfort women is not only a neglected aspect of history but an issue of gender, class and race; an issue of mostly Asian women from predominantly poor and uneducated families.

If Japan destroyed most of the relevant documents immediately after the war and continues to lock away whatever was spared in order to hide the sexual slavery, the Allied Forces, especially the United States, did little to seek justice for Asian atrocities committed by Japan. The Tokyo Tribunal (1946-1948) when General Douglas MacArthur was the Supreme Commander, knowingly swept this issue under the rug for political expediency.[5] The Peace Treaty of San Francisco in 1951 which recognized the sovereignty of the Japanese people showed remarkably little interest in justice for peoples of Asian origin. Only the Dutch held trials about interned Dutch women forced to become sex slaves for the Japanese soldiers. Held in Batavia, known as Jakarta then, Dutch women's cases were prosecuted and the offenders sentenced. However, notoriously missing was any discussion of Indonesian comfort women.

No society and no period in history has been free of prostitution and human history is replete with gruesome rape stories, especially during wartime. Horrifying military rape stories are not just history; they are current and on-going. The stories about Serb soldiers raping ethnic Albanian women and girls in Kosovo continue to make front page news. (For example, see *the New York Times* article, "Deny Rape or Be Hated: Kosovo Victims' Choice," by Elizabeth Bumiller, June 22, 1999).

To be sure, it was not just the Japanese soldiers who raped. So why take issue with the Japanese? This is precisely what a professor of education at Tokyo University, Fujioka Nobukatsu said on camera when I interviewed him in Tokyo in 1997. "The liaison between prostitutes and the military has existed from ancient times to the present. Even today, no matter how hard you preach moral lessons, the problem of prostitution in the army is never solved. It is unnecessary to compare the level of morals among countries. Human beings are neither lofty nor low. Human nature is more or less the same. The issue of comfort women is a problem humans have not solved. It is unfair to criticize only the Japanese Army's misconduct of more than 50 years ago."[6]

It is true that the comfort women is but one of countless military rape stories stretching back to antiquity. Though the Japanese experience is different

7

from victorious soldiers raping the women of the defeated country, even today similar cases are found in Algeria, Sierra Leone and Uganda; there young women and girls are abducted from their schools and homes for the use of the rebel soldiers as sex slaves. However, that rape is so widespread does not make the horrendous rapes by the Japanese any less evil. Of greater importance, Japan officially institutionalized sexual slavery on a massive scale. It was not just random, bold violence; it was a systematic and carefully thought through system ordered and executed by the Japanese military.

Scholars and activists grapple with questions of how to define "rape," and with the question of the authenticity of stories told by the victims. Some are eager to stress this as a "woman's issues" and others to make comfort women truly a global issue. Rape, especially wartime rape, is a global issue but I focus on Korean women because they were the majority of the women taken as sex slaves and I could talk with them, rather they talked with me, as a woman born in Korea. Further, for these women, rape is neither a matter of definition nor of nationality; it was a massive and deep personal pain. For the majority of victims, the questions of nationalism and/or feminisim are afterthoughts imported from scholars and activists. First and foremost, it was a human experience that was dehumanized by fellow human beings.

I travelled to the Republic of Korea, China, and Japan in a search for former comfort women and other firsthand witnesses, including former Japanese and Korean soldiers, recruiters and traders. I found one even in the United States. I tried to visit the Democratic People's Republic of Korea for two years but to no avail. The majority of my interviewees live in the Republic of Korea (South Korea). I was fortunate to spend countless hours with many of them, visiting some twice, others three or four times. When I talked with them, the pain hidden beneath their wrinkled faces was so deep that it often struck me like electricity.

Their stories, the stories of the Korean comfort women, are the core of this book. The stories they told me, which are neither neutral nor objective. Anyone knows that human memories are by nature limited and subjective. Oral history is a subjective recollection of the past. Further, as I listened to these grandmas' stories, I quickly became aware that these women had learned how to adjust their stories to be more politically compelling. That, too, is expected. Clearly, nobody can swear by the truth and accuracy of a single story in its entirety, yet bound together individual accounts can form a collective truth.

What's more, I make no pretense that my response was or is objective. I listened and responded to their stories as a woman born in Korea, and with overflowing sorrow, outraged by the violations inflicted by the Japanese on Koreans, by men on women, by the rich on the poor, and by the powerful on the weak. At times, my response may have been even more subjective than their stories. No one can deny a streak of self-righteous indignation in people with passion. I am no exception.

I did not conduct systematic interviews with a set of questions; often my questions were provoked or evoked by their stories. The amount of time I spent with them frequently depended upon circumstances, including their availability, and emotional as well as physical conditions. Frequently pure luck dictated the setting and the length of our talks. Inevitably, the stories presented in this book are uneven in length and depth. You will soon find out, for instance, that Chapter Four, Grandma Bae's story is much longer than others. I do not embellish their stories. None of this, however, means that I was totally incapable of disengaging myself whenever needed in pursuit of truth; to do justice to their stories. I am simply admitting a strong connection—intellectual as well as emotional—between myself as a listener/writer and the reality represented in the book.

Talking with these women, frequently our feelings were entangled, pure shock vibrating in my raised voice. I had such emotional battles with Grandma Bae Gok Gan when she told me over and over again that she would prefer marrying a Japanese. Thinking back, I feel genuinely happy for my raised voice. In fact, I am astonished how I could have been so totally oblivious of the Stockholm Syndrome which delineates the emotional bonding of victims with their victimizers if for no other reason than the pure desire for survival. Easily, this woman is a classic example of that Syndrome, down to the point of her desire to become the willing tool of the Japanese and her grateful rememberance of small kindnesses in the midst of so much brutality. Had I remembered it, I might have remained a neutral observer and studied this fascinating object. I am glad that I was unable to make her an object of my study but rather wrestled with her person to person.

Most oral accounts in print of the former military comfort women are primarily summaries of interviews conducted by scholars or journalists with a focus on their years as comfort women. If those women told stories beyond "that period," that information was not included in the majority of the oral histories. It is as if their existence is justified solely by the horrendous years they suffered; nothing before or after that seems to matter. Saddest of all, the women themselves are convinced of that. Further, in the name of objectivity and scholarship, much of their stories are refined, hence taking away the raw pain and feelings from their stories. They have largely become issues, numbers, things, and objects of studies, not full blooded human beings. It was important for me to present their lives — before, during and after—as much or as little as they told me.

This book is, then, a product of double subjectivity. These are their stories which I could not hear without fumbling on occasion in the welter of my emotions, nor report from a neutral position. The stories of these women frequently made me a captive of unruly and turbulent feelings. I often felt my entire personal history becoming entangled with the history of my land of birth, Korea, coupled with that of humankind. I include myself in the story in order to remind the reader of the double subjectivity. If you are distressed by this, I urge you to think about all those carefully selected "objective" accounts written as "official" histories in the Japanese text books. And think of all those conceptual frameworks imposed on their stories in the name of scholarship.

Anything I have to add would be like water that runs off whereas their stories would, hopefully, penetrate you to the marrow. Hence the first chapter is Grandma Hwang Keum Ju's story, who initially got me into this journey. However, in Chapter Two, you will find a brief history about Japanese colonialism in Korea, followed by comprehensive information about the sex slavery—why and how comfort houses were established, and who and how women were recruited. In Chapter Three, accounts about their lives during and afterwards are presented, primarily based on my firsthand interviews. Then, four more individual stories follow, only to be interrupted by Chapter Five in which brief accounts of breaking the long-kept silence and of the ongoing legal issues.

I finished the first draft of this book in September 1996. Then, I launched a documentary film on the same subject. I wanted to leave the faces of these women for posterity to see and to hear their own words. For my film, I talked with some of the same women and added a few others. Now the book and film are companions, designed to complement each other but also to stand on their own. I have not, hence, altered the manuscript drastically; I have simply added information I obtained in making the film.

The film as well as the book tells their stories. In the film, however, I meddled more with my subjectivity. Initially conceived as a one hour documentary, I struggled to complete it as such but the paucity of direct visual material drove me to dramatize some of their stories. As in the book, in making this documentary, I rely on the collected voices of these grandmas but by the time I moved to the dramatized scenes, it no longer became important for me to keep track of who said what. Feeling the power of their stories as a common experience, and for dramatic impact and effectiveness, in some cases, I made composite characters but the stories are theirs, not fiction. I simply mobilized their stories and integrated them into a powerful narrative, their own voices narrating under dramatized images.

Both in the book and film, I try not to romanticize or glorify these grandmas. Heaven knows they have plenty of problems and faults. Above all, however, to me these grandmas represent the human spirit that can overcome the most horrendous atrocities. They made me mourn the wrong committed against them, celebrate their resilient spirits and add my voice, however feeble, to theirs to bring the silenced past into the present and to a future that should never repeat the unspeakable crimes against ourselves, humanity. Throughout the wrenching conversations, they were the ones who made me laugh and gave me a lesson or two that I will carry deep in my bones for the rest of my life. I am proud that they are my grandmas, Korean grandmas of my gender, female warriors.

I call them grandmas because it is a Korean custom to so refer to any woman old enough to have grandchildren. More importantly, I call them grandmas because I feel as if they are my own grandmas.

I bow to them in deep respect and affection.

Chapter 1

I WOULD RATHER DIE THAN . . .
Hwang Keum Ju

Prelude

Till the day of death
Not to have one speck of shame
Toward the sky up there

I grieved
Even by the wind on a leaf.

With my heart singing for the stars
I resolved to love
All those on the way to death

And to walk the road
Destined to me.

Again tonight
Stars are grazed by the wind.

After her first visit in 1992, Grandma Hwang Keum Ju was invited back to Washington to join a protest rally in front of the White House in June 1994. The occasion was a state visit by the Japanese Emperor Akihito. I was summoned again to be her translator. I spotted Grandma Hwang in Lafayette Square. The crowd of roughly 600 local Asian Americans — Chinese, Filipino, and Korean — demanded atonement for wartime crimes, shouting "Japan apologize," "Japan Liars," and "Japan must confess; no more hiding." The crowd also demanded that President Clinton back away from his effort to obtain a permanent seat for Japan on the United Nations Security Council. I ran to her, put both of her hands into mine and helped her climb up the stairs to the platform. I translated for the emotion charged crowd. "My peace of mind is forever taken. How can I ever restore it? That is not possible even if they gave me all of Japan! There is no way that they can bring my life back. They can't make up for the terrible way they ruined my young life."

A year later, I called her in Seoul and asked if I could visit her. She gave me detailed directions to her apartment, warning me about the importance of remembering the building number as well as that of her own apartment. "It is a government subsidized complex. It is huge. Remember my building is 705." It took me more than two hours to find it. When I rang the bell, she came to the door, gazed at me and then produced a sound of vibrating delight, "Aigo (O, my, my . . .),[7] It is you, really you." I was pulled inside her apartment, my eyes sweeping the clean but small space. She sat me down on a straw mattress in her sitting room (which is actually an all-purpose room; sleeping, eating, and everything is done here as it is larger than the other one, supposedly a bedroom, but only the size of our king sized bed back home in the States). "Look," she pointed to a framed picture hanging on the far side of the wall. "Do you recognize it?" It was the picture of the two of us standing on a platform in front of the White House. Of course. I remembered how I was swirled into her passion that day as I put her words into English. It was the fire of pain, anger and sorrow . . . further inflamed by those who were crying for justice on her behalf and for many others whose lives had been so brutally violated.

"Let's have lunch." She was already setting up a small, square table in front of me. "I cooked hot rice for you." She put down small plates and bowls, filling the table in no time at all. As she dished out the steaming rice into two bowls, my eyes travelled across the table, with my mouth already watering. "Three different kinds of Kimchi!" "Of course, all homemade. Did you know that these days young people no longer bother making kimchi at home. They all buy it," she said stifling a sigh.

She tried to lure me into eating a pork casserole with squash and tofu, in a soup made of bean paste, fresh from the stove, still boiling. "Not much meat, mostly vegetables but they are fresh. Nothing much, but I know you have not tasted a home prepared meal like this for a long time." Clearly she thought pork was a special treat but I was in seventh heaven gobbling her vegetable dishes. How times have changed, I thought to myself. When I was growing up, this was poor people's fare but now it's health food. We made small talk about where she buys her groceries, how often she goes downtown, etc., but inevitably she brought up her past.

"So you are going to write a book about us. I think that is a good idea. It should be known to as many people as possible. Tell me, do you think Americans would be interested in our stories?" "I think so, especially women." But you have already heard my story twice. What would you like me to tell you?" "Anything that comes to your mind. Don't worry about repeating yourself. In fact, I wouldn't mind hearing the same story again. I doubt, though, that it would be the same." "What do you mean? Facts are facts." "Oh, I know, but this time I am sitting in your apartment, eating your Kimchi and listening to your story alone." "That is true." There was no need for me to explain what I meant. Her story began.

I was born in a family where learning occupied an important place. My paternal and maternal grandfathers were both learned men. Though they did not live in the same region, they knew each other. When my grandmother was pregnant with my father, my grandfather said to his friend, (my maternal grandfather), "If it is a boy, let's become in-laws." But my grandfather died before my father was born. So my father was brought up without a father. My grandmother raised him alone.

When my mom was five years old, my father was born. You have heard about "engagement in the belly," haven't you? My mother was engaged while her future husband was still in his mother's belly! Two men determined her fate.

When they were married, my mother was eighteen and my father thirteen. Wait a minute. You have a different way of counting ages — you don't automatically become a year old when you are born, right? I like that better. So, according to the American way, my mother was seventeen and father twelve. You know, it was not unusual that the wife was older in those times. My mother's family brought my father up. Everybody loved this smart, handsome son-in-law. They sent him to junior high school in Seoul. He graduated with flying colors.

My father's hometown was further south, the village of Puyeu in Choong Chung Province. I was born there on August 15, 1922 (*lunar calendar*) as the first daughter. I had one younger sister and a brother. Oh, you want to hear more about my growing up. Well, what is there to tell? When I was born, my father was fifteen. I know he was proud of me and secretly loved me. But if I called him Dad when his friends came to the house to visit, he would spank me. He was embarrassed to be called Dad. So I called him "third Dad," just like my cousins. He was the third son of his family. So my cousins called him "third Dad."

After completing junior high school in Seoul, my father went to Japan for further study. A relative on my mother's side, about twenty years my father's senior, was a law clerk and helped my father with some of his expenses in Japan but father had to work — shining shoes, delivering newspapers, any job he could find — to make ends meet. I remember his coming home twice a year in his student's uniform. He looked so smart. He was the only one in our village who went to Japan to study. He glowed with self confidence. People used come to him with questions, to read their letters, etc. Whenever people came, pride welled up in me.

You want to know how my mother was when he came home for vacation? No way for me to tell. You know, women at that time were not expressive. Emotion was all bottled up inside. I never saw them together. He didn't talk to me much either. He spent most of his time with his books. My mother rarely spoke about him. She just said that as soon as he is finished with his studies, we would have our own home. You see, we lived at my uncle's house. I didn't go to school! How could I? We were so poor — we lived in asshole splitting poverty.[8] My mother worked in other people's fields and rice paddies as much as she could but we were largely under the mercy of our father's brother who had a hard enough time feeding his own family.

About the time when my father finished his studies, he fell ill and came home. I didn't know then but now I can guess. What he had was a venereal disease. While he was doing odd jobs in Japan, he came in contact with, you know, those women, prostitutes, who gave him that! Japanese women! Speaking of irony. . .

He came back to Korea very sick. He received what treatment he could, occasional shots and drugs. His medical expenses made us poorer, as if that were possible. My father was bedridden and spent most his time reading newspapers and books. One day, I saw him crying, reading his Japanese newspapers. You know, he was the only one in our village who could read Japanese. I learned that he had found an ad in the paper about a medicine that could cure his disease, but it would cost 100 *won*. Where could we get 100 *won*? That was a huge sum of money. That's why he was crying. Imagine my father shedding tears. It tore me apart. Day and night, I racked my brains, try-ing to think of the ways to get that money for my father. But to get 100 *won*? It was harder than plucking a star from the sky.

One day, a friend of my mother came to visit us. I asked her if she knew a way I could get 100 *won* for my father. "Will you do what I tell you?" she asked. "Anything, I will do anything at all to help my father." Roughly a month later, she came back from Seoul and said something to my mother. Then, my mother started sobbing. How can I tell you everything? Just the thought of it pains my chest. I was only twelve. I knew nothing. Then, my grandmother started wailing. I thought someone had died or something.

There was a Mr. Choi in Seoul who was a friend of this woman's husband. He was originally from Ham Hung, far north of Seoul. He was looking for a girl whom he could adopt, and take to his concubine's house in Seoul to help with the household work. So this woman had told him about me and was asked to bring me for an interview. That day, in the midst of all the crying and sobbing, she took me out. I followed her barefooted, in worn out clothes. She bought me a new out-fit and black sneakers. I was transformed. At the sight of me, my grandmother started weeping again.

I had seen that my father always kept his diploma from Japan under his quilt. As I stood there in my new outfit, confused, an idea came to me. I need-ed to prove to this man that I come from a good family, something that would impress him. I waited until my father went to the bathroom. While no one watched, I took the diploma, replacing it with a 100 *won* bill, and put it inside of my clothes.

Later, I learned that my grandmother hanged herself seeing the 100 *won* under my father's quilt. You remember my grandmother was a widow. She had three sons but the two older ones were adopted by our relatives. My father was the only one left to her. He was her life. But upon seeing the money a small granddaughter left for her sick son, she went berserk.

When I left home, I hardly had time to put my new sneakers on proper-ly. I didn't want my father to find out what I took, his diploma. I ran, choking until I found the woman under a huge bowery tree, waiting for me. I was only twelve. I sat down beside her, took a deep breath, picked up a stone and threw it toward my home, and made a secret pact with myself. I swore that I would not return home until I had made something of myself. I told no one about this.

> After a long silence, she mumbled, "I was imbued with a sense of purpose, so determined to make something of myself . . ."
> Her sigh was deep enough to make a hole on the ground.

My mother's friend took me directly to Mr. Choi's house in Seoul where his concubine lived. He was in his office attached to the house. I was struck by how handsome he was. I was just a kid, but it was clear that he was an important person with lots of money. I bowed a deep bow to him. He gently told me how glad he was that I had come. "Please go inside, take a bath, and have a good supper." Instead of leaving him immediately, I lingered. "What

16

is it? Do you need anything?" I took out my father's diploma and showed it to him. His eyes swept it and turned to me, surprised. "How did you bring this? Why did you bring this?" "I wanted you to know about my father." He held both of my hands and squeezed them. "You are a smart, thoughtful girl. Your father is a lucky man to have you. You will be just like my own daughter. Now I am lucky. I am so sad that your father has such a bad disease. Let's all hope that he gets better." I saw this proud man's eyes all watery.

When my mother's friend came by to see how I was doing in Mr. Choi's house, I gave her my father's diploma, carefully wrapped in rice paper, in a brown envelope. "Please return it to my father. This is his life." She told me that they took the whole house upside down, with everyone looking for the diploma after I had left. My father was still alive when his diploma was brought back but shortly after that, he passed away. The medicine did not cure him, I learned later.

Mr. Choi's concubine was ill tempered (*lowering her voice as if someone was listening, she said, "just between you and me, she was a bitch"*). She whipped me often for no reason at all. I curled up on the kitchen floor and cried until I fell asleep. That life was incredibly hard. I was often a cause for their fights. He didn't like the way she treated me. After three years, Mr. Choi, whom I called "father" by then, said to his concubine, "Pack up all her things. I am sending her to Ham Hung." That's where his first wife lived. I was fifteen years old.

They had two sons and two daughters. So they already had plenty of their own children. That's why I was registered as the concubine's adopted daughter. Mr. Choi said to this wife, "Now, you must treat her as your own." To me, she was my adopted mother. She was very kind and insisted that I be educated. She sent me to night school when I became 17 years old. That was a women's night school, run by a big church. A large room was divided by curtains and students belonged to one of four classes, from first to fourth grades. I attended the first and the second year classes and learned Japanese and math. They taught Korean only two hours a week. I was good at knitting and sewing.

After attending two years of night school, I stayed home.[9] The times were already changing — we no longer got married to younger boys who did not know how to wipe their runny noses. So none of the girls in the family was married. The family was on the lookout for proper young men for us. In the meantime, the whole society was in a big stir — army and labor recruitments in a variety of forms were rampant. Young students were taken into the military, and girls were drafted to work.

The president of our neighborhood council was a Japanese man. He lived in a rented house behind ours. I rarely saw him but I ran into his wife and children once in a while. His wife went around the neighborhood spreading a rumor about a Japanese ammunition factory where one could go with a three year contract and earn a huge sum of money. She also made the threatening remark that at least one from each family should go there. I had heard that a Japanese government official sent his own daughter to such a factory.

There were three unmarried daughters in our household, including myself. The family received a notice that the oldest daughter, Keum Ja had to go to work in a factory. We called it "virgin work recruitment" *(virgin often meant "an unmarried girl or woman")* but it was also called, *Kunro Jungshindae* (Voluntarily Committing Body Corps for Labor). If you received this notice, you had to go. It was an official labor draft. Mrs. Choi's face turned ashen. At that time, the first son was attending a university in Seoul and the second son one in Japan. The second daughter was in a high school in Ham Hung and the first one, Keum Ja was preparing to go to a college in Japan after graduating from high school.

Mr. Choi was summoned from Seoul. The whole family was in great turmoil. Nobody knew what to do. Everyone was crying. I thought and thought about it and decided that I should go. It didn't make sense that my older sister should give up her chance to study in Japan and work in a factory. Besides, I still had a debt to pay, 100 *won*. That money had always remained a debt in my mind. It wouldn't hurt to earn some money. Well, three years would go by fast, I thought to myself.

I went to my father and mother and told them that I would go. Their mouths dropped wide open, their eyes becoming teary. "Father, please go back to Seoul and tend to your business. You don't have to worry about it anymore. Three years will pass fast." They were moved and felt proud of me. They said that when I returned from this work, they would arrange my marriage to a fine family.[10] It was February 1941 (lunar calendar).

There was one other person from my neighborhood. When I went to the Ham Hung train station as instructed, there were about twenty girls from various regions. Most of them were about 15 to 16 years of age. There was no farewell party but many family members came to the train station to see us off. I wore a navy blue skirt and a Chinese cabbage color top, made of fine material. I braided my hair and tied it with a red ribbon. And one thing I will never forget, I wore a black cape. At that time, there were very few who could afford a cape but my mother had it made for me. I even had a wrist watch which had been given to me as a going away gift by my older brother who went to school in Seoul. I was in top form. I also packed clean underwear, cosmetics, soap, a tooth brush, a comb, digestives, and enough clothes for three years.

Did you know that of all the women who registered as former comfort women, very few went with an official draft notice like mine? My case is significant because it points directly to official lying by the Japanese government.

She looked into my eyes, making sure that I understood. I nodded.

Where did I leave my story? Oh, yes, at the train station. We were met by a Korean man about fifty years of age who took us to a Japanese soldier who led us to a military train with a number of cars, many occupied by Japanese soldiers. The car where I was placed had about fifty women, mostly strangers. I sensed that there were other cars with women but I wasn't absolutely sure. I noticed that an oil-paper blind, all black, was drawn over the train windows. Everybody was drenched in sadness because they were leaving home.

I looked out the window through the cracks of those black blinds. I saw the Japanese soldier who took us to the train exchanging rolled papers with a Japanese military policeman.[11] A sudden chill grabbed my chest and pain cut through my body like a knife. I somehow knew that my life would never be the same. Sure enough, that scene became an unforgettable image for the rest of my life. Even today, the image of those men exchanging rolled papers is so vivid . . . No doubt, our names in those papers turned us into sex slaves. Life and human fate — all so fragile.

I heard a whistle blow and the train started to move. I slumped in the corner with my knees up and buried my face between them. We were guarded by two Japanese military police officers, one in the front and the other at the back. Total darkness surrounded us inside the train because the black blind was drawn and there was no artificial light. However, feeling the way the train moved, I could tell that it was heading north. It was strange, you see, I had thought that the train would go south toward Seoul. I didn't know what was going on but I could not ask anybody.

The train stopped frequently in tunnels and did not operate well during the nights. Many times we had to get off the train and hide ourselves in barn like places. I think we were transferred to another train but I can't be sure. They gave us a rice ball, the size of a fist, (so it was referred to as "fist-rice"), twice a day with some water. I could not eat them. I am not absolutely sure but it must have been about two to three days when the train came to a final stop. We got off the train and heard a voice over a microphone, "Killim," "Killim." It was the name of the station (*the northeast part of China, old Manchuria*).

We came out of the station and found trucks, covered with dust and torn canvas. They assigned us to different trucks. Those trucks were horrible. Today, we would not transport even animals in them. Each of us clung to a bundle of our belongings, bouncing along on a rough road, a dirt road. You could feel the rocks under the wheels. Over and over again, the truck made our bodies literally jump up from our seats and touch the canvas top, as we rode it about half a day.

Finally, the truck stopped and we were told to get off. "At least, I will not die inside of this miserable truck," I felt relieved. When my feet touched the ground, evening dusk brought night shadow and I found myself standing in a Manchurian field, earth without human warmth. Can you imagine my feelings? I can't describe how I felt. "Fear embodied loneliness?" I can't. It's no use. No way I can describe it.

No sign of civilian houses, just endless rows of military tents. We were brought to a small cottage, called *goya*, a round, tin plated cottage. A wooden board covered the floor on which a Japanese mattress, *tatami*, was placed. We were given a blanket and a quilt. At least we didn't feel the direct wind inside but the sound of wind, you know that sound? It makes you feel bone chilling cold, your soul trembles with sorrow. "This must be a temporary place for one night," I thought.

We put down our bundles inside of *goya*. All of us wanted to wash but there was no water. Everything was frozen solid. I put my hands on the ice in a bucket and rubbed them. Then, I went where they pointed to get our meal. They gave us some rice, soup, I think it was bean sprout soup, I can't be sure, and a couple pieces of yellow turnip pickle. I looked around for a spoon but there were no regular spoons, only wooden chop sticks and wooden spoons. You know why? Don't you? Everything, steel, brass, all metal things, whatever they were, the Japanese used for manufacturing planes and weapons. The rice felt like sand in my mouth. I could not swallow it. I just drank some soup and went back to the *goya*.

It was so cold that we had to warm ourselves with each other's body heat. I thought that we had been brought there to cook and do laundry for the soldiers. We met several women who had been there for some time. They said to us, "You people are also going to die. My heart aches for you." I asked, "What kind of work are we going to do?" "You might call it a kind of work but not really. Just do as you are told. Otherwise, you will be beaten to death," was the reply I received.

She got up abruptly, stood by the window for a while and turned around.

Did I tell you that I tried to report about the Korean comfort women, you know, women like me, long before Kim Hak Soon went public?

I shook my head, almost startled.

When I lived in Kang Won Province, I had a couple of adopted kids. Life was hard. I used go to the mountains, pick lots of edible plants, many different kinds, and sell them. That's how I was able to put food into our mouths. When was it? Anyway, it was after Korea and Japan signed the now infamous 1965 Treaty. I heard that Mrs. Park, the First Lady, was going to be in the area to visit her family. She had given an enormous amount of money to restore a Buddhist temple, Bong Won Sa Temple, near where her parents lived. On the 8th of April, you know, the Buddha's birthday, there was to be a celebration with all kinds of people coming from all over. She was staying with her parents and planned to celebrate Buddha's birthday at that temple.

At that time it wasn't easy, actually impossible, to have any kind of hearing at the Presidential Mansion, Chung Hwa Dae (*Blue House*). So I thought it was my chance to get close to the President's wife. I cooked all kinds of mountain vegetables, packed them neatly and set out on a trip to meet the First Lady. You see, I knew where her folks lived. If you went around the house, there was a toilet. I stood near the toilet where I wouldn't be seen. I don't know how long I had been there. It must have been several hours. Then, I saw her going into the toilet. I waited until she came out. Then, I knelt, grabbed her skirt touching the ground, presented my gift and said I had an urgent matter to discuss with her. She had this incredulous look on her face. I was afraid that she was going to call for help, yell or something, but she allowed me to talk.

I told her briefly about myself and the women who served Japanese soldiers and asked why the Korean government did not do something for us. Her face became ashen and she grabbed my hands and said quietly, but with the ring of urgency. "Please don't ever repeat this story. You must not talk about this with anybody else. Korea and Japan have already signed a treaty to take care of the matters concerning the two countries during the colonial period. When times are better, when we have true peace, perhaps, something like this could be discussed and resolved. But now is not the best time. Korea needs to move forward. This is a matter of the past that should not be brought up again now." She looked into my eyes and stressed again, "Do you understand? You never told me this story and you will never mention it to anybody else. This is a dangerous story." So I put my story under my feet, turned around and went home crying my hearts out.

Then, in 1991, I saw Kim Hak Soon on television urging us to report. I wrote down the number and called her. We arranged to meet. She helped me to report at a nearby police station. Since then, I have been going to places wherever I was needed and testified. You know, that's how I went to Washington where you live.

> *"I know," I said. What an amazing story . . . If the First Lady was willing to do something about her story as a fellow woman . . . But this story is between Grandma Hwang and the former First Lady who is dead. The ground for verifying it rests entirely with Grandma Hwang.*

It is pretty incredible, isn't it? That's why I don't tell this story. What's the use? I know people won't believe me. (*Damn . . . it was uncanny the way she could read my mind*). You know, these days, I am pretty free of fear. Actually, I am not afraid of anything. That's why every time I go to Japan, I yell at them. People are still careful not to offend the Japanese. Well, I can't worry about offending them, can I? They ruined my life; they tore it into a thousand pieces and did the same thing to countless other women. No matter what I do, there's no way I could match them. I once took up the fingerprinting issue. You know about that, don't you, the Japanese fingerprinting Koreans living in Japan as if they were criminals. I said, "What possible reason could you have to fingerprint Koreans living in Japan? You should fingerprint yourselves, not the Koreans. You are the ones who stole innocent virgins and inflicted unimaginable cruelty and pain. Let me fingerprint you and see if you are worthy of belonging to the human race. If you continue to mess around with the Koreans living in Japan, I swear to you that I will kill every Japanese over sixty who ever appears in Korea." I understand that my speech shook up quite of few of them.[12]

> *She laughed, her laughter filling the room. I felt small . . . so much potential crushed and stepped on. I sighed, thinking of the image of Asian woman in the United States, "submissive woman, eyes always avoiding direct contact . . ." She poured more barley tea in my cup.*

I know that many other women don't feel this way; they are not like me. I know that there are some women who say they like the Japanese, and talk about their past loves . . . Some even want to marry Japanese. If that's the way they feel, they should not talk about "compensation," those mother fucking bitches. I will never understand them, not even in a million years.

> *I saw her frown darkly and a curl appearing about the corners of her mouth. No doubt emotion was boiling inside.*

My body can't follow my passion. I am old as you can see. You know, people talk about making movies about us. Actually, there is a documentary, recently made. It doesn't begin to show what it was like. Then, there is this long television series, eighteen hours or something. I watched it. Even with the eighteen hours, it doesn't begin to show the hardships we had to endure. No way any movie can depict our past . . . How can anybody or anything convey our suffering and pain? Did I tell you that till this day I can't drink rice wine, *Makgulri (looks like milk)*? Do you know why?

> *I had an idea but I had my mouth shut. Then, with her eyes coming alive and with some sort of hope surging in her body, continued.*

I actually want to throw out an idea—see what you think. You might consider it vain but I want people in the United States to do something that would publicly acknowledge my past, to recognize the hardships I had to endure and the humiliation I had to suffer. Admittedly, it is not like an award in recognition of one's great achievements but perhaps just celebrating the fact that I am still alive. Maybe, they can give me an honorary doctorate in "hardships." I want to give testimonies about the human strength that endures . . . You might call it a miracle of survival. Am I silly? Am I vain?

What she said was so unexpected that I honestly didn't know how I felt then but said anyway, "Oh, I don't think you are vain. In fact, such a thing could be a great source of inspiration."

Let me go back to my story. Where was I? Yes, I spent a night in the *goya*. The next day the soldiers came and took each of us. I was taken by an officer who brought me to his quarters. The officer sat by the bed for a while and then told me to come closer. He tried to pull me close to him.. Scared, with my heart pounding like crazy, I said, "I would rather do laundry and clean," I said, avoiding his eyes. "We don't need that kind of work." Saying this, he snatched me. As I pulled away with all my strength, he slapped both my cheeks hard. Kneeling, and with my forehead touching the floor, I begged and begged, "Please, please, my life is in your hands. You can save me; you can let me live." "If you want to remain alive, do as I tell you!" "I would rather die." I was wearing a black skirt and a white top and had long braided hair. The officer grabbed my skirt with such force and tore it off. A string from my black skirt hung on my shoulder and only underwear covered my body. I knelt and pleaded with him, and repeated that I could not possibly do what he wanted. He grabbed my braid and ripped my underwear with his military sword. I fainted. When I became conscious after a while, I found the officer wiping sweat from his face as he put on his uniform top.

Soon a soldier came and took me out of the room. I gathered my underwear and wrapped my skirt around me. I followed him, crying. Pain cut through my body as I took each step. A woman who had been there for some time saw and said, "See what I mean. We can't get out of here alive."

Because we newcomers were virgins, only officers had the privilege to take us. For about two weeks the officers ordered us to come with them several times a day. One day, an officer came and ordered that I lick his thing. "I would rather die than do that, you son of a dog! I am a daughter of Korea, not a dog!" He screamed like an animal, "*Konoyaro koroshitei yarou ka*?" ("Shall I kill you, bitch"?) He kicked me and threw me around like a bundle of clothing. I fainted. When I regained consciousness, my friends told me that I had been unconscious for three days. I wasn't happy to be conscious. I just wished never to wake up.

After that incident, I had no choice but to do whatever they told me. Some of those men, even before I put their thing in my mouth, white stuff started dripping. To me, it was horrible. Even now, at the sight of any white liquid, I feel like vomiting everything inside of me.

On one of my trips to Japan to give testimony, a reporter, named Nagano, came to see me. He had been in Korea, I think three times. I treated him to meals. He is crazy about Korean food. He handed me an envelope. I opened it; there was money inside. I threw it back to him. He said, "When I visited you in Korea, you gave me such splendid meals. I just wanted to pay back a little." I yelled, "You came to my country and I treated you as a guest. I did not feed you to get money. You want to give me money for my food? If you want to offer us money, compensate us what we deserve. Not this chickenshit money." So many Japanese are afraid of me; they are afraid to talk to me, especially because I tell them that they say two utterly conflicting things with one mouth. At the sight of them, curses run out of my mouth like a river. I can't help it. If Emperor Hirohito were alive today, I don't know what I would do with him. Lots of my friends tell me not to curse like that but I can't help it. Curses just flow out of my mouth. I have no power to stop them.

> *The telephone rang, a chance for me to stand up and stretch. I went to her tiny balcony and saw flower pots, one of which drew my attention. It was Bong Sun Hwa, pink balsam flowers with delicate petals, which we crushed when I was a little girl and put around our fingernails and slept with overnight. In the morning, the fingernails would be red, more beautiful than any modern manicure I have seen on any woman's nails. Hum, Grandma Hwang, with all that tough image, she raises Bong Sun Hwa . . .*

That was Kim Hak Soon. She said that she would be happy to see you. Here's her number. She is expecting to hear from you. We all have stories to tell. Such gruesome stories, tales that would curdle your blood.

The soldiers didn't wash their feet, let alone take a bath. They didn't brush their teeth; clothes were unwashed for days and they didn't take off their shoes. The only thing they took off was their uniform top. They didn't want us to see their names. The nameless animals exploding on top of us. They stank. You can't imagine how they stank. The rotten stink. Nauseating is not the word. I used to put soft grass I had picked in my nostrils to avoid the smell. Till now, just the thought of that smell makes me feel as if the entire intestines are turning upside down.

The soldiers were ordered to use condoms but often they didn't and many women became pregnant. Much of the time, we didn't know we were pregnant. While they were pregnant, the doctors gave them strong shots called 606^{13} to treat them for venereal disease. The women found their bottoms drenched in blood. Then they were taken to the infirmary and the doctors scraped their uteruses. So the shots, 606, killed the babies inside and also prevented them from being pregnant again. You see, if this is repeated three or four times, women could no longer get pregnant. At first, I didn't know what was happening to me but I believe I, too, was pregnant three times. The third time, I skipped my monthly thing for three months. In the fourth month, my bottom was all bloody and I felt such pain that I wished to die.

After two weeks in the *goya*, they took us to the comfort stations. They were temporary wooden barracks. Each barrack was divided by thin boards, making five or six small rooms. Each room had a door made of a torn blanket and the floor space was large enough to put a single bed with barely enough space for one person to pass by. I heard there were many comfort stations on the base. We were supposed to return to our *goya* to sleep after our job was completed. However, because soldiers came all night and because we were so exhausted, often we slept in the comfort house. Under a thin quilt, we almost froze to death.

We ate at the military mess hall. The soldiers cooked food. Usually, the meals were rice, bean paste soup and pickled radish. When we first arrived, they gave us a supply of clothes: a pair of tight slacks, called *mompei*, a short Japanese style top called *haori,* army socks, a cap, black sneakers, a quilted overcoat, a pair of quilted slacks, and what looked like army sportswear. Later when supplies became short, we wore discarded soldiers' clothes. Beginning in 1945, we had hardly any supplies — no clothing, not even soy sauce or bean paste. We ate a couple of rice balls a day and boiled water with salt. They called that soup.

They could come and go any time, but not many officers came because they were fearful of venereal disease. On the average, about 30 to 40 soldiers each day came to every woman but on holidays the numbers increased. Often many of them waited outside the door in their underwear. Some just walked in the room stark naked in the middle of intercourse with another soldier. Sometimes they shouted, *"Hayaku, Hayaku,"* "hurry up, hurry up." Some soldiers, before they went to the battlefront engaged in the act as if their life depended on it but others wept doing it. I felt sorry for them. Some had a condom on and others brought it. They would ask me to put it on for them. Yet there were others who did not bring a condom or wanted to wear it. At first they distributed each of us a box of condoms. Foolishly, I thought that if I did not have condoms, they would not come. So I threw them away but, alas, they never stopped coming. Nothing, nothing stopped them.

You want to know if there was anyone for whom I felt anything. Are you kidding? No time for feelings. I bet you have heard about those, haven't you? Those things usually happened if you were at different kinds of comfort stations, you know, the ones run jointly by the military and civilians and not located in the military compounds like mine. At first, when you were young and still pretty, usually officers were the ones who came. Then, when you were all worn out and ready to be discarded, soldiers just came and got on top of you until you died. I don't think we know how many of those virgins died . . . beaten to death, sometimes shot to death or rotted to death with venereal disease, not to speak of suicides. Oh, they would give you shots and medicine if you were sick not because they gave a damn but because they had to repair the sexual commodity . . . when the sickness became hopeless, those bodies just disappeared.

Dense silence followed, both of us battling our feelings . . .
I sat still . . .

I don't ever remember being paid during my comfort woman years, not in cash, not in any form of paper that would enable me to get paid later. Besides, what would we have done with money? Nothing to buy with, nowhere to go to, no one to give it to. . .

At first, they conducted regular medical examinations two or three times a month in the hospital. In less than a year, every woman found something wrong with her body; they became ill one way or the other. Many got pregnant twice or three times and were infected with venereal disease. If the disease became serious, the sick ones were isolated and kept in separate rooms and were instructed to use different bathrooms. If they got better, they were brought back. If this kind of treatment became necessary for the third time, the soldiers came and took them away, never to return. Some women were swollen with yellow ooze from their vaginas to their navels. You should see their faces. . .they were puffed and yellow. These women simply disappeared. I was the only one left of the twenty who boarded the train at the Ham Hung station. Some disappeared because of their illness and others were transferred to other military bases. A lot of new arrivals also disappeared and only seven remained in our *goya*. All seven were Korean. We were all so sick we could hardly move.

It is hard to describe how they beat us. One of the women was ordered to lick the thing. She bit it hard and he fainted. She was beaten and kicked until she passed out. Then, they brought a coarse straw mat, put her body on it and dragged like they would drag a dead dog. They dumped the half dead body on the ground and shot.

Did I see it? Of course. If I didn't want to see it, they would make me see it. They did those things to show an example. They told us, "Remember, this will happen to you if you behaved like she did." You know, all those politicians, I mean Koreans, do you think they have any idea what happened to their people like us? No way. If they did, those fucking bastards would have done something for us long time ago.

At first we were given some kind of absorbent cotton to use as sanitary napkins. About a year later, this supply simply stopped. So we were forced to make sanitary napkins out of anything we could get hold of, like soldiers' gaiters, torn and abandoned by them. If we were found using their gaiters, they would beat us, and cursed. They said it would bring them bad luck.

We were not human beings to them. We were beaten every day. If we looked at the moon, they would beat us, asking what we were thinking; if we just mumbled, they would beat us, accusing us of bad mouthing them. The best thing to do was to pretend that you could see and hear nothing. So I walked around with my eyes covered with my hands. However, because I was more rebellious than others, I believe I was beaten more. Until this day, I feel the impact of those beatings — half of the time, I have trouble hearing.

We were not allowed to leave the military base. That is why I do not know the name of the base and don't remember any faces or ranks of those soldiers. One day we were told that we could go with troops moving to some other place. I thought that nowhere could be as bad. So I got into the truck with several other women. I was so carsick; I had no idea where we were going. It's possible that we were on a ship for a while. When we got off the truck, the comfort station looked very much like the one before. I had no idea where it was. Because of the severe bombings at night, we could not turn the lights on. There were other women who had been there, all Koreans except for two Chinese. They told me that even if we were let go, we would end up in the sea and die. Most likely it was a naval base. Soldiers were worse there than before. If they came before they were sent to the battlefront, they were incredibly cruel. It was truly unbearable. About eight to nine months after I arrived there, I noticed that some troops were withdrawing in the direction of Killim. I hid myself in one of the trucks, risking my life in order to leave with them. So I went back to where I had been before.

One day, it must have been evening but no one called for supper. Nobody came and there was no sign of people. I went outside and looked around but there were no trucks, no horses. Some worn-out cloth was on a wire fence, flapping in the strong wind. I tiptoed to the mess and found it in utter chaos with nobody there. I was getting a drink of water when a private appeared. He told me that he had just returned from a "messenger" job and found a memo from an officer in which he was instructed to leave the place as soon as possible. He told me, "A bomb was dropped in Japan. Japan had to surrender. You better go back to Korea. If you stay here, you will be killed by the Chinese."

I returned to our quarters and told the seven remaining women that we had to leave. They were so sick they could not walk. They urged me to go alone. One of them said, "Most probably, we will just die here. You go and tell our parents what happened to us. People have to know." The pain I felt for leaving them there. . .how could I describe it. . . my chest felt like as if it were being torn into thousand pieces. I had no choice, though. I went back to the mess but the private was gone. It was August but it was cold. I grabbed anything I could find — I put on soldiers' abandoned underwear, shirts, anything and tied my hair full of lice with a piece of cloth. Then I ran.

The military base was much larger than I had expected. The whole place was surrounded by a fence with three layers of electric wire. So you see, there was no way for us to escape in a hurry. It took some doing to pass through that fence. I walked a long time before I saw any people. After a while, soldiers, laborers and families filled the streets, all of them with bundles on their heads and backs. Some Japanese families carried quite a few bundles. When they became too heavy for them to walk, they discarded things. So I picked some to wear. Some kind people let me cook rice with them once in a while and make a fire during the night. Most of the times, I begged. Imagine begging from those people! Whatever I could find on the street, I put on. I also got some abandoned shoes.

You want to know how I felt when I learned about our independence. What was independence? You don't get it, do you? You still think we were human. We had no feelings left. I had no feelings. I didn't understand what the hell was happening. I didn't know who defeated the Japanese.

Even when I was in Korea, I didn't know much about the relationship between the two countries, Japan and Korea. I had heard about the names of independence fighters like Ahn Jung Gun but I didn't know how Korea was swallowed up by Japan. Nobody bothered to tell me. Even at school, they taught only the Japanese language. I knew that Koreans and Japanese were different but didn't know how or why Japan took Korea. My adopted father was a highly learned man but he hardly spoke about those things to me. His wife, you know, as a woman, concentrated on raising the family, nothing else. Actually, it was from my birth father that I learned bits and pieces about independence movement but not much.

So the only thing I knew was that I could leave that dreadful place. I just wanted to get the hell out of China and come back to the place where I could at least speak my own language. So I walked with the crowd. Somewhere in Kang Won province, I saw American soldiers. They spread DDT all over us and dead lice dropped from everywhere. Even now, whenever I dream about those times, I scream and yell but I can't move. I fight with the soldiers. I wake up, frightened by my own scream.

From there, I was able to get on a train transporting coal. I got off the train at a small station in the outskirts of Seoul. It was Chung Yang Li. It was early December. I went to a small eating place to beg for some food. When I told the owner that I came from Manchuria, she gave me some rice. I went inside and cried while eating. I did not want to go home the state I was in. I told the owner that there was no way that I could find my family or relatives. She told me that I could stay there and work. I took a bath, had my hair cut, spread DDT again on my hair to take care of the lice, and put on the owner's used slacks and sweater. I worked there for three years. As soon as I saved some money, I got a job in a textile factory in the neighborhood. I was twenty seven years old.

I treated my venereal disease with shots of penicillin smuggled out of American army bases. It took me ten years to cure my disease. The Korean war broke out about three years after I started working in the textile factory. I became a refugee with only my bank book and my signature seal. During the war, I took care of two orphans whom I eventually left at an orphanage. I took care of three other orphans whom I also entrusted later to an orphanage. After the war was over, I farmed for four to five years. During that period, my orphans all came back to me. I married them off and they are doing okay. They still come see me. I can't tell how many times I wanted to kill myself; it was an ordeal simply to survive.

You want to know how and why I took care of five orphans? You are old enough to remember the Korean war, aren't you? I was among the refugees walking in the bitter cold headed south. One day, I saw something wrapped in a green army jacket on the roadside. A strange feeling crept through me and I was drawn to it. I squatted and carefully looked. I felt something moving. Well, I found a baby inside the army jacket. I could not just abandon it, could I? What crime had he committed to be deserted like that? No way I could leave the baby. . . I would be hit by the lightening. Have you any idea how many babies were separated or abandoned by their parents during the war? I took care of them as much as I could and when I found an orphanage, I left them there. But they all found their way back to me. When I came back to Seoul, I sold tofu for a while. If I sold twenty, I got one tofu. You should have seen all of us in a single square room with a roof over us, made of tin from a variety of cans. We ate whatever food we could get from selling tofu. We starved more than we ate. Can you imagine what it was like?

After tofu, I sold vegetables, then noodle soup. Finally, I was able to run a small eating place, which helped me to make ends meet, but barely. When I came to Washington, I was still doing that. I did it all by myself. I could not afford to hire help. Twice a week, I had to get up at five-thirty in the morning and go to a wholesale market to buy food supplies. I tried to stay awake on coffee. My uterus was removed and my knees constantly hurt. Until today, there isn't a part of my body that doesn't hurt. Aches are everywhere in my body. I always want to lead a dignified life without other people's contempt or pity.

Choking silence.

I left home for sick father. I agreed to work in "a Japanese factory" or wherever it was to live my life with dignity. But look at what happened to my life. No matter how hard I try, it is impossible to describe what Japan did to me, to hundreds and thousands of young women. It is even more difficult to describe how I feel. Japan tore my human dignity into shreds and through no fault of mine, Japan inflicted pain and shame on me. Nothing they can do now can make this up.

> *Her hands were folded in her lap and her eyes were full of unshed tears. The sky outside her little balcony was stone gray. I writhed at my own feelings of helplessness. "Well, perhaps, you might want a little something for supper. I had no idea that the time had gone by so fast." Once again, she came to my rescue. Politely saying no with my head, I gathered my things and stood up. She followed me to the bus stop and waved good-bye. I left, promising to return before I left Korea.*
>
> *I did go back for half an hour two days before I got on a plane at the Kimpo International airport to go to Japan in search for some more grandmas. That was late June, 1995. In November, I went back to Seoul for the screening of my film, "A FORGOTTEN PEOPLE: The Sakhalin Koreans," at the Seoul Short Film Festival. I called her and she recognized my voice right away. "You are coming to see me, aren't you?"*
>
> *When I rang her bell, there was no answer. Discouraged, I turned around. Then, the familiar voice, "Aigo, it's you. I was just around the corner to put out the trash. Imagine, I nearly missed you. Come in. Come in."*
>
> *We ate grapes and shared sighs, talking about former President Roh Tae Woo who took all those bribes. While we talked, I could not let go a question I was itching to ask, a question about her mother. I knew that her father died a couple of years after she had left, but on and off, I had wondered about her mother. If she saw her at all after her return.*

I never did go see her. She came to see me one day. A relative of mine told her that she thought she had seen me; she wasn't absolutely sure. So the two women came looking for me when I was selling tofu in Seoul. My mother stared at me from a distance. I recognized her but could not move. She walked toward me and asked, "Are you Keum Ju by any chance?" I simply nodded my head. After a moment of unbearable silence, I said, "Please don't ask me anything but tell me how father died." I was hollow, no other feelings, not even sorrow. That was the only time I saw my mother alive. Even when I was informed of my mother's death, I didn't go to my hometown. Why? I didn't want to set my feet in it. How could I go back? I swore that I would not come back unless I made something of myself. All those dreams of a twelve year old girl, throwing a stone . . .

You know what? I do feel grateful these days. For what, you might ask.

For being independent. Whatever life I have left, I want to live a dignified life without burdening others until I die and to bear witness to the horrible past if it kills me. It should be faced so that it would never be repeated.

Postscript

In April 1997, I took my crew to film her. As I entered her apartment, I noticed a picture of her with President Clinton in front of the White House, a cardboard cutout of the President! I laughed, pointing out that picture to the crew. Grandma Hwang sat me down, ignoring the crew. "Listen, if you are going to make a film, do it right, not like some other ones already made. You have to do your research right. For instance, in my case, you must stress that I went with an officially drafted notice. This is important because it means Japan's deceit was official and systematic—the draft notice was from the government just like an army draft. With some other women, it is not always clear how they went. Don't make a film that will bring shame to you, you understand?"

Chapter 2

JAPANESE MILITARY SUPPLIES

Colonial Master in Korea

Japan colonized Korea and dominated its people for thirty five years, 1910 to 1945.

Before 1910, the Korean peninsula, primarily due its strategic location, had long been coveted and fought over by Japan, China and Russia. For centuries, Korea had been a dependent or vassal state to China. In the 19th century, modernization and economic development from the West changed the dynamics of this rivalry and stirred the land long known as the hermit kingdom. The arrival of the European and American expansionists along with Western style capitalism and industrialization altered politics, economics and social life in Japan, China and Korea, feudal, agricultural countries.

Following the first major shock of the Opium War of 1839-42 in China, the European and American powers entered East Asia. Commodore Matthew Calbraith Perry led a fleet of American ships to Japan and secured the Treaty of Kanagawa in 1854. He opened Japan's door to the West with "gunboat diplomacy." By 1858 Japan had signed similar treaties with Great Britain, Russia, France and the Netherlands.

Shortly after the coming of the West, the power of the Emperor was restored in the Meiji Restoration (1868), with the collapse of the Tokugawa *Shogunate,* the military dictatorship which had ruled the country with an iron hand since the mid sixteenth century. The Meiji leaders were aware that the treaties were "unequal" but, caught in the Western expansionist surge, they steered the country toward modernization, adopting Western techniques and industrial improvements. Western imperialism offered Japan a model which the Japanese were quick to learn and to pursue relentlessly. By the turn of the 20th century, Japan had emerged as a modern, industrialized, military power, with feudalism dissolved and a constitution promulgated. In the mid-19th century, Korea was not yet a target of foreign attention, but the developments in China and Japan caused the hermit kingdom to close its doors even more tightly. Isolated, Korea faced enormous internal problems due to the gradual collapse of the traditional class structure, chaos in the royal families and economic hardship. Determined that Korea should not come under the control of the Western powers or any other, and with an additional impetus by a weakened China, Japan decided to open the hermit kingdom. Japan in 1875, according to most historians, incited conflict by sending a warship, *Un'yo* which landed on Kangwha Island and Korean guards fired on it. Three months later, Japan sent naval vessels to Kangwha Island ostensibly to settle the incident but with the real goal of opening Korea. The result was the Kangwha Treaty of 1876, with which Japan began its gradual domination of its neighboring peninsula.

Soon ports were opened and Japanese merchants enjoyed a near monopoly on trade, with an inundation of Japanese goods, and an outflow of rice. As Japanese power in Korea escalated, China came back, taking every opportunity to re-assert its former suzerainty. Then came the Westerners. In 1882, the treaty with the United States, Korea's first with a Western country, was signed at Chemulpo (In'chon). Other nations followed — Great Britain, Germany, Italy, Russia, and France — all between 1883 and 1886.

By the early 1890's, Japanese economic activity had reached such astonishing proportions that no other nation could rival. Japanese traders, mostly from depressed elements in their own society, would routinely loan Korean farmers the money to buy seed and other items and then, at harvest time, would collect a large part or even all of their crops. The opening of the country to Japan exacerbated the already extreme hardship of the farmers.

Tonghak (Eastern Learning), a populist movement and a direct protest against economic distress, emerged around 1860. Anti-foreigner as well, *Tonghak* sought to protect Korea from *Sohak*, Western learning, but it was especially anti-Japanese. Expelling "foreign barbarians" was one of the top priorities. Among a number of specific demands the *Tonghak* Movement made, two stood out; equitable taxation and the halting of rice exports to Japan. This fiercely anti-foreign movement attracted two competing foreign powers, China and Japan, each wanting to take advantage of this unrest. Desperate to suppress the *Tonghak* rebels, King Kojong appealed to Ch'ing China for help and within a month, 3,000 Chinese forces landed at Asan Bay. In response, Japan sent troops ostensibly to protect its legation. The *Tonghak* rebellion was crushed and the Korean government demanded the withdrawal of all troops. China, backed by the United States, Great Britain, Russia and others, proposed simultaneous withdrawal of all troops from Korea but Japan insisted on staying. Japan saw an opportunity to drive the Chinese out of Korea, even at the risk of confronting China in a war.

With Korea caught helplessly in the middle, the first Sino-Japanese War broke out in 1894. Japan attacked Chinese ships in the Yellow Sea near Asan Bay. With a swift series of victories, Japan emerged triumphant, dominating

Korea. Japan's exploitation of Korea was in full force under the pretext of modernization. The Japanese took the rights to build railroads and telegraph systems and controlled most ports. More importantly, a military alliance was signed which in effect made Korea a source of Japanese military supplies.

Then Russia, which had already been in conflict with Japan over China and Manchuria, appeared actively on the Korean scene. Japan, in anticipation of an inevitable clash with the Russians, concluded an alliance with Britain, a long time foe of Russian expansionism. This prompted Russia to ally itself with France. The forces of imperialism, Western and Eastern, were entangled in political machinations and struggles, with the stronger and weaker nations shaking hands one moment and pointing guns the next. Korea was coming dangerously close to being colonized by any of these imperial powers, including Great Britain and the United States. However, Korea was too small a potato for them; they gave a free hand to Japan, which they considered a model of Asian modernization.

Japan demanded that Russia withdraw its troops from Manchuria. Upon Russia's refusal, Japan attempted negotiations, asking that Russia recognize Japan's preponderant interests in Korea. In return, Japan would acknowledge Russia's special position in the operation of its railway in Manchuria. In the absence of serious compromise on the part of either party, the negotiations went nowhere. Just as they had done to China in 1894, and as they would against the United States in 1941, the Japanese opened fire without warning on Port Arthur on February 8, 1904 and declared war two days later.

Japan won a series of decisive victories, depriving the Russians of any remaining power in Korea. With the fall of Mukden, an important Manchurian city, and with the help of Great Britain which denied the Russians the use of the Suez Canal for its Baltic fleet, the defeat of Russia was only a matter of time. Japan became the first nonwhite nation to subdue one of the great powers.

Complete Japanese domination of Korea was in sight but Japan had to insure that there would be no Western interference. In July 1905, a secret meeting in Tokyo between the Japanese Prime Minister Katsura Taro and William Howard Taft, the American Secretary of War, produced an agreement calling for the free exchange of colonial interests. The United States recognized Japan's interests in Korea and in return Japan would stay clear of American rule in the Philippines. Japan bargained with Great Britain as well for similar arrangements; Japan would support British rule in India. The Westerners clearly did not yet see any threat from Japan.

The Taft-Katsura agreement was not the only U.S. support for the colonial ambitions of Japan. In July, the Emperor of Korea secretly sent Rhee Syngman to appeal for help from President Theodore Roosevelt. When Rhee visited Roosevelt at his summer house in Oyster Bay, Long Island, the

President promised to work on behalf of Korea, but he, as was subsequently demonstrated, had no intention of helping. Then, Roosevelt negotiated peace between Russia and Japan. Russia lost control of Manchuria, Korea and half of Sakhalin Island, a few miles off the Eastern coast of Siberia. In the Treaty of Portsmouth in 1905, Japan still "recognized" Korean independence but in fact gained control of Korean foreign relations, thereby denying the sovereignty of Korea in the eyes of the international community.

On November 17, 1905, with Japanese troops in Seoul on the main street leading to the old palace, a treaty was signed, which the Japanese called *hogo joyaku*, the Treaty of Protection; Koreans called it simply "the 1905 agreement." A protectorate was a device widely used for domination by the Western powers in the late nineteenth century, e.g., the French in Tunis and the British in Egypt. Japan used that device and became the protectors of Korea. That this was done legally is widely challenged. According to Lee Tai-jin, curator of the Kyujangkak archives at Seoul National University, the emperor's signature and his seal are missing in the original text of the treaty. Scholars at the Center for Research and Documentation on Japan's War Responsibility in Japan agree that the treaty was invalid since it was never ratified either by the Korean or the Japanese emperors.[14]

With the five articles of the Agreement "to serve until the moment arrives when it is recognized that Korea has attained national strength,"[15] Japan took control of all Korean foreign relations and the Japanese Residency General *(tokanfu)* was established, supposedly to direct matters relating to the foreign affairs of Korea but practically to rule the country. In March 1906, the first resident-general *(tokan)*, Ito Hirobumi, arrived in Seoul with a free hand and full control over all military forces in Korea.

Emperor Kojong extended his efforts to plead the Korean case to the international community, starting with the Americans. The United States, together with Great Britain, supported Japan with not only a free hand in Korea, but also a helping hand. Koreans protested through riots and uprisings throughout 1905 and 1906. The newspapers mourned the 17th day of November 1905 as "a lamentable day"; countless petitions were sent to the Throne; and many killed themselves. Guerrilla forces called "righteous armies" *(uibyong)* rose throughout the country to fight against Japan. All the uprisings and protests by Koreans at home and abroad simply accelerated the establishment of the Japanese military and civilian police networks. Japanese suppression extended to freedom of speech and all spheres of intellectual and spiritual life. Further, they used Koreans to subjugate their own countrymen. Some Koreans willingly allied themselves with Japan, convinced that the future of the country would be better if they cooperated, and others were merely opportunistic.

The formal annexation of Korea by Japan came on August 22, 1910. Japanese troops surrounded the palace and forced Emperor Sunjong to approve the Treaty of Annexation, which had been signed already by Prime Minister Yi Wan-yong. The Treaty proclaimed that the Korean government "has not proved entirely equal to the duty of preserving public order and tranquility," and that the purpose of annexation was "to maintain peace and stability in Korea, to promote the prosperity and welfare of Koreans, and at the same time to ensure the safety and repose of foreign residents." Article I of the Treaty declared, "His Majesty the Emperor of Korea makes the complete and permanent recession to His Majesty the Emperor of Japan of all rights of sovereignty over the whole of Korea."[16] The Treaty deprived Korea of all sovereign rights. Korea was a colony.

The new colony was ruled through a Japanese Governor-General, appointed by the Emperor. The Governor General ruled as an absolute dictator, exerting iron control over the administration, legislature, judiciary and military, and answerable only to the Emperor.[17] The military dominated colonial policy; of the total eight Governor-Generals, seven were army generals and one a naval admiral. The first, General Terauchi Masatake, put into effect the "military administration" and united the regular police and military police (*kempei*). The most striking aspect of the colonial government of Korea was the role of the *kempei*, enforced under a heavy handed military policy. With the largest allocation in the Governor-General's budget, the police force covered every sphere of Korean life: in addition to regular police work and the suppression of Korean independence movements, the police guarded mail, supervised rice production, enforced tax collections and even the spread of the Japanese language.

Control of the Korean mind was considered of major importance. Scholars, cultural agencies, newspapers and journals were strictly controlled and people who protested were placed under surveillance or imprisoned as "thought criminals." Newspapers published in Korean (*hangul*) were banned. The cultural policy and programs were carefully designed to insure the complete Japanization of Korea, often under the banner of constructing a "joint" community. Simultaneously, Japan emphasized "Korean backwardness" or low cultural level (*mindo*), and Japan's mission to civilize its colony.[18] Consistent with this policy, the primary purpose of education was to transform Koreans into loyal and obedient subjects of the Japanese Emperor. Study of the Japanese language was compulsory in all public schools. Korean history and geography were banned. At first, Korean language instruction was merely discouraged but by 1938 it was forbidden in all public schools and Japanese was required. Textbooks were revised to promote the Japanese spirit and ideals. The indoctrination of Koreans penetrated the religious sphere. After 1935, attendance at Shinto ceremonies was compulsory. The intent to destroy Korean identity was best expressed in Ordinance No. 20 of 1939 under which Koreans were required to change their family and personal names to Japanese.

Thus the opening of Korea by Japan evolved from free-trade imperialism to a protectorate and finally to full colonial rule. Japan, extending the successful industrialization of the Meiji Restoration to Korea, installed a "developmental" colonial regime. Prior to annexation, the Japanese government pushed a policy of "concentrating overseas migration in Manchuria and Korea" to consolidate and expand Japan's economic and political influence abroad.[19] And the government wanted settlers in Korea to be "colonists" (*shokumin*), not "emigrants" (*imin*), designed to serve the national interest even while pursuing their own interests. With the "colonists," the government proceeded to "develop" the colony.

In agricultural development, a central goal of Japan's development scheme, the government accelerated Japanese landownership by changing the legal status of foreign landholding in Korea, and made Korea an important source of Japan's food supplies, which made already poverty stricken Korean farmers even more miserable. The majority of farmers, many of them tenants, were still without the benefits of modernization and worked small holdings of less than one *chongbo* (2.45 acres). By the time they had paid high rents—an average 50 percent of the crop proceeds—taxes, and other fees, including those for water and transportation, they were often left with less than 25 percent of their harvest to live on.

The countless peasants who refused to till the lands for absentee landlords, or those who did not have any land to farm, were forced to become *hwajonmin*, cultivators of fire-fields. They burned wasteland and hillsides, made fields, and planted corn, sweet potatoes and millet. They roamed the country to find hillsides to burn in order to grow a few potatoes or vegetables while Korean rice went to the colonizers. All natural resources, fishery and forestry, were Japanese controlled. Many farmers had resorted to fishing after losing their land or rights to farm but the Japanese expansion of the fishing industry with their superior boats and equipment made it difficult for Koreans to compete. Koreans in large numbers were forced to leave their motherland and went to Manchuria or Siberia. When Manchukuo, the Japanese puppet state, was established on March 1, 1932, a large Korean population was found there, reaching nearly one and a half million by 1940.

Under an overall plan for industrial and commercial development, Japan also controlled industries and commercial markets. Korean owned firms and businesses grew fewer and smaller with Japan's eye on having Korea's commerce for itself. The shrinking numbers of Korean owners had to operate under tight restrictions. For the Koreans to obtain government licenses, they were required to have Japanese as co-investors or as managerial staff. Additionally, most business activities were operated with state sponsored loans.

With the Manchurian Incident of 1931, Korea became an even more critical base for heavy industry development. They extracted Korea's large mineral reserves, including gold, silver, iron, lead and coal. As Korea became a critical base for Japan's continental expansion, communication and transportation related work expanded. The South Manchurian Railway Company, a state company set up in 1906, built many railroads, roads, telegraph and telephone lines. Thus the last fifteen years of Japanese rule witnessed the beginning of Korea's industrial revolution; the uprooting of the peasants from the land; the emergence of a working class; and urbanization accompanied by population mobility.

With the Sino-Japanese War in 1937, Japanese demands on Korea increased and the production of chemical, machine tool, and iron and steel industries was pushed a step further to meet the need for military supplies. The war also pressed Japan to mobilize human resources in Korea in order to establish "the New Order in East Asia." The Japanese collected data on labor resources — skilled workers, engineers, farmers, technicians, etc. — all to use according to Japan's priorities and needs. Hundreds of thousands of Koreans were mobilized to work in mines, factories, airports and dam construction sites, etc.

According to the Fact Finding Team for the Truth about Forced Korean Laborers, formed in 1972 jointly by Koreans in Japan and Japanese, "the forced drafting of Koreans was classified into the following categories: 'recruitment' (March 1939 - January 1942); 'government sponsored recruitment' (February 1942 -August 1944) and 'manpower requisition' (February 1944 - August, 1945)." The team further reported that "about 1.5 million were taken to Japan, 4.5 million were forcibly recruited in Korea and worked there, 330,000 were sent to Southeast Asian countries, and many were sent to Taiwan, Sakhalin, and Northeast China."[20] Estimates of the total number of laborers vary widely, the lowest figure being roughly 750,000. Generally, the Japanese government cites lower figures.

Included in Japan's labor mobilization were women. From the onset of colonization, Japan saw Korean women as easily exploitable and inexpensive labor. Japanese employers both in Japan and Korea actively recruited young Korean girls from rural areas for a variety of manufacturing jobs. Promises were made of secure jobs and good wages, but the female workers were paid only one quarter of what Japanese male workers received.[21] The mobilization of female labor was carried out mostly under the pretext of voluntary participation, force and well crafted lies. Countless women were drafted in the name of the *Kunro* (labor) or Yeoja (women) *Jungshindae*, meaning "Voluntarily Committing Body Corps for Labor," a Japanese coined term meaning devoting one's entire being to the cause of the Emperor. Numerous women who went under this voluntary work system were made sex slaves for Japanese soldiers at the comfort houses.

Origins of Comfort Houses: Why and How

The Imperial Government of Japan established comfort houses, and shipped girls and women like military supplies. The most often cited reasons for establishing comfort houses in official reports of the Japanese government are: 1)to prevent soldiers from raping local women and incurring local opposition; 2)to protect them from venereal disease and thereby avoiding the disablement of fighting men; and 3) to protect military secrets.

During the battle of Shanghai in 1932, following the invasion of Manchuria, Japanese soldiers committed brutal rapes and murders, provoking fierce anger among the civilian Chinese. Clearly, soldiers had raped local women long before then but from the diaries of Generals Okabe Naosaburo and Okamura Yasuji, both on the staff of the Shanghai Expeditionary Army, we learn that the two generals ordered the establishment of "army comfort houses" in Shanghai in March of that year.[22]

Following the second Sino-Japanese War of 1937, comfort houses were established rapidly in all war zones in China, especially after the infamous Nanjing massacre. After the outbreak of the Pacific War, the Southern Expeditionary Army issued orders to supply comfort women everywhere in Southeast Asia and the Pacific. The highest division (the staff division) of each expeditionary army (the operational army) ordered the establishment of comfort houses and each expeditionary army belonged directly to the Emperor.

The authorities considered it essential to supply sexual comfort to officers and soldiers for the war effort. In order to continue the war, they needed to keep the soldiers on the battlefields for long periods of time. They recognized the value of a leave system but rarely were the soldiers allowed to return home, even briefly. Soldiers suffered from a dreary as well as dangerous life in the battlefield. One military doctor, Lt. Hayao Torao, wrote, "there was no other measure than letting them embrace women."[23] The comfort women were not only to satisfy the momentary physical needs of the soldiers but also to provide their spiritual comfort.[24]

The soldiers' use of private brothels and the rape of local women made control of venereal disease difficult. Nearly every comfort woman testifies that medical examinations in the comfort stations were fairly routine. The venereal patients would endanger the fighting power. The soldiers were there to fight; the women were to help soldiers fight. Further, they did not want to see the Japanese soldiers return home and produce disease infected babies; the government was concerned about the future of the Japanese nation. However, based on testimony of former comfort women as well as some documents, nothing stopped the infections.

Finally, they were afraid that military secrets might leak out through "pillow talk."[25] *Kempei* (military police) watched military comfort houses closely, providing direction and control. The majority of the former comfort women testify that they were not allowed to leave the premises. I asked several of them if the soldiers and officers ever talked about the war and was repeatedly told "no." According to Grandma Hwang Keum Ju, it was out of the question that the soldiers would discuss the war; most of them didn't even reveal their name or rank.

According to official documents, including those cited above as well as those from the United States, the Netherlands, and Australia, military comfort houses existed in China, Hong Kong, Amoi, French Indochina, the Philippines, Malay, Singapore, British Borneo, Dutch East Indies, Burma, Thailand, East New Guinea in the Pacific Region, the Okinawan islands, the Ogasawara islands, the Chishima Archipelago, Sakhalin and Hokkaido. Comfort houses were established wherever the Japanese troops went, from the border of Siberia to equatorial New Guinea. Toward the end of the war, in anticipation of a decisive battle on the mainland, comfort houses were set up in Japan as well as in Korea.[26] No wonder that Japanese soldiers joked that on every battlefront women arrived with the ammunition. They were nothing more than the military supplies of the Emperor.

Recruitment: Who and How

It is impossible to determine the exact number of comfort women but estimates range from 100,000 to 200,000. It is also difficult to establish with any precision the nationalities of the women, but it is generally agreed that roughly 80 to 90% came from Korea, then a Japanese colony. Women were also recruited from Taiwan, yet another colony,[27] and other Japanese occupied territories such as China, the Philippines, and Indonesia. Some Dutch women in Indonesia served as comfort women. Japan attempted to force Australian nurses to serve as comfort women.[28]

In Korea, according to a former official of the Japanese colonial government, a Korean who does not want to be identified, the Japanese compiled detailed data on all available girls in every village, town, city and province and pursued them under the official pretense of *Kunro Jungshindae,* part of human resource mobilization by Japan for military purposes. People often called it "virgin recruitment," because efforts were made to take single girls, young and healthy. However, the government recruiters frequently altered the women's ages and snatched married women and even mothers if they could not meet quotas specified by their superiors. Official draft papers were not always presented. According to studies of fifty six women conducted by Professor Yun Chong-Ok, the average age at the time of recruitment was seventeen.[29]

Due to the lack of official documentation, it is difficult to provide complete information about the actual recruitment process, especially those who were not drafted under the pretext of *Jungshindae*. However, largely based on testimony of the victims, former soldiers and recruiters, we know that there were no clear procedures; deception, coercion and lying were common. Korean villages were raided frequently to seize women. Numerous Korean females, especially in rural areas, were vulnerable to promises of stable jobs and wages in urban areas and abroad. Frequently, young daughters of poor families were willing to work not only to help feed their poverty stricken families but also to support the education of their brothers. Government officials, often aided by the police, recruited girls and women. Japanese military officials employed traders[30] to recruit women directly or through intermediaries. Often, male members of the family sold young women, daughters and wives to brothels.

In some cases, especially toward the end of the war, schools were pressured to provide the girls. In 1997, I interviewed a Japanese woman in Tokyo, Ms. Ikeda Masae. In her seventies, her back slightly stooped but covered with a knapsack and her face still retaining a girlish charm, Ms. Ikeda rode the train for six hours from Nara to Tokyo to talk with me on camera. Polite to a fault, she relayed this story. "I was teaching sixth grade children at Housan National School in Seoul. The principal told us that in Japan even small kids were working to win the war. He said, 'Korean children also have to work. I have received a request from the Board of Education to send Korean children to Japanese military factories. We have to send female junior high school pupils and sixth grade students.' That was the command. Every day I tried to persuade girls to volunteer. The school principal asked me about volunteers every day, but he insisted that I not force them. I had to induce them to volunteer. By letting them apply for the job, the Japanese government and the Japanese Army could insist that they were volunteers. One day, five students volunteered to labor in Japan. I suspect that those who volunteered were forced to become comfort women." Ms. Ikeda's talk was a confession to absolve her sin. As she parted to catch her train, her eyes were filled with tears.

As early as 1938, a Japanese doctor, Aso Tetsuo, examined 80 Korean and 20 Japanese women. By his account, all of the Japanese women had been prostitutes, but the Koreans were virgins, thus fit to be gifts to the Emperor.[31] It is no wonder that in Korea in the 1940's, so many girls and women over the age of fourteen married almost anyone they could find in order to avoid virgin recruitment. It wasn't unusual that fifteen and sixteen year old girls married widowers twice their age with lots of children from previous marriages. This reduced the chances of their becoming the sexual prey.

Grandma Kim Bok Sun, a former comfort woman, told me how she was taken.[32]

"I was born in a family of three girls. My father disappeared when I was a baby. I don't remember him at all. Whenever I asked about my father, my mother told me that he had passed away but I heard later that he had just disappeared. I have no idea why but I think he abandoned us. My two older sisters went to live with my aunt, a well-to-do sister of my father and they married fairly young. So I was the only daughter left with my mother. She was good at sewing and she did that for a living. She even sent me to school for four years. We were inseparable and were happy together. But my mother died of uterine cancer when I was twelve years old.

"I was left all alone. By that time, my sisters had their own families to take care of and I didn't want to bother my aunt. So I went to a small village in Cholla Province where my uncle lived, my father's brother. From the time I was about fourteen, my uncle encouraged me to marry. I was fair skinned, tall and mature for my age. But I said, 'Well, I am too young to get married. I would like to live with you a bit longer.' But when I turned seventeen, my uncle told me, 'Well, well, I heard that the Japanese take away all the virgins, you know, the virgin recruitment. Many girls are taken away whether they want to go or not. No choice. You are a mature girl, already seventeen. You are a beautiful woman now. I know you are a prime candidate for this virgin recruitment. You must get married. They only take virgins, single girls.' So I had to say, 'I will get married, if that's the case.' What choice did I have? It was 1944.

"So, at his urging, I consented to be interviewed by this man. But I didn't like him at all. No feeling for him. I refused. They brought another man, a farmer. The same thing. I had no desire to marry. So I couldn't eat; I spent lots of time crying. My uncle then said, 'I can't force you to get married. You can wait a little longer.' Relieved, I felt like flying.

"Most farm houses had a small attic for storage. One day, my uncle came home and ordered me to hide in the attic. I had to obey. It was better than getting married. Once in a while, I came down to eat but spent most of my time in the attic. At night, I came down and slept. I did that for three weeks but no one came.

"One day, my aunt told me to come down for lunch. It was summer. We were having lunch on the open veranda. Suddenly, a Japanese policeman in a dark uniform, a long sword dangling at his side and accompanied by a Korean man, rushed up. The policeman sat on the edge of the veranda, exclaiming, 'Look, here is a girl, a pretty girl.' We stopped eating. My heart was beating hard and I was trembling all over.

"My uncle returned home. The Korean man said, 'If that girl goes to Osaka and works in a factory for only one year, she will be able to make lots of money. It will be good for all of you. She will be able to send you money every month.' 'No,' my uncle protested, 'she can't go anywhere. She has no parents and I am responsible for her. She is just about to marry, anyway.'

42

"With his eyeballs bulging, the Japanese pushed the Korean away. 'What are you talking about?' Then he kicked my uncle so hard that his body rolled across the yard. They grabbed me by force and I was dragged out of our yard. We rode a bus for two hours to Kwang Ju where I was taken to an inn. There were four other girls waiting. One of them just had a baby. Her breasts were dripping with milk."

Here is Grandma Kang Soon Ae's story.[33] "I was born in Tokyo, Japan. You see, my father had been recruited for labor and sent to Japan to work. I was so proud of my father; he was a self-educated, smart man. I remember my father telling me that he had mastered one thousand Chinese characters by the age of five. He was a skilled construction worker and a surveyor but in Japan, he had to do so many different things—worked in a mine, built bridges, you name it. As I remember those days, I remember hunger and forever packing worn out quilts, you see, we moved around so much. We moved so many times a year that I could hardly keep track of where we had been. As a little girl, I used to watch the Japanese kids eating food. You can't imagine what it felt like to watch them eat . . . My mouth watered and it felt as if all my intestines were dried up and stuck together. I cried all the time; there was nothing else I could do, I was so hungry. My father used to wipe my tears and say, 'Wait a bit longer. One of these days, I will be able to provide all the food your little belly can hold. But you know, he died young because he was beaten so much. He was thrown into jail so often, it felt as if jail was his home. You see, my father was a proud man; he could not tolerate injustice and unfairness. When I was 12, after my father died, my family came back to Korea and settled in Masan, a southern port city. But the starvation continued. In fact, I don't remember when I wasn't hungry growing up.

"When I was fourteen, news abounded that the Japanese were drafting virgins. In desperation, I wore a married woman's hairdo, you know, hair all gathered at the back, and held together by a long pin called *pinyo*. I also stayed home. In those days, food was rationed once a month at a designated place. When my grandmother went to get the rationed supplies, she was sent back empty handed. In order to receive the goods, we were forced to sing the Japanese anthem, *Kimi ga yo*. My grandmother didn't know the words.

"I decided to go and sing *Kimi ga yo*. I was given more rice than the usual amount. They also gave me two pairs of rubber shoes. One I gave to my grandmother and the other to my younger sister. Shortly after that, I was taken to comfort the Imperial soldiers."

While virgin recruitment was more common among the poor and uneducated, it knew few boundaries. Professor Yun Chong-Ok often explains why she became a pioneer researcher and activist for comfort women issues. "In December 1943, when I was a freshman at Ewha Women's University, the entire Korean peninsula was stirred up by Japan's draft of single women for the war effort. Frightened, many students quit school in order to get married in a hurry. Desperate to prevent a mass exit of students, school officials announced, 'The school will take full responsibility on this matter. No student will be drafted.' Not long after that, however, we had to sign a document declaring that we, the students, would cooperate in this effort to mobilize human resources for the war. Personally, I narrowly escaped the fate of joining hundreds and thousands of sexual slaves because my parents persuaded me to quit school."

Many girls/women were cheated or coerced by military purveyers. Private operators with permits and instructions issued by the military, often came to Korea and recruited comfort women on their own and/or with the help of the military and police. In many cases, Koreans collaborated with the Japanese.

Grandma Lee Yong Nyeu who was born in 1926 in Yeu Ju, Kyunggi province, told me how she was talked into going.[34] "I come from a family of five children. Our life was unbearably poor. In our farming village, I didn't know any one who wasn't poor; it seemed everybody was poor. All the rice we grew, the Japanese took. Not just the rice, though, even the brassware in which we put rice. We were all hungry. I had an older brother and I was the second child. We were so poor that from the time I was eight, I had to do all sorts of work to help my family. In desperation, our family moved to Seoul when I was eleven, looking for work. No such luck. I did anything and everything I could to earn a few pennies for my family. We starved more than we ate.

"Then, I started to work for a family as a live-in maid. When I was sixteen, a woman came and said that she had wonderful information for me. The Japanese were looking for young girls who could be trained to work as nurses. She said that once we started working as nurses, we would be fed well and earn lots of money. Well, it was the heaven sent opportunity that I had been waiting for. There were about fifty girls like me who gathered at a Chinese restaurant. They fed us Chinese food. I still remember what I ate. Sweet and sour seafood. The very first time I had put such food in my mouth. Even now, my mouth waters when I think of it. Then, they took us to the Seoul train station and we went to Pusan where we stayed about a week. You cannot imagine how happy I was. Imagine being happy?! This bubbly girl, finally given some hope of putting food into my mouth and helping my starving family! Had no inkling about the fate awaiting me. Do you know that I persuaded two of my best friends to go with me? We ended up in Langoon, Burma and became sex slaves for Japanese soldiers! One of the two girls disappeared. Till this day I don't know what happened to her. Imagine she went because of me!"

Asked how she felt about the Japanese who put her into that fate, she said, "You must remember: the one who took us there was not a Japanese; it was a

Korean man. Some Koreans must share the responsibility. So even now, we demand that the Korean government also look into this issue."

Grandma Ha Gun Ja whom I met in Wuhan China said, wiping tears with her fist, "When I was seventeen, you know, at the time Korea was in such a pitiful state because of the Japanese. They took us to Kyung Sung (Seoul). They told us we would go to Manchuria and earn lots of money. Work in a factory. That's how I came. What could I do? I couldn't go back. Japanese made us sell our bodies." Grandma Hong blurted out in halting Korean, "When I came to China, my mother couldn't walk. After a baby, my kid brother, no walk. No money at home. So I came to earn money. But the Japanese came and sold my body. No money, they didn't give me money!"

Then, there is Grandma Shim Mi Ja whose life was ruined by cherry blossoms. "When I was in the fifth grade, my teacher visited our house and saw a Korean map on which a Rose of Sharon[35] was embroidered. She praised my talent and asked if I would embroider flowers on a map of Japan. I talked with my mother and we decided that morning glories would be better than cherry blossoms. It took me a long time to finish it because I was careful with every stitch.

"The teacher hung the Japanese map with morning glories on the wall of the huge room shared by all the teachers. One day, I was called to the principal's office. A Japanese policeman was waiting for me. He asked, "why did you embroider morning glories instead of cherry blossoms?' 'Because morning glories are very beautiful,' I replied. Ignoring my answer, he repeated the same question. Angry and provoked, I said, 'I did it because I want Japan to perish just like morning glories fade in the evening.'

"He took me to the police station. All the way to the station, he yelled that my spirit was corrupt and that my thinking was rotten just like my father's. You see, my father was always away. I had no idea where he was; I was only told that he was fighting for the independence of our country. The officer took me to a room where policemen stayed at night and he rolled my skirt up. Instinctively, I bit his ear. He tortured me with electricity, thrust bamboo needles under my finger nails, and pressed a hot iron on my shoulder and neck. I passed out. When I woke up, I was in Hukuoka, Japan. Cherry blossoms took my life away."[36]

I met Grandma Chung Seo Woon in 1995 at the NGO Forum on Women in China held in conjunction with the Fourth World Conference on Women. She had this story to tell. "I was born as the only daughter without sons in the family of a wealthy landowner in southern Korea. I know that the majority of the women who suffered my fate came from poor and uneducated families but I was a protected child of a well-to-do family.[37] In those days, the Japanese took all of our brassware to use for the war, for weapons, etc. My father dug a deep hole in our rice field and buried all of our brassware. He said that it wasn't because we had such an attachment to them but he was opposed in principle to contributing to the Japanese war effort. One day the police came and took my father away. I learned that the police took him to the hiding place and made him dig it up. When they found all that brassware, they kicked and beat him. I don't know how they found out about it. My father was put into prison. We asked to see my father every day but each time we were refused. One day, however, the president of the neighborhood association (*Ijang*) came and asked if I wanted to visit my father in the prison.

"When my father saw me coming to his prison cell, he almost fainted. Gathering himself, he said, 'You should never have come here. This is not a place for a girl like you. Please don't come back at all and you must promise me never to tell your mother what you saw today.' I stood there with tears streaming down my cheeks. My father looked so frail; he looked as if I could blow him away. Going closer to him, I grabbed his hands but he groaned. Frightened, I pulled away, and saw his hands covered with bandages. 'I didn't realize. . . What happened to your hands?' I saw blood marks on his finger tips. I begged him to tell me what happened to him. 'They pulled all my fingernails,' he said, 'Also my toenails.' 'Do they torture you every day like this? What else did they do to you?' 'You don't want to know and you should not trouble yourself anymore. I wish you hadn't come but don't tell your mother.' 'Is it because of the brassware?' I asked. 'It is more than that but I can't tell you. Please go back and take good care of your mother.'

"My feet would not move but I had to leave him there in that horrible prison cell. Then, *Ijang* came to our house. 'You could work on the thousand stitch belts in Japan for two years. If you go there, I will see to it that your father is released from prison. Immediately after you leave, he will be released.' After seeing my father, I didn't think I had a choice; I was only glad that I could do something to save my father.

"My mother was horrified. She said I couldn't go. She pleaded and begged. 'You are the only one I have left. How do you expect that I can live if you also leave me? Besides, you are only fifteen and you have never been anywhere. Two years in a Japanese factory! It's unthinkable.' Of course, she didn't know the true state of my father. It was bad enough to leave but to persuade my mother was something else. Finally, resigned to the situation, my mother quietly packed my clothes made of fine materials, occasionally stopping to wipe her tears and pointing to some as special items she had prepared for my wedding someday. I can't tell you how I felt when I followed *Ijang*, leaving my mother behind. Every step away from home was prompted by the image of my father, especially the bandaged hands and feet. His pain was mine; we were so close. Even if I were a girl, I was the only child. I was my father's baby. This stubborn man whose facade was as stern as rock had unlimited tender love for me.

"Of course, you can guess the rest of my story. My father was never released from the prison and I ended up being a sex slave for Japanese soldiers for seven years in Semarang, Indonesia."[38]

Grandma Song Shin Do, the only former Korean comfort woman living in Japan suing the Japanese government, lives in the country, about a day's journey by train from Tokyo. In 1995 I talked to her for a couple of hours in a Tokyo inn where she was brought to appear in court. A woman of laughter that rang out, with her body as sturdy as a tree trunk, she was at once reliable and intimidating. Putting down my recorder carefully in front of her, I said, "Grandma, please tell me where you were born, how you were brought up, what you remember about your mother. . . "I never think of my mother." Her reaction was swift and sharp. Startled by the force of her reaction, I looked up with my eyes saying, "Why?" "I hate my mother. She was a mean woman. I don't ever want to think about her.

"I was born in a rural village in Choong Chung province in southern Korea. My father died when he was fifty two years old. I was only twelve. He left a will about Shin Do, that's me, to my mother. He told her, 'Once a daughter is married, she becomes an outsider. Don't make Shin Do an outsider too soon. Keep her at home until at least she is twenty.' You know, my father used carry me on his back, wrapped in a soft quilt until I was seven years old. I was his favorite child. But my mother couldn't stand me.

"Even before the three year mourning period for my father was over, my mother fell for some fellow and she wanted to get rid of me and my younger sister. She wanted to marry us off. She didn't care about my father's will. She went ahead and forced me to marry when I was sixteen. You wouldn't believe this but I had no inkling about what marriage was all about. I remember asking my mother about it. Most of the time, she ignored me, calling me names, "stupid," "naive," whatnot. Other times, she said, 'it is something where you do exactly as you are told by your husband.'

"On the first night, this man, supposedly my husband, looking like somebody who would steal someone's fire (when I went back to film her, she described him as someone who would steal cows), told me to take off my clothes. When only a slip was covering my body, he knocked me down, got on top of me and started being weird. He said, 'Let's do it.' Whatever it was, I knew I didn't want to do it. I pushed him and quickly told him that I had to go to the toilet. With the thin slip covering my naked body, I ran through the rice paddies, listening to the soulful cries of the frogs. When I reached home, I was afraid to go in. I stood in front of the door a while. My younger sister came out and finding me, her eyes rolled. 'What are you doing here? You should be with your husband.' She said that I could not come in but brought me her clothes. I put them on, went to the kitchen, got on the clay kitchen counter by the big rice pot.[39] The counter was still warm. Can you imagine what it was like when my mother found me? She grabbed a wooden stick we used to pound the laundry and tried to beat me, screaming and yelling. I ran away.

"I had no place to go. I had several cousins but I knew I would not be welcome. I did odds and ends and wandered around. One day, I met a well-dressed woman from Pyong Yang who told me how I could get away from my miserable life and make some money fast. That's how I ended up being a sex slave for countless Japanese military men for seven years in China. I was sixteen."[40]

In the summer of 1995, I went to interview Yoshida Seiji, former chief of the National Service Labor Recruitment in Shimonoseki, in the office of attorney Takagi Ken'ichi. In 1983, he became the first Japanese recruiter to confess publicly and apologize to Koreans. A slender man, looking nervous, he informed me that he did not care to talk about the comfort women in detail. He explained, "You know some people are skeptical regarding what I had said about my helping to forcibly draft Korean women on Cheju island, providing trucks and soldiers from Army headquarters. But I want you to know that I stand by what I said. Even now, my life is threatened by some Japanese; they think I betrayed my motherland, Japan. Under the circumstances, why would I make up a story? When the Japanese mass media sided with my accusers without hearing my side of the story, I was so disappointed. Some Japanese Americans in the United States are concerned about my life. They are trying to help me move to the United States. I intend to arrange a press conference and tell my story all at once. I will invite you to come then. In the meantime, it will do you good if you looked into papers in the United States Archives. At the moment, you can learn more from them than from anything the Japanese can offer." Then, he compared the mind set of the Japanese during the war with those of a modern day cult. "You will not be able to understand what went on at that time anymore than you can understand those tightly knit cults. If you are inside, everything makes sense but from outside, no way to comprehend." "At that time all Japanese thought alike, listened to the same things, read the same newspapers and received the same kind of education. The War propaganda. Labor was needed for the war. At the time when I was recruiting laborers and comfort women, what I did was right; that's what I believed. It was long after the war that it hit me how wrong I was. But even now, there is something like a neo-Nazi mentality in Japan, very strong. That's why my life is in danger."

In his book, *Chosun Yeoja Jungshindae*, (Korean Women Voluntarily Committing Body Corps for Labor, published in 1992), Yoshida Seiji relays his experience recruiting comfort women. The Korean labor draft was regularly referred to as "Korean hunting." The Japanese literally hunted Koreans like animals — from the toilets, beds, rice fields and closets, anywhere they could find them. Once ordered to draft 100 Korean women in Japan to be sent

48

to Singapore, Yoshida decided to recruit, rather than "hunt." He crafted lies, selling points, that would be attractive to potential candidates: 1) location, close to Korea; 2) wages, high; and 3) nature of the work, an army hospital. Immediately hooked by these lies, one 50-year-old Korean woman volunteered to go. "No, you can't go," he said. "Why not? I am a good worker. You will see. I could work twice as well as any of those young women you chose." "But you are over 35. I can't take you." Persisting, the woman said, "In that case, take my daughter. She is only sixteen, but like me, she is a strong worker." They took the daughter. A sad story of deception and also a prime example of crossing from recruitment to cheating, anything that works![41]

In sum, the Japanese military was involved directly in recruiting, coercing, and abducting women for sex slavery. Normally, this took the form of orders and instructions from the military, often through the military police. If the officials, military or police, were not directly carrying out the task, it was given to the local leaders and/or traders. These people worked together, sometimes individually and at other times collaboratively, but always under a keen military eye. Comfort women came largely from the colonies and the occupied territories, the majority with no prior record of prostitution. The Japanese military never proposed using Japanese women other than known prostitutes.

Chapter 3

SLAVES OF SEX

Life in Comfort Houses

There were three types of comfort houses or stations: 1) military; 2) private houses regulated by the military and open only to the military and its civilian employees; and 3) houses open to ordinary citizens with priority given to soldiers. The Japanese government was directly responsible for the first and second types. Responsibility in the third type depended upon the extent and the scope of use by the military. The second type was the most common. Usually, the military provided the accommodations and posted detailed regulations for soldiers, traders and women. "Comfort House Regulations" specified who could visit, the schedule, fees, and rules regarding disease prevention.[42]

Comfort houses under direct control were located within the military compound and the accommodations were shabby. The size of each room was usually five to seven square meters, hardly enough space to walk around after allowing for the bedding. In some instances, comfort houses were newly built. Mr. Kawakubo Toshio, a former Japanese soldier, told me in 1995 that he was ordered to build mobile barracks that followed the soldiers on the front lines, much like a MASH unit. Tents were used as well as shelters and trenches. Grandma Song Shin Do told me how the soldiers forced sex in the shelters during the air raids and, when they were moved with the troops, in the trenches!

Most private comfort houses were set up in facilities confiscated by the military or abandoned by civilians, including hotels, houses, shops, restaurants, schools, churches and public halls. Spaces were often divided by plywood into small rooms with blankets as doors. Those not run directly by the military were managed by traders under supervision of the military, observing the same regulations. They enforced the regulations through manipulation and force.

None of the women seemed to have known what their destination was; they might as well have been blind folded. The women I interviewed all found themselves in a strange land surrounded by alien faces and languages. Moon Pil Ki, a grandma I interviewed in Seoul Korea (in 1995) said, "I had no idea where we were going. Wherever it was, when we arrived at our destination, it was pitch dark, the middle of the night. I couldn't see anything and I wasn't going to ask anyone where it was, either. I didn't want to be beaten ."[43]

On camera, in 1997, Mr. Kawakubo Toshio told me how he transported comfort women. "When we were drafted by cheap post card, we had no choice but to go to the front since everything was the Emperor's order. I was an interpreter and information agent in the 24th Regiment. At that time I was stationed at Shogun military base. I brought Korean comfort women by truck to the base. The Japanese soldiers greeted these women with 'Banzai! Banzai'."

The comfort houses were virtual prisons. They were watched closely, with every precaution taken to prevent women from escaping or leaking military secrets. Comfort houses could turn into battlegrounds at anytime depending on the war situation. It was virtually impossible for the women to escape, not knowing where they were or where to go. Still, they were watched twenty-four hours a day by guards standing at the exits and by military police who patrolled and supervised. They were normally not allowed to go anywhere except to hospitals for medical check-ups.

In some places, the women were allowed to take walks during designated hours, within restricted areas. The soldiers were forbidden to take these women outside without permission. Sometimes, officers took them out in their cars and some were allowed to go shopping as a group for basic necessities but never alone. Most of them say that they had no energy or desire to go anywhere.[44]

Visiting times and fees varied according to military rank and location. Usually, morning to early evening was reserved for enlisted men; a couple of hours in the early evening for high ranking civilian military employees and then nights for officers. Frequently, officers were allowed to stay overnight.

Quite a few women told me that they preferred dealing with soldiers because they were quick but the officers often stayed all night with cruel as well as weird demands! Grandma Bae Jok Gan had this to tell me. "The soldiers just went bang, bang. Many ejaculated even before that thing went inside of me but the officers, I hated them. The things they made me do I wanted to evaporate, just disappear." Grandma Chung Seo Woon relayed her experience. "The soldiers had to return to their quarters by 8:30 p.m. Then, officers came. In comparison with them, the soldiers were harmless. Because there were always lines outside the door and because they were not given much time, the soldiers had to hurry and go, but the officers—they were something else. They had more time, and those high ranking ones, they could stay overnight. They demanded such unspeakable things! When I didn't obey them, many of them took out swords, threatened me, and used them on my body. When they did, they made sure that I bled. Did you know that the Japanese believed that once the sword was out, unless it sees blood, it would not fit back into its case? Such strange people. . . To this day there are so many scars on my body from sword wounds."

Nothing could stop them. All of the grandmas told me in detail how they had to receive the soldiers even while they were menstruating. Many of these women with their bottoms drenched with blood half of the time didn't know from where and why the blood was coming. Holidays were virtually non-existent. Grandma Hong in Wuhan said, "I hurt, I bled. But still had to sell my body. One came, another came. I cried, cried so much. I was young, so young. If I cry, they say, 'why you cry?' then beat me to sell my body. Can't tell you all—the hardships. When I think of it, Japan compensate. Do you know what 'compensation' is?"" Grandma Ha chimed in, "They came even when blood came out. Hurt so much down there. When I peed, it hurt. Even when I peed in the toilet, they came and ordered me to hurry, to come out quickly. Can't tell you all. No way."

How many soldiers did they have to comfort a day? Almost every woman tells the story of soldiers' lining up in front of their rooms, often yelling, *Hayaku, Hayaku* (hurry up, hurry up). Grandma Moon Pil Ki said to me, "I was just lying there like a piece of wood. I hardly noticed any of their faces. They just came in one after another and did their thing." Does it matter if we know exact numbers? Many scholars took a great deal of care to determine the numbers, but it is impossible to be precise. Suffice it to say that anywhere between 20 to 40 men, some days more — Grandma Chung cited 100 on week-ends — violated these women.

Mr. Kawakubo, a former soldier discussed above, explained what happened after he brought the women to the base. "Four or five went to the high ranking officers. The rest went to a shack. It was divided into sections. You rolled down the partition and could see the other side. They spread one or two blankets and the women went in. Ten or twenty soldiers lined up and one after another, they had sex. It was not human. It was like sex among beasts."

The harsh life in the comfort houses extended beyond beastial sex. Regulations prohibited drinking. They also banned violence, especially drunken violence. However, many relate stories of cruelty and brutality. The women were not only the objects of sexual desire but objects to be thrown around, kicked, tortured and discarded out of anger, fear, sorrow and the crazed attempt to forget the war. According to these women, beating and cursing were routine, with soldiers often drawing bayonets. The women were not equipped with the language skills to express themselves. They were not allowed to speak in their native tongue. They were beaten for speaking Korean and for not understanding Japanese. Each of them was given a

Japanese name but frequently they were simply identified by their room number.

Talking about the private houses, some report that the managers were brutal, but the soldiers were not. Grandma Lee Young Sook who was taken to Taiwan told me: "The Japanese owner was really cruel. He beat and kicked us all the time—when we failed medical inspections and when we didn't earn enough money. So much so that I was used to his beatings. But not the soldiers. In fact, they were kind and protective. No reason for them to be cruel to us. They were thankful that we did that for them."[45] On the other hand, Grandma Park Oak Yeun boasted that she was never reprimanded or beaten by the manager. "It all depended on you. The women who were drunk and did bad things were beaten sometimes but not me." Grandma Lee Yong Nyeu said, "In the middle of all that hardship, I could not eat. And I was grief stricken with the thought that I would never be able to step on the land of my birth. I had a nervous breakdown, you know, I became crazy. For almost six months, I was a woman without a mind, just staring outside . . . There was this kind Japanese who came to me and took care of me. He didn't even tell me his name but he was so kind to me. He was an army doctor and he is the one who nursed me back to health."

The fee system varied but regulations indicate that the visitors were supposed to pay according to their rank. The accounts I was given by the grandmas vary: most didn't know anything about fees; they didn't and couldn't think about that; they received military currency; handed over the fee to the managers and never saw it again; or were told that the money was saved by the managers. Some grandmas told me that the account book was lost and others said it was stolen.

Civilian traders/managers were experts in selling women's bodies and masterfully insuring that the women incurred debts in advance. They added every conceivable item of expense to the long and growing lists of debt: travel costs (which were in fact military expenses); clothes, cosmetics, food, etc. Grandma Song Shin Do told me, "What's the use of talking about money? Everything was charged as debt. The food I ate from the time they brought me from Korea to Wuchang, China, the kimonos and dresses they wanted me to wear for my 'work,' and anything and everything. As long as I owed the trader money, he took sixty percent of my earnings. Did I keep my forty percent? How could I? I had to use it to pay my debts. During my seven years of that horrible life, I was free of debt only a short while toward the end. Even then, my manger took some of my money and said that it was used for a 'defense contribution'." Even before the forced sale of their bodies, these women were deep in debt, often without their knowing it. Under the traders' methods, money disappeared before it was in the hands of these women.

The mangers used force when they didn't see enough money for themselves. Grandma Moon Pil Ki told me, "My owner posted a big chart on the wall. He used red ink to draw lines. The more soldiers one accepted, the higher the lines went up. Mine always went down. I was not strong. I could not deal with too many of them. Oh, he used to get furious with me. He often made me stand barefoot on the frozen ground for a long time. Whenever it gets cold, I still suffer from frostbite after all these years." She went on telling me how cruel the soldiers were. "Once a soldier came in and, after he had done that, he attacked me again. I felt so much pain down there that I pushed him away. So he became like a mad dog, drew his bayonet and struck my naked body but that didn't satisfy him. He went outside, grabbed a burning coal and burned me. It took more than three months for the wound to heal but did they leave me alone until it was healed? No way. How can I describe what they did to me? You know, I still have nightmares. Tonight, after you are gone, I will not be able to sleep. I will be chased by the images and voices of my past."

There were undoubtedly cases in which a manager in fact kept their money in good faith. I talked with Grant Hirabayashi, a Japanese American currently living in Silver Spring, Maryland, who served as a U.S. Army interpreter in Burma. When Myitkyina, Burma fell on 3 August, 1944 to the army led by General Joseph S. Stilwell, they found some twenty girls still there. "I don't know how many had been there. I am pretty sure that some of them tried to raft down the Irrawaddy and were killed by Allied marksmen and by fleeing Japanese troops. Anyway, when those girls were picked up by our forces, someone called me and said that there were a 'bunch of girls.' That excited many Chinese and American soldiers who had not seen a woman for quite some time. But the military police quickly separated them from other prisoners of the war and put them in tents inside guarded barbed wire, which made me think of my parents in the internment camp in the United States.

"I was called in to interpret and interrogate. Though dressed in baggy pants and shapeless tops, many in fear, anxiety and bewilderment, they were quite good looking and some really pretty. An elderly woman wearing a traditional Japanese kimono was with them. I spoke with the *Mama-san* who translated into Korean. As far as I could tell, all of them were Korean including the Mama-san.[46] She spoke Japanese with me but it was heavily accented.

"I noticed that the elderly woman's *obi* (the traditional sash) was full as if she were pregnant but I knew that she wasn't. She was too old. I cautiously asked her to unwind the *obi* which she did and out came neatly wrapped bundles of paper currency. She explained that she kept all the girls' money on her person for safe keeping. I picked up a bundle. The bills were still warm but they were Japanese scrip, military issued currency. I felt such pain to see the anxious faces of the *Mama-san* and the girls. I spoke to the woman as gently as I could, 'Because the Japanese were defeated, this is worthless.' I can't possibly describe the total disbelief slowly turning into despair on their faces."

In addition, a few women told me that they were able to hide a little money given to them as tips and/or gifts by the soldiers and officers. In most cases, however, it is clear that the women ended up with no money. A former soldier, Tokuda Masanori telling me on camera at Yasukuni Jinja in 1997 did not agree. "I can completely deny recent reports that comfort women were forced to work for the Imperial Army. Because women could earn more in war zones than in their home towns, there were many applications to work near the front lines. Thus the Imperial Army set up the limited terms for the women, and after their terms were up, they had to go back to their hometowns. The comfort women working at the front could live more extravagantly than Japanese. There was no discrimination against Korean or Taiwanese comfort women. They were Japanese nationals at that time. It was nonsense to discriminate against them. Korean and Japanese comfort women were all equal." Off camera, he explained how, compared to poor Japanese farmers like his family, comfort women enjoyed more affluent lives and how some of those women whose terms were over wanted to stay longer. Professor Fujioka Nobukatsu also had this to say, "The price of a woman was a third of a soldier's monthly pay. So they could not frequent comfort centers. They saved money for many months, and then used those places."

According to Regulations, examinations for venereal disease were required.[47] All bear witness that they were examined fairly regularly. When there were not enough military doctors to go around, corpsmen conducted the examinations. The frequency varied according to the region. The soldiers were supposed to wear condoms. Sometimes they brought condoms with them; other times, the women provided them. Many soldiers asked the women to put condoms on for them. "I felt so humiliated!" said one grandma to me. When supplies of condoms were short, the women had to wash them. Grandma Kim Bok Sun told me that it was when she washed the condoms that her life hit the bottom. Sadness and despair seeped through every cell of her body and she couldn't even cry. Others thought that they might not have to accept the soldiers if they ran out of condoms. So they threw them away. The result? Venereal disease! The women were ordered to clean themselves, often with salt water. Moon Pil Ki said, "After each intercourse, I washed myself. After a while, I didn't know if it was my body. It was just flesh with no feeling."

Despite the check-ups and wash-ups, venereal disease was not easily suppressed. The women were infected by soldiers and the soldiers got it from the women. All testified that whenever there was a sign of infection, they were given shots called 606.[48] Further, when women reported that the pain was too much for them to continue their work, they were given drugs and shots. Many of them were given opium and they took it without knowing what it was. Two grandmas told me that they did not know that they were drug addicts until after the war.

Grandma Chung Seo Woon had this story to tell. "Much of the time, both my body and spirit felt numb but when the bodily pain became unbearable, I screamed. Then, they would give me shots; sometimes several times a day. Each time the shot soothed my pain and I was again under those soldiers. I didn't know it then but they made me an opium junkie.

"When I returned home, our house was full of dust and spider webs, completely deserted. The neighbors came with brooms and cleaned the house. They told me about my parents. My father was never released; he died in prison. The Japanese had come to the house and tried to rape my mother. Humiliated, she killed herself. Then, the Japanese took the house and used it to entertain important visitors from Japan.

"You know, we die once, only once. It matters how we die. I was immensely proud of the way my parents died. The Japanese took our country away but they could not take the spirit of my parents. The Japanese defiled my body through and through but not my spirit. I locked up the house and decided to get rid of the opium addiction. It was my personal battle to regain my dignity as a Korean woman, as a human being. I gnashed my teeth so much that my gums bled and I could not eat. I crawled around the room, ripping off the floor paper until only the mud underneath showed. Then, I dug the mud. I chewed off all my fingernails. It was a desperate scream to be free of the opium and to be human. It took me seven months to get rid of it."

Infected women were usually segregated and treated. If cured, they were brought back. When the women's bodies became unsalvageable, they disappeared. Clearly, many women became pregnant but often they did not realize it. Strong shots like 606 was so toxic that it caused miscarriages without the women knowing it. Grandma Hwang told me that it was only when she was pregnant for the third time, four months, that she realized that she had been pregnant twice before. Grandma Chung Seo Woon, however, in Bejiing confided in me, "Those women who talk about pregnancy are telling lies. They could not have been." Puzzled, I said, "What do you mean?" Then she told me what happened to her and other girls when they reached Jakarta after sailing from Japan to Taiwan, Canton, Thailand, Singapore, and Saigon. "In Jarkarta, twenty three of us were ordered to get off. There I saw a sign, 'Army Hospital.' Nowadays it would be called the gynecology department. Whatever they did to it, my belly felt pulled and torn apart. The pain I felt then, I can't tell you. On the ship, I had my first period. In my whole life I had just one period. I believe they did something to prevent pregnancy. All twenty three of us were the same. They also did not menstrate after that." When I told her that not all other grandmas have the same experience, she nodded but her expression remained skeptical. When women became pregnant and when miscarriages didn't happen, fetuses were aborted. If the babies were born, they were taken away.

As I was putting my recorder away, I asked Grandma Song Shin Do, "If you had children of your own, what would you like to tell them about all this?" "If I had children of my own?" Her eyes wandered out of the room and I knew she was oblivious of my presence. I sat quietly waiting for her to come back from wherever she was in time and space. "You know, I did have babies. Three of them. Actually, I could have had four but one of them died in my womb. You know, even while you were pregnant and your stomach looked like a mountain, they told us to do that thing. They were all over you, crushing and banging you. One baby died before it saw the world. The rest, three, they were all taken from me and given away. I don't know where they are."

In 1997, when I went to her house for my documentary, she told me about the dead baby. "In China when I was about twenty, a baby got into me. I didn't know. The baby died in my belly. The dead baby wouldn't come out easily. I was hungry. So I ate a couple of bowls of seaweed soup and I put my own hand inside and pulled it out. The baby was dead. I went to the mountain, dug a grave and buried the baby myself." After this story, she fed her birds. I asked, "Grandma, why do you raise birds?" "Because I don't have kids. They are like my kids."

Was there life outside the bedroom? I asked them. Hardly. "We could not seek pleasures even with eating. Half of the time, we were starved," said one. Meals consisted usually of some rice, soup (bean sprouts or other vegetables) and a couple of other vegetables such as pickled turnips and radishes. Even then, the food supply was always short. So they could rarely fill their stomachs. Grandma Park Oak Yeun, who was at Rabaul, told me that they had to live without rice for days every time the military supply ship was sunk by air raids. Often she gave her cigarettes to the islanders who came to do household chores in exchange for bananas and papayas. Frequently, skipping meals was used as a form of punishment. During my production trip in 1997, Grandma Hwang Keum Ju told me about how she ate human flesh. "I bet I was the only one of the women of the 160 who registered as former comfort women in South Korea who has eaten human flesh. When they were cooking, I went there and asked for some more. The person who cooked hit me head-splittingly hard with a soup spoon and said, 'Do you know what this is?'"

In the military run comfort houses, these women usually ate with the soldiers. However, whenever they had time free from the soldiers, many were forced to cook and do the laundry. Grandma Song Shin Do said, "Sometimes when the soldiers were all out on the battlefield, we had to wear their uniforms, hat and all, and guard the place. They taught us how to use rifles and swords in case we saw the enemy." Another grandma reported, "We were slaves, not only for sex but for other things as well."

Of the women I interviewed, the length of time they served varied from two months to seven years. According to Prof. Yun's study of fifty six women, most of them stayed two to four years. Rarely were they able to return home before the defeat of Japan in August 1945. I did meet two grandmas who were sent home before the end of war. Grandma Kim Sun Duk, one of the two, told me how it was possible for her.[49]

"I was taken to Shanghai, China when I was seventeen under the pretext of 'virgin recruitment.' A high ranking Japanese officer, actually a general, (I think he had five stars) liked me and often sent for me. A person of his stature did not come to the comfort house. He was about fifty years old. I was infected with venereal disease and bled severely. Once he sent for me from Nanjing. There, I confided in him that four other women and I wanted to die and often discussed whether we should jump from a cliff or hang ourselves. He said, 'No, no. You should never kill yourself. I will help you and your friends to return home so that you can treat your disease there.' He handed me a long letter and other official documents which we used to get on a ship and then a train. That's how we came back to Korea before the end of the war."

I saw this beautiful grandma again. Asked what she would like to be if she were reborn, she said, "I would like to be born as a male." Taken aback, I asked, "Why?" "I would like to become a soldier and defend my country. So no one, no country would take away our country like the Japanese did."

Life After Comfort Houses

Most of these women were released in August 1945. Nearly all learned accidentally that the war had ended. I asked Grandma Moon Pil Gi what she thought when Korea became independent. "I had no inkling of what was going on, especially about Japan's defeat. For three days, no soldiers came. On the third night, I felt scared and spooky. I moved into the room of an older woman and we slept there. In the morning, we woke up to the sounds of a strange language. It was Russian. We saw Russian soldiers. 'Oh, my, first it was Japanese. Now it is Russians!' we said to each other. Sure enough, a couple of them snatched our watches and tried to get on top of us. I don't know where the strength came from but we pushed them away and ran.

"In desperation, we ran to a house somewhere. It belonged to a Chinese family. There was a Chinese grandma, a kind woman. She explained that the Russians had come and it would be best if we ran away as soon and as fast as we could. She warned us that if we were caught by the Russians, we would have to serve them. You want to know how I understood Chinese? Don't forget we had been there for three years. And our cleaning person was Chinese. Of course, we understood some rudimentary Chinese!

"We left the house and walked without knowing where we were headed. Soon we joined a huge throng walking back to Korea. I was nineteen. Did I feel happy that Korea had become independent? I had no feelings. I knew nothing. On the way, we met a kind Korean men who helped us cross a stream on his back, get food and other things. When we finally reached Shin Ue Ju, a city in northern Korea, close to the Chinese border, the older woman whom I called sister and I had to part.

"So I followed the Korean men who were also headed south. When we reached the Seoul train station, we were given a ball of rice, the size of a fist, rolled in sesame seeds and salt. Until this day, I can almost savor the taste of that in my mouth. It melted in my mouth, so delicious. Then, someone gave me a train ticket to go home further south. That's how I went back home."

Grandma Lee Yong Nyeu had this to tell. "One day, I remember being ordered to come outside to take a look at something. There was this white thing lying on the ground. I went closer. It was a dead man, a corpse, with all the blood drained and the body looking so white. It was a white man. The Japanese soldier said, 'you had not seen a dead white man, had you?' He laughed with all of his teeth showing. Shortly after that incident, the war ended.

"When I got off the ship in Inchon harbor, they gave me some money. I don't remember how much it was. By the time I arrived at the Seoul train station, it was night —dark. No way I could try to find my home. I spent a night in a cheap inn near the station and the next day I went to look for my family, the last place they had been. But there was no one. Not a trace of my family. After all, I had been gone for five years.

"Our house was on top of a hill. I remembered a small Mom and Pop shop near our house with candies, and few items of groceries, bean sprouts, bean curds, you know. I used to go there, begging him to give me some groceries on credit. I found the shop; it was still there at the same spot. The owner saw me, and almost fainted. He took me to my older brother's place. My sister-in-law was dismayed to see me. She believed that I was dead. For sure, she was not happy to see me alive. There was no way I could stay at my brother's place. So I became a live-in maid for a family in Seoul.

"What had happened to my parents? They had left Seoul, unable to make a living and moved to the country. My brother took me there but my father had passed away. He died in December 1944. My brother told me, weeping, how my father had waited for me everyday. My mother, when she spotted me walking with my brother, just fell on the ground. One brother ran toward me with a small A frame on his back; he was on his way to pick some dead branches in the mountains to use for fire wood. Another brother, who had become a cripple, wounded in a textile factory, made this desperate effort to hasten his steps toward me. The whole family was stirred as if a war had broken out. You cannot imagine how we clung together and cried, blowing our noses, wiping tears with dirty skirts and sleeves, until all the tears dried.

"Again, I had to work until my bones felt crushed in order to help feed my poor family."

Grandma Kim Sun Duk relayed her experience when she came back home. "When I found my mother, she was wearing a coarse cotton top and a skirt, white but soiled with patches everywhere. Seeing me, she wiped her eyes to make sure that it was indeed I. Then, she grabbed me with such force and said, 'Tell me it is not a dream. I never thought I would be able to see you again. Tell me you are back, really back.' Then, she let the tears stream down her brown face. No way that I can describe . . . I can still see the image of my mother . . .

"But my conscience did not allow me to stay with her at home. I was there less than a month and then just went to Seoul. 'Mother,' I said, 'please consider me a lost daughter. Forgive me for leaving but there is no place for me here. So many people tell me to get married but I can't get married—I have neither courage nor confidence. I will go to Seoul, work at whatever job I can get and try to earn some money.'"

Grandma Kim struggled but after a few catastrophes in small business ventures, she ended up living with a man with a family. Her life was anything but easy or normal.[50]

I asked Grandma Kim Hak Soon, if she wasn't tempted to get married again.[51] "What's the use? I didn't want to try again after my experience with that Korean man who rescued me from the misery of that place in Manchuria. You know, this man, more than twice my age, came there and I begged him to take me with him. He was Korean and took pity on me. I ran away with him. He was a pretty understanding man. Even then, every time when he got drunk or we had a fight, he would not fail to mention my past . . . 'It shows,' he would say, 'It was wrong of me to expect anything good from you. After all, you couldn't help it, could you? After all that sex with the Japanese . . .' Whenever he uttered that stuff, I felt as if he had stuck needles in my cells.

"Worse still, I had a terrible time with any activities involving sex. The horror of that experience took any desire for sex away from me. Just the thought of it sent cold sweat through my spine. So every time this man wanted to have sex with me, I was miserable." She paused. "People talk about the pleasure, enjoyment and excitement of sex. I knew none of those, only the horror and fear." Another pause. "I don't like the male species. I don't have any desire to depend on men for anything. Every time when I tried to protest, those Japanese soldiers would say, 'This, too, is the order of the Japanese Emperor. You have to obey!' Whatever feelings I had and could have had, they took them away from me. I don't like the male species!"

The life awaiting them was not much better. Worse for many. Worst of all, many had been killed or died of disease and/or other catastrophes, never to tell their stories. Further, some grandmas told me about how they narrowly escaped massacres the Japanese had planned. *The Korea Daily* (May 8, 1990) reported about a former Korean comfort woman who witnessed the killing of forty Korean women in the Truk Islands.

The majority of those who survived and can tell their stories have not been able to lead normal lives, not to mention the inhuman hardships they had to endure. Many did not return home. Grandma Ha and Hong in Wuhan are among the countless women who could not come home to Korea, their land of birth. Grandma Hong said, "Japan lost the war. I marry Chinese. No food there, though. Husband good man. Lots of struggle again. Bore two sons. One died. So much hardship, so much struggle. My kid brother still alive, I learned. My kid brother, I took care of him on my back. His wife died and he hurt legs. I can't go; he can't come. No money. I miss him. I cry. Going back to Chosun (old name of Korea), I think about it in my dreams. At night I think about it. Then I cry myself to sleep." Grandma Ha, "Japan lost the war sometime in August. The Chinese beat the Japanese. The horrible things the Japanese did to the Chinese. I was happy. How could I not be happy? I want to tell Japan—'had it not been for you, we would not have left our hometown and come here. We are stuck here and can't go back to our own land. You must bring us back.' And I want to tell Koreans not to ever become like us."

Grandma Song Shin Do relayed her story how she ended up living in Japan all these years. "One day Japanese soldiers stopped coming but I didn't know what was happening—who had lost the war and who got liberated. And nobody said anything about what would happen to me. I was completely abandoned and forgotten in China. If my father had been alive, I would have tried to find a way to go back to Korea but . . . Then, one day a Japanese soldier whom I knew asked me if I wanted to go back to Japan with him. He even tempted me with a proposal of marriage. It didn't take me long to make up my mind to go with him.

"When the ship pulled into a Japanese harbor, I could see the change in that man. I didn't know one soul in Japan and I had no idea how I could survive. I desperately clung to him. I even followed him to his hometown, knowing full well that he now did not want me. Finally, he said to me, 'Well, why don't you try to be a whore for Americans now?'

"Totally alone in the world, I got on a train with no destination. At some point, when a train was passing through a village, I jumped from it. I wanted to kill myself." For one split moment, she looked as if she might reveal her emotions, but quickly dismissing it, she continued with her voice unshaken. "Do you know what I feared most during those miserable seven years in China? Death! I didn't want to die. I wanted to live. That's how I was able to endure the unspeakable hardships. But in Japan after the war, a total sense of loneliness and abandonment drove me to pursue death. Can you imagine it?" I shook my head. "You'd be surprised at how resilient human life is. I didn't die but the jump killed a baby in my belly. You see I was pregnant with his baby, the one who threw me away like a piece of garbage."

Grandma Song has lived in Japan all those years. During the couple of hours we talked, she wanted to deny all sentimentality; she dismissed all emotion. I couldn't expect that she would open her heart to me in that inn in Tokyo. Even then, feeling exasperated about her attempts to hide her emotions, I asked, "Do you have anything you enjoy?" "Drinking," she answered instantly. "When you drink, especially when you are drunk, I am sure you sing. Would you sing a song for me, one I can listen to when I return to America and think of you." "What do you want me to sing?" "Anything, You claim that you don't like Korea. So sing a Japanese song, a drinking song, anything. I don't care." She looked into my eyes. Then, she put her head close to my small microphone and sang, "Life in a strange land." A Korean song. The vibration of her voice was all emotion, so rich that it shook my being. To hell with her not liking Korea! Her song betrayed her. The lonely life of a Korean woman in Japan, one who didn't or couldn't come back but still the land of the father who carried her on his back![52]

"Write that book of yours in Korean," she ordered me, "I can read Korean; I can't write but I can read. Be sure to write that book in Korean. I want to read it."

CHAPTER 4

I WOULD RATHER MARRY A JAPANESE
Bae Jok Gan

Sorrowful Tribe

White kerchief around black hair
White rubber shoes dangling on rugged feet

White top and wrap covering her body
White cloth knotted around her slim waist.

In the same government apartment complex where Grandma Hwang Keum Ju lives, I was told that there were at least three other grandmas. One morning, I was able to get in touch with one of them, Kim Bok Sun, and off I went. After my talk with Grandma Bok Sun, she telephoned someone she called "older sister." "I am going to send her over to you but she says she will have lunch first. So you don't have to prepare anything. Just make sure that you are there when she arrives."

I went to a small, greasy Chinese restaurant and ordered a noodle dish. I ate half of it without enthusiasm and waited a little, making sure that enough time had passed to assure this grandma that I did have my lunch.

I rang the doorbell and found a grandma, about four feet tall, stylishly dressed. "I was expecting you. Please come in. I just cooked steamy rice for you." "Didn't Grandma Bok Sun tell you that I would be coming after lunch?" "Yes, she did but it doesn't matter. It is lunch time." "But I just ate noodles. I can't take another bite of food.. My stomach is so full that it is going to burst." "You can't mean that. How can you eat noodles when hot rice is waiting for you? I wouldn't eat that . . . her voice trailed off but I could

feel her disgust. "What do you have against noodles?"
"Well, that's a long story," she said and led me to the front
room with a balcony.

"You know, after the war, many of us had to wait a long
time before we could go home. During that time American
soldiers gave us nothing but flour. No rice, just flour. I got
so sick of flour then that anything made of flour still makes
me ill. You have no idea how much I missed rice." No disgust
this time, just smiles which were contagious. "Do you know
what? I had an entirely different experience with American
flour. During the Korean War, our family had to go to a
farming village at the foot of a mountain. I used sit by a tree,
listening to the grumbles of my own stomach. Whenever I
heard American airplanes fly over, I dreamed about flour
sacks falling from the sky. I had a fantasy of picking one of
them up and running to the thatched roof house where our
family rented a small room. "Mom, look what I found, a sack
of flour!" "My, my, don't we all have stories to tell?" We sat
down, she gave up on her rice and allowed me to place my
recorder in front of her.

"So when you want me to begin from the beginning, you
mean when they took me, don't you? "No, I mean from the
beginning of your life, as far back as you can remember."
"What for? I thought you wanted to know about what hap-
pened to me when I went there." "I do, but I want to know
everything about you, as much as you can tell me." "That
will take years." "I know but let's see how far you can go
today."

My hometown is Northern Cholla Province, a small farm village called
Kon Ham. My father was a farmer who didn't know the first letter of the
Korean alphabet. They had two girls before me but my uncle adopted the
older one and the second one died when she was little. I was the third daughter and after me, my mother bore a son, my little brother. Some fortune-teller
told my mother that her son's life was meant to be very short, that he would
not live long. My mother became wacky. She was desperate to do something
about my brother's supposedly "short" life. My mother just left her husband
and went to a temple. She took us with her. Even that did not save my brother. He died soon after we left my father.

What happened to my father? Well, by that time, he had no land of his
own to till. So he worked for others and waited to see what happened to my
brother. When he heard about my brother, he went back to his hometown and
got himself a second wife. She bore him a boy and a girl.

64

In the meantime, my mother left the temple, dragging me along. We walked over many hills and arrived at a village. She settled there, did anything she could find, tilling other people's soil, doing odds and ends like cooking, taking care of babies, you name it. Then, she was able to get a place of her own for a business, a small eating place. She sold meals and rice wine. It was from that place that they took me.

The reason why I was taken. Well, those were hard times. I used to roam around in the mountains, gather dead wood for fire and cooking, and dig edible mountain plants and berries. Believe me, we had nothing and life was hard. I had heard here and there that some girls got jobs in a textile factory and earned lots of money. Naturally, I often thought, "Wouldn't it be nice if I landed on one of those jobs."

You know, we attracted a lot of people, Japanese and Koreans, to our eating place. You'd be surprised the trouble people took to drink the stuff. People came from a distance to drink. There was this Japanese cop who frequented the place. It was because of him that I was taken.

They took every virgin in sight, you know. One day, he came and forced me to leave home while my mother was out. "Come, you will get lots of money. You will be working in a factory." I cried and wanted to wait for my mother, but no use. He forced me to go. I didn't know where I was going but when we arrived at some designated place, there were other women. Later, I found out that the place was an inn in Pusan. They kept bringing more girls. We got on a ship in Pusan and went to a small harbor somewhere in China, then to Shanghai.

When we arrived in Shanghai, I saw Japanese policemen everywhere. Then, all the girls were lined up and we were sent to different cities and places. There I began to realize that something was odd. First of all, it wasn't Korea; we were somewhere in China and we could not even pee without being under the sharp eyes of Japanese policemen. Everyone cried, wailed, and sobbed. Still, we didn't know what was really waiting for us.

I was ordered to go to Gusi.[53] Other women were there when I arrived. I was the only one from my village. I was all alone, not a soul whom I could call a friend. It was a huge Chinese hotel, an abandoned hotel. Because of the war, people had deserted the hotel and gone away. I can't tell you how many rooms there were. It was huge. There was a big sign, number 3, posted on my door. They didn't bother to use our names; they often identified us by our room number. It was a two story building with a large gate. The compound was large enough for a car to drive in, with water fountains in the yard and flower gardens. There were guards at all times on both sides of the gate.

I knew no Japanese. I had no idea what year it was. Remember, I was literally a mountain girl. So you can imagine what it was like when the soldiers showed up in my room. We had nothing, no quilts, no mattresses. There was a kind of bed in the room, if you could call it that. And it was fiercely cold. Bone chilling cold. There was a coal stove but the coal fumes made our heads ache so much. I thought my head would burst open and I would die. It was in that situation that the Japanese soldiers attacked you. If you said, "no," they would kick and beat you. It was god awful. You want me to talk about how I felt when it first happened? How can I talk about such a thing?

A pause, her eyes avoiding mine glancing and lingering on plants outside the door on her small balcony.

You know, my thing was already picked *(deflowered)* by that Japanese . . .Then, he sent me away. How do you expect me to talk about a thing like that?

My eye brows were raised with a big question mark on my face.

By force. Against my will, by that Japanese cop. He was chief of the village police station. He was the one . . . By force. Against my will, by that Japanese cop. He was chief of the village police station. He was the one . . .Have you seen old coins? Some of them had holes in the middle. He put thread through lots of those coins, made it look like a necklace and tempted me with it. While my mother was asleep, he sneaked into my room, put that money thing onto my lap, patted my back gently and told me that he wasn't a bad person. The third night he came to my room, he no longer bothered to be gentle with me. He just did that to me. My mother didn't have the faintest idea about what was happening.

Of course, I didn't tell my mother. How could I? I was afraid of her. I was seventeen. Sure, I was frightfully unexposed to the things of this world in that small mountain village. Still, I could not have been so totally blind. I sort of knew about things between men and women. I was scared that my mother would be furious. She would get mad at me . . .

As a result, a baby got into my belly but I didn't know it. I didn't know what was going on. I couldn't put food into my mouth and if I did, all I wanted to do was to throw up. It must have been morning sickness but I didn't know. My mother must have suspected something because she said, "Hum, it's weird. What's happening to you? Why aren't you eating?" "There is nothing wrong with me. I must have some kind of stomach virus. It will go away."

You know it was that policeman who forced me to leave home and go to this "factory" to work. He was responsible. So he took my thing *(virginity)* and then threw me in with the wolves. When I arrived in Pusan, lots of us went to a public bathroom. One of the women who was with me stared at my belly and said, "There is a baby growing in your belly!" "What baby?" I yelled. "You know, baby. You are pregnant." "No, no. I can't be." "But I know. My sister-in-law, I saw her when she was pregnant, her belly and her tits. I am certain of it. Go see a doctor."

66

I was five months pregnant, the doctor told me. They rented a small room for me and waited until I had a baby. It was a baby girl. She looked exactly like him. In fact, so much so that it felt spooky. Even before I could breast-feed her, they took the baby away and the next thing I knew, I was on my way to that place in China, only at that time I didn't know where I was going. I learned later that the baby died within a month. So it was a Japanese police-man who picked my thing for the first time. I didn't feel any pleasure at all when he did that to me. It just hurt me down there.

Then, in China, the Japanese soldiers, they went "bang, bang. You know, those men were starved. One look at the women made them go crazy. It did-n't take long for them to do that, you know. So bang, bang . . . you can't imag-ine how many of them came . . . Thirty, fifty a day. Men came in constant suc-cession every single day. They didn't take off their clothes. They just took out their peppers and did that thing. Who could count? So many came and went so fast that you could not see their faces. You know, peppers, don't you?

> *Her voice was high pitched, excited at my ignorance, even a*
> *little disgusted. Suddenly remembering, I smiled. "Of*
> *course, you know what peppers are!" Relieved, she offered*
> *her analysis about why Korean virgins were drafted.*

You know, the soldiers cannot fight without doing that. So they would just grab any woman in sight, even Chinese. Then their peppers would become rotten. They couldn't fight well with rotten peppers, could they? So the solution was Korean virgins. Do you understand?

> *I nodded, making a mental note to myself, "even the*
> *Chinese." I said nothing. Satisfied, she continued.*

After a while, we had to move to another house, also huge. At first, I did-n't know any Japanese. I felt so stupid. I lived like a mute. So I decided to learn some Japanese. I started out with simple expressions like "*Ira Shai mashai*" (*Please come in*) and "*sayonara* (*good-bye*)." Of course, I knew, "*bagayaro.* (you, idiot)." Everyone learns cursing words first. My vocabulary increased as the time passed but until this day, I don't know any difficult Japanese.

Of course, they were brutal and cruel. Some of the women got sick, you know, venereal disease like gonorrhea and syphilis. If the women couldn't be cured, they became a useless commodity. A burden. So they were killed. They just disappeared. I didn't see the killings myself but they disappeared and no one knew where they went. So what do you think happened to them?

I wasn't tortured or severely punished myself. But I did get venereal dis-ease when I was 19. Everyday we had to clean the room. The smell was worse than anything you can think of. I can't describe it. They also ordered us to

67

clean ourselves with some kind of disinfectant. That smell, you can't possibly forget it as long as you live. They were fairly keen about medical examinations. Those things were done as a service, no charge.

Did I get paid? What money? The only money I saw came from the soldiers,. Some of them gave me money once in a while, which I saved. Then, they would ask us to contribute money for the cause of the *Dennohekai* (the Emperor). I gave all the money I had. For that, they gave me an award certificate. I wish I had saved it. There were some Japanese and Chinese women but we did not stay at the same place.

The soldiers supervised us directly. It was a military operation. No doubt about that. It was the soldiers who guarded us day and night and it was the soldiers who distributed our food. We were often starved. Our food supply was not much to start with. Even that was stopped quite frequently. You don't know how often we had to hug our empty stomachs.

We were at the front in a small Chinese village, a farming village with fields. The place was called Jin Sung. The house was not big; there were about 30 of us. We started at 9 in the morning. From 9 at night till midnight only the officers were allowed to come. Those officers, they made such weird requests! "You want me to talk about them?" Yuck, how can I?

The soldiers didn't have much time but it was different for the officers. Yes, they did all kinds of things. I can't bring myself to talk about them even though you are a woman. I hated it when they used their fingers on me. I just wanted them to do their usual thing on top of me and go away. I just wanted to get it over with.

There were some officers and soldiers for whom I had some feelings but what's the use? It was a war; it was a military operation. Some of the soldiers stole food and blankets for me but they were transferred soon. No one stayed long enough to develop feelings. They rotated the soldiers. They did the same thing with the women.

Yes, I was at the front with the soldiers and I did see actual battles. I saw people killed! We were with the Japanese soldiers and on the other side of the mountain were the enemy soldiers, you know, the Chinese. We didn't have electricity. We used candles. They guarded us every minute but sometimes they made us guards if manpower was short.

Every time new soldiers came, the Chinese soldiers attacked. The Chinese thought the new ones wouldn't be familiar with the area. Countless Chinese soldiers would surround us and shoot. Then, there would be no one in the compound; everyone was out fighting and smoke was everywhere. We couldn't see anything. I couldn't even see a friend right beside me.

Whenever a battle was on, many Japanese airplanes came. During the day if the airplanes came and dropped bombs, there was a little less shooting but at night it was incessant — da, da, da . . . Then, it was like we were all dead.

How could you consider yourself alive? You might as well be dead. When the fighting got worse, relief soldiers were sent from places like Shanghai.

I did see so many wounded soldiers with their legs, and arms cut off, bleeding like crazy. I also saw the Japanese killing Chinese civilians. Sometimes, they ordered us to line up. All the officers and soldiers had already been lined up. Once, they brought five Chinese who, they said, had committed crimes. One looked old and the other four looked so young. Their eyes were covered with black cloth and each of them was tied to a stick, held by a Japanese soldier on either side. They would say, *"ichi bang ike."* Then, they would draw bayonets[54] and march toward the criminals.

The soldiers were trained. So they knew how and where to put the blades into their bodies to kill them instantly but did they do that? No way. They practiced killing on those Chinese bodies. If the blade touched the bones, it would not go through the body. If that happened, they were told to try a second time. Then, the sword would go through and come out at the back of the body. The groan, it was a groan, he couldn't even yell, when the blood sapped out of the body. That noise, no way I can describe it . . . I couldn't bear to hear it. I couldn't watch it, either. Who could? But I was ordered to! They told us to open our eyes wide and watch.

The most cruel thing — they didn't die instantly, their necks dangling. They lingered on. Four of them, however, died by the blade. The last one, they shot to death. It wasn't the only time. They regularly practiced killing by swords with real bodies, you know human bodies, supposedly Chinese criminals. They practiced killing, "yap," "yap," "yap." They practiced killing with swords like people practicing shooting.

When I was in Japan the last time, I told them all this but they still say it was not a war of aggression. They drafted virgins, took away all the good crops, took away anything brass and beat and tortured anyone and everyone who protested. But still, they insist that it was not a war of aggression. How can they say that?

Sometimes, I hid myself and saw what the Japanese soldiers did. They would crawl, and kill the Chinese guards with their swords. Then, a fierce assault would start. If too many people died, they couldn't do anything with the dead bodies. Soldiers were often left on the battle field, dead and nameless, but if officers died, the Japanese cut off their thumbs which they brought back.

I also saw them piling up corpses, pouring gasoline on top and setting fire to it. Individual cremation? Forget it. They would put some ashes in a box, attach a name on top and send it back home. No way of telling what and whose bones? The leftover bones, they buried and burned with some scent, and prayed for their souls. So many young men rotting in a far away country.

You want to know how I felt about the war between the Japanese and the

Chinese? And how I felt about the Chinese? I was young and immature and didn't know how the world was going around. There were some Chinese, older women, who felt close enough to me. They told me stories about the Japanese raping them. The Japanese didn't care whether old and young. Even those who had gray hair, the Japanese raped the hell out of them. The worst part, most of the time, the raped women were killed.

How did I feel about the Chinese hearing stories like that? If you mean whether I felt sorry for them, well . . . I didn't have room to feel sympathy for the Chinese. I didn't want to be close to Chinese, either. I was on the side of the Japanese. I wanted Japan to win. After all, they were the ones who supervised us, ordered us around. How could we want the Chinese to win? We did everything the Japanese told us. If I had any sympathetic feelings, they were for the Japanese, not the Chinese. I am not lying! I wouldn't tell you lies. I cheered for the victory of the Japanese.

They were almost to the point of taking all of China but the Japanese made the mistake of involving the Americans. That's how they lost the war. The American airplanes, when they came, it was something else. Even then, I was thoroughly on the side of the Japanese. They were the ones who took me there. That's all I knew, nothing else. All I knew was that I was there for the Japanese. I devoted my entire being to them. If the Japanese had wanted me to die, I would have.

When the food supplies ran out, I used to take a basket and walk around the fields looking for beans, zucchinis, anything I could find. Sometimes, we would find Chinese cabbage and make soup. Everybody fought for a few more pieces of the cabbage in the soup. Sometimes, we walked to Chinese homes, knocked and took whatever they had. You should have seen the looks on their faces when they saw us. The Chinese were scared of us; they too thought we belonged to the Japanese military. So you see, we were also nasty to Chinese civilians.

Another time, there was a notice on the bulletin board about another execution ceremony of the Chinese. They ordered us to come out and watch. This time, the captured people were well dressed Chinese. There were lots of them. Even the Chinese villagers came out to see what was going on. The soldiers took them to the bridge and sat them with their heads stooped down toward the water. The soldiers put their swords on the neck from the back, counted, one, two, three and then struck. Sometimes, the head was not completely cut off and it would just dangle. Then, they would hit hard one more time so that the head would fall into the water. Otherwise, the blood would just go up as if you would put a water hose up. It rained hard that day. The persons, both dead and living, were all soaked in rain. Don't know what they were accused of. The most common crime cited was spying, but who knows?

They killed countless Chinese like that. Even with all of that, some survived. The Japanese did not make sure every time when they kicked a body into the water. A few of them were still alive. If some were shot, they were just thrown into a big hole. Among a pile of corpses, some who were still alive found a way to crawl out, avoiding the eyes of the Japanese. In a few cases, when that happened, some were reported by the Chinese. Can you believe that? There were Chinese spies who reported on fellow Chinese. Then, after the liberation, those Chinese who had collaborated with the Japanese were killed. Killings and killings . . . endless killings.

While all this was going on, I had no one to talk with. No, no friend. Even among us women there was a difference between the ones who had been there and the new arrivals. We were separated. I belonged to the older camp and we did as we were ordered. Not much contact even among ourselves. At first, I cried a lot but the longer I stayed there, the stronger I believed that I was to die there. I didn't have the slightest hope that I might be able to go back. Not one bit. I was just there. No outside news. Nowhere to come and go. Sooner or later, I would die. That's the only thing I knew. And I became a real bitch with nothing to fear. I was waiting to die. Naturally, there was nothing to be afraid of. I became so bad tempered and rotten, I could hardly recognize myself. It was as if an evil spirit was up to my neck. Sometimes, I just wanted to end it myself instead of waiting. I tried to jump into the water or poison myself. How can I describe it all? No way.

Then, they told us not to steal things from the Chinese, not to pick things from their fields. And the killing stopped a while. Shortly after that, we became independent. Did I have an inkling about the war coming to an end? You could tell from the soldiers. You could just tell from their looks that something had happened. They didn't stand or walk straight with their heads upwards. Lots of whispers and crying. Then, I heard that Japan was defeated. After a few days, there was no one left. Every soldier was gone.

One morning when I got up, I saw a red mark on my door. It was a mark made by the Chinese. They were going to kill all those who worked for the Japanese. So I fixed my hair like a Chinese woman and wore something that looked Chinese and left bare handed, with nothing, toward a ship. Was I happy that Korea had become independent? Are you crazy? No way. I was sad that Japan had been defeated.

> *"What?" I felt as if a rock had banged my head and made my mouth crackle. Ignoring me, she continued.*

I was able to get on a ship and it went somewhere. It was Shanghai, I believe. There were lots of people waiting to go home. Men and women were separated. Japanese and Koreans were all mixed together, but there were more Koreans. People couldn't tell who was Japanese and who was Korean. So we each wore our flags. The Chinese would not sell things to the Japanese but if we Koreans went, they were kind. They said, "we are all human beings." But soon all of us ran out of money. None of us had much to begin with. That's how we got the flour ration from American soldiers. You know the story I told you already.

It was a long waiting period. We had to wait our turn. It was a year before my turn came. I had nothing, just my body. It took us 15 days to reach the Pusan harbor. In China, where I was, American soldiers did no weird things to women, but when I got off the ship in Pusan, I saw American soldiers trying to approach women on the street.

When I got off the ship, I didn't have a penny. I think I was able to ride a bus free. So I went to my mother's village but there was no one, not my mother, not one soul waiting for me. Because our family wandered around so much, I could not find anyone I knew. In order to put food in my mouth, I looked for work. I weeded rice fields with bare hands and I planted rice. My waist felt like it was breaking or something. After squatting so much, I couldn't stand up, let alone straight. Sometimes I had to beg for food. I often ate resin from the tree trunks.

Then, I decided to go to the mountains and look for a temple. There, I practically slaved for them, worked and worked. And all I got was some food. That's all. They were mean people. I am not lying. You better believe me. No, I wasn't in a Buddhist temple, nothing like that. It was a small place, a shrine run by a couple who claimed they could connect up with the gods. I tilled the fields for vegetables, chanted, cooked . . . did everything. But the husband wanted to make me his concubine. I couldn't stay there, could I?

So I wandered into another small place, this time run by an old woman. She made me her wailer, you know someone who would wail for her when she dies. She had no money. I was her slave. I worked until my bones felt like crushing into pieces. There wasn't a thing I didn't do. Not a thing. You better believe that I am not telling you lies. There, again, I was not left in peace. People tried to matchmake me and the old woman wanted me to get myself a man. One day, I just left there and ended up in Dae Gu, a large city.

I managed to get a temporary shack and polished other people's brassware. You know what I am talking about? All this brassware Koreans use. Have you any idea how difficult it is to polish day and night? I worked until my arm didn't feel like mine but the income was so meager. Then, someone told me about an American military base near by where lots of whores were swarming around. Do you know what I mean? We called them "western whores," sometimes "western princesses," Korean women who served American soldiers. They are still around, you know.

I did laundry for those women. I washed their dirty things, day and night. I was able to save enough money to get myself a small cottage. Then, I became very ill and a fortune-teller told me that it was *sinbyong*, spirit sent illness. I was a little over thirty then. Because of this *sinbyong*, I became as thin as a stick, nothing but bones. She told me that the ghost of family members had something to say to me. That's why I had *sinbyong*. I checked it out with two other fortune-tellers who confirmed this. They all told me that the only way for me to get rid of my sickness was through *gut.*[55] I had no choice but to do *gut* (shamanistic ritual). It was awfully expensive; it cost me 40 *won* which was a lot of money.

We went to a mountain with five experienced *mudangs* (shaman). While they performed exorcism rituals, my throat felt funny and I felt as if words were going to pour out but I repressed them. Then, one of the senior shamans shouted something and put bamboo in front of me. When I grabbed it, it shook uncontrollably. "Let's go to an open space." These words came out of my mouth and I had nothing to do with them. I didn't say them, if you know what I mean.

So we all went to an open field and continued our ritual. At the height of it, I grabbed the bamboo. At that moment, my mother's soul entered my body and she wailed with so much sorrow. She said, "Oh, my daughter, oh, my daughter, the things you had to endure and suffer are so enormous. You had to overcome so many valleys of death and life. You had to cross the water and travel so far. But you are back because of my prayer." My feet were stuck to the ground and I could not move them. Then, my dead sister's ghost entered and my body jumped high up and down. Then, my grandfather. It was around 9:00 at night. It was so dark. We all had candles in our hands when we came down the mountain.

When I returned home, I felt no change at all. I was exactly the same as before the ritual. About a month or two later, though, words just poured out of my mouth and I jumped up and down in the room without willing it. I didn't say anything but words just tumbled out. Then, my neighbors came knocking at my door. They all wanted me to predict their future. I told each and every one of them what was awaiting them and what to do. If a soul of a child entered my body, I behaved like a child, if my mother's soul came, I sounded like her and if the mountain spirit came, I smoked a long pipe. It was truly strange, something I could not begin to understand. Because the ghost entered my body, I became a ghost. When they left me, I was myself, the old self.

After that, an old lady believed that I was a possessed *mudang* (*shaman*). I became possessed as a result of the spirits descending into my body. She wanted to take advantage of that. She adopted me as her daughter and took me around. I performed *gut,* you know the ritual ceremony for people, playing drums and chanting. Of course, we charged money but my adopted mother took all the money and didn't give me a cent. She didn't buy me one set of decent clothes. I was around thirty five or six years old. So many people tried to rip me off. It is all true. I am not telling you lies.

When I was a possessed shaman, I was determined that I would remain single, not get married. So I adopted a baby, a baby girl whose mother died at her birth. She cried day and night. I could not sleep a wink at night but I felt such a human bond with that baby. I took care of her with everything I had and didn't have. You have no idea how I took care of her. However, she got sick in her stomach and died in five months. When I buried her, I cried and cried . . . until my tears dried out.

Then, someone brought me a five year old kid. I let her sit on my lap and poured out all my affection. A year later, her mother came and claimed the girl back. She said she missed her too much. I went to see the girl once but she ignored me totally as if she had never seen me before. Can you imagine? I had taken care of her for a year! Then came a 12 year old boy. I picked him up from the street, a homeless boy, nowhere to go. He was very smart. I sent him to elementary school and saved every penny and gave him tuition to enroll at middle school. He ran away with that money. He went to Seoul.

Once again, I was left alone, totally alone. But I was able to make a living by performing *gut*. I was a shaman, after all, I was a possessed one. People would not leave me alone. Lots of people wanted to be my matchmaker. I wouldn't give in, though. I didn't want to marry. Why? Well, there wasn't much choice. If the man was smart, he was already married and wanted me to be his second wife, a concubine. If he had no wife, he was poor with so many children. In some cases, I simply didn't care. I could not fall for them. I didn't feel attracted to any of them.

Then, one day a matchmaker came and told me that there was truly an outstanding candidate for me. He had come from Kang Won Province, looking for a good woman to take as his wife. He was a learned man and handsome. He came to see me with the matchmaker. He was indeed good looking, very clean cut and refined, a world apart from all others. I could not make up my mind, though. So I went away from the house, visiting friends and neighbors. I tried to avoid him. I didn't know what to do with him. Whenever I returned home, he was still there waiting for me. He pursued me doggedly.

He had several things going for him — he was good looking and a widower with only two kids and apparently enough money not to worry about daily living. I still couldn't make up my mind. Then, my adopted mother said to the matchmaker, "Well, knowing her, no response means 'yes'. So why don't we set the wedding date for them? The wedding date simply meant that I would go with him. Don't even fancy that I actually had a ceremony!

On the day when I left with him, my adopted mother who had taken all my earnings didn't buy me one new dress, not even a new pair of rubber shoes. I followed this stranger, a few steps behind him with nothing but my small body. The hardships I had to endure, I don't think anyone can imagine. It is simply unimaginable.

We walked and walked over the mountains and fields, deeper into the mountains. We went through one valley after another. My legs didn't feel like they belonged to me; at first they hurt and then they were numb. On top of everything else, it started to rain and I became soaking wet. At last, I could see a few thatched houses and he led me into one of them. It was a mountain village in Kang Won province.

There was a woman waiting for us, apparently a relative. Once inside, I took a quick glance around. There was no furniture to speak of; one old chest in a corner of the room and few brass bowls for rice. That was all. I couldn't believe it. Then, I saw a straw sack, half full of barley. I could not breathe. I sat there dumbfounded for a while. "Well, this must be my fate, nothing I can do about it. I will accept it and make the best of it." Then, came the best part, you know what I mean? The worst! I had been told that he had two kids but I saw six coming in to be introduced. They came one by one and bowed to me, four boys and two girls. I thought to myself, "Surely, four of them must be cousins or some relatives." But alas, they were all his children, the youngest about four years old and the oldest son was in his teens.

For three days, I would not go into his room. You know, that man, the groom, begged and pleaded with me to come in but I wouldn't. I was trying to decide whether I wanted to stay there or not. But where could I go? I had no one waiting for me, nowhere I could go. No transportation, either. It was such a deep valley. He lit a long pipe and inhaling deeply, tried to drag me toward him on the third night. I pushed him away. He got so mad that he just threw a coarse straw mat in the yard and lay down, putting his head on a wooden pillow. He coughed, clearing his throat so loudly. I could see that he was all fury and anger. About five days passed and he wouldn't even look at me.

Alone, I felt as if my entire insides were going to break loose. I didn't know whether I should live or die; come or go. Then, I saw him staring at me. I thought killer rage flashing in him. I was literally afraid. "Please come in," I said. So he did. For a while, he lay on one side and I on the other. You know, ever since I returned to Korea, I had not had any man. So I could hear my heart beat and I jumped at the slightest move or noise. It was hard going at first. After a while, it became better.

He later told me that he had thought I had known lots of men but after sleeping with me, he thought otherwise. The way I was behaving, so easily frightened and acting awkward. Besides, if you do not do that for a long time, that hole becomes smaller; it must shrink. It was small. So he thought he had been mistaken. Talking about irony . . .

God, how tough it was. All day, from the crack of dawn to night, I worked, in the fields, in the kitchen, and in the mountains digging medicine plants. By the time, I was able to lie down my small body, I was so exhausted. I didn't know if my body belonged to me . . . or what. (Pause) You know what? He got on top of me three or four times each night. It was as if he had

75

spent all day thinking only about that. He must have waited all day to do that. . . Can you imagine what it was like?

> *I felt my lungs might collapse; couldn't pull the air in. I*
> *wanted to ask, "How come? Didn't he have to work, too?"*
> *but no need to ask. She knew what went through my mind.*

No, he didn't have to do the same kind of work. He fancied himself a scholar. He sat around and read. He ordered me to do all that rough work while he sat playing scholar, smoking and drinking. He knew nothing about daily chores and he didn't want to know. I was 42 years old when I became his wife and he died when I was fifty eight. All those years, I had to raise six children and earn enough money to put food in those mouths and pay for my husband's drinking and smoking. You wouldn't believe what I had to go through. Those sons, after I raised them to be grown men, all left home and left for Seoul. They didn't stay around to help. I was stuck with everything in that mountain village. For me, there was no winter, summer, fall and spring. Made no difference. I had to work at all times. Sometimes in the winter I would wander around the mountain, digging medicinal roots, selling them and paying for my husband's drinking expenses.

Those kids didn't call me "mom." Actually, they didn't call me anything but they had to obey me. Did I tell you that I raised those kids like an army? I gave them strict orders every morning. Otherwise, they would not know what to do. For example, early in the morning, I would tell the No. 1 and 2 sons, "Today, you have to go to a field over there, set fire and plant potatoes." If they didn't obey, I would line them up and spank them. Sometimes, I would use a stick and whip their legs. The third one was rebellious. He would grab my hands and protest, "What right do you have to beat us like this?" Then, I would beat him harder. Many times, he simply ran away from me. "You are not my own kids. You didn't come out of my own belly but don't you see I am trying to raise you all like my own?" Sometimes, I just broke down and cried. I just sat, unmindful of tears trickling down my cheeks, mixing dirt on my face.

With the older ones, I had no choice but to be strict. For one thing, I had to get some work out of them. The younger ones, the two youngest ones, I treated as if they were pure gold. Whenever they got into a fight, which was often, believe me, I was always on the side of the younger ones. The older girl used to say, "Do you know that you are spoiling those brats? You are always on their side. It doesn't matter if they are right or wrong!" I knew she was right but my heart went out for those little ones who had lost their mother. I felt such sadness for them. Sometimes, I would tell them not to fight until my voice would give out and could not even yell any more but they would go on fighting. Then, I would just sit on the ground and say, "It was your mother's *karma* that she had to die so young and now it is my *karma* that I am stuck with you!" And I cried.

You can't imagine the trials and tribulations I had to go through with those kids. I used to get up before the dawn cracked open, get things going for them to eat, and set out for a far away field. Once I was there, it wasn't easy to come back. Just a waste of time. Besides, I wanted my girl to come and help me till the field. So I would arrange for her to bring my lunch. By the time lunchtime arrived, I had worked many hours and would hear my stomach making noises, but no sight of the girl. Then, I would watch the others eat and gaze in the direction where her little head might pop up but still no sight of her!

On my way back, I would find her playing with her friends with my lunch basket still sitting beside her. As soon as she saw me, she would literally crawl, fearful that I might beat her. At least she knew that she deserved a beating. "Had I been your own mother, you would not have done this. You would have worried about her empty belly. Do you make me starve because I am not your mother?" Then, I would whip her. I always ended up crying to see her cry. The image of that little girl pained me.

I will never understand this but you know what? Those kids who had more rods from me than the others, they are the ones who are still good to me. That daughter of mine is now married and has a good family. She is not well off or anything like that but has enough to feed her family without daily worries. She is married to a nice man. She lives in Kang Won Province. She calls me and says, "Mother, do you know that I just made hot bean paste just like the way you taught me. I make everything the way you taught me. I am just about the only young woman around here who can make all these things without asking older women in the neighborhood. Maybe all that beating was worth it." Then she giggles.

> *Pride and affection seemed to iron out the lines on her face as she talked about her step daughter. "Life is strange, isn't it?" She looked up at me and I nodded.*

Eventually, we also moved to Seoul with my husband, but none of our kids helped us with our living expenses. There isn't one factory in the neighborhood where I didn't work. I had to earn enough for my husband's drinking, smoking and medicine on top of our basic living expenses. No one helped us. By the time my husband was about sixty, he started showing signs of senility. When I came back from work, he would say strange things. He would accuse me of having affairs with other men every morning when I went to work. Sometimes, he would chase me out with a large stone in his hand, demanding to know who the man was.

Then, his entire body started to swell. I could not stay in Seoul. We decided to leave Seoul and went back to Kang Won Province, not to our place but nearby. We rented a room and I worked for other families. We gave him painkillers. Then, one leg started rotting. Then, he could not go to the bathroom. He crapped on the floor and urinated everywhere.

One evening, I cooked him barley. He enjoyed the meal and tried to say something. He stuttered but I could recognize his words, "Now, its time for me to go. I hope you go and live with the children." I cleaned him and dressed him in a new outfit which I had prepared and put him down. But he didn't die. He just lay there. Around eleven at night, I thought I had to let his children know. I sat with him all night, barely breathing. He was like a corpse but he did not go until morning. Then, the children came from Seoul.

On the third day after his death, we buried him. No one wept but me. I wailed and sobbed, not so much for him but for myself. How on earth was I going to live? Now that he was gone, there was no one in the whole wide world. When I returned from the funeral, the landlord told me that I had to clean out the room to chase away the spirit of the dead. The expenses for redoing the room were enormous. I was so desperate that I had to work as a shaman and earn enough money to pay the landlord for completely redoing the room. Then, I packed whatever we had and gave it all away to one of the relatives because there was no place to store it. All this time, no one, not one soul tried to help. None of the children I raised offered to help.

Then, alone, I went to be a live-in maid for a family of five children. The work was incessant. Never a moment to rest my tired bones. My body was a machine, a work machine. But I saved some money which I put in a bank. Someone told me that I should go to Seoul and work as a live-in maid. They said it would be much better. I had been told that I was to work for two people, a husband and a wife, but no such luck. There were about ten people I had to slave for. That's not all. They didn't pay me. Then, I found out that the family had to declare bankruptcy. Because I wasn't paid a penny for my work, I found myself following a bankrupt family. I was digging a deeper hole. Talking about an incredible fate. . .

The couple went all over the place and tried to start a new business. It didn't matter, though, where they went and what they did; they failed over and over again. With each move, things became worse and I was in a deeper hole. I should have left but I kept hoping that they would make it and give my wages, all the piled up debt they owed me. In the middle of all that confusion, the woman became pregnant and a baby boy was born.

> Grandma Bae stood up and brought a framed picture of a
> boy and said, "Look, that baby is this boy in the picture." A
> good looking boy with sad eyes.

The couple went to work in a factory every day and left the baby boy home. Who is going to raise the boy? I was stuck. Then, the couple started to sell clothing with a small vendor in the South Gate market. The baby knew no one but me. He followed me around calling me, "Mom." I loved the baby . . . I did everything for him. I lived with that family for 18 years. Can you imagine? I was practically the head of the family. I raised the boy and saw him through elementary school.

They got into so much debt, the debtors chased them every single day. They took away every penny I had, even the money the government gave to help when I reported. Then, finally they just disappeared. They had to hide. The boy is with his aunt. He doesn't know where his parents are. He calls me every single day and asks me, "When can I come and live with you?"

How do I live now? You know the government helps us women, with 200,000 *won* a month (about $200)[56]. Out of that, I have to pay 80,000 *won* for this apartment. With the rest, I try to cover living expenses, including medicine bills. From time to time, some Japanese invite me to come and give testimony. Then, they pay me. That's how I make out.

I have no idea how much the Japanese should compensate. I hope enough to help my sons and for me to buy a small cottage in a country area. I want to spend the rest of my life and die in peace in a place like that. This apartment belongs to the government. It doesn't look good, though. Even today, the Japanese say that it wasn't a war of aggression. Then, they are talking about the private funds. Even now, I think there's quite a bit of money raised but I think most of it goes to paying expenses for all the activities and movements supposedly on our behalf. So not a penny comes to us directly. Sometimes, we victims think we are being used.

What gets me angriest? I see no end, no children, no hope, no nothing, nowhere to go. Ah, you saw a name of a Church posted on my door. Does the Church teach me something about hope? I am not much of a church-goer. I just believe in God by myself. I pray to save me from sin and ask him to forgive me.

What sin? How can you ask that? This is sin. My life is sin, don't you think? I was not able to marry in a normal way, like everybody else. I told you all my suffering. This is all because of my sins in a previous life, *karma*. Without that, how is it possible that I had this kind of life? Same with the blessings of wealth and children. It is because of your previous deeds. You bring your own blessing. I was stepped on, trodden and had all that suffering because of my previous sins. This is what I believe. That's why I don't blame. I offer food to those who are starved and offer clothes to those who have nothing to wear. All those things happened in China because of my sins in my previous life. I believe that.

In my next life, I would like to be born so that I could live with a peace of mind, live a life of dignity and honesty. Even now, I give away what little I have to cover the expenses for medicine of my sick friend. You know there is this woman who was also a former comfort woman. She is very sick and she needs money for medicine. It means nothing if you share because you have it left over. You have to share when you do not have enough for yourself. That's the only meaning of true sharing. You don't offer food after your stomach is full.

I sound like a saint to talk like this? No way. I just talk to you, though you were a total stranger when you came through that door, because you seemed sincere and honest. So I wanted to open myself and tell you the truth as much as I could. I don't tell lies. You better believe that. But I do know that there are some who exaggerate or even make up stories but not me. For instance, there was this woman who went to Japan to testify. I heard her say that she had been drafted as a worker and then forced into being a comfort woman and that she killed a Japanese officer. That is impossible. That's simply not credible because a Japanese officer was treated as more precious than a piece of gold. No way that a comfort woman could kill an officer and get away with it.

According to her, this officer took his sword out because she didn't obey. She snatched that sword and pushed it into his body. He was rushed to the hospital and she was sent to prison. Later he died and she was released. Now, any fool can understand that this couldn't be. If you killed an officer, you would have been killed instantly. It was war.

She mused . . .

Then, we were also soldiers. We were not prostitutes. We helped the soldiers to fight. Do you understand?

I shook my head.

You do know why the women were taken, don't you? If the men couldn't do that thing, they couldn't fight. That's why we were also soldiers. We helped them fight. Do I think what Japan did was evil? Not really. After all, Japan was at war. They wanted to win the war. They could not have done that without doing evil things. Actually, I blame Korea most. The fact that our country was weak. Were we a strong country, it would not and could not have happened. So if I am to blame anything, anybody, it is Korea.

Of course, I understand why Japan did what they did but I blame Korea for being a weak country. Japan was able to do what they did because our country let them do it. Japan was single-minded about winning the war. When Japan came to Korea, they made sure that everything Korean was wiped out and crushed our country completely. They killed an awful lot of Koreans whom they considered dangerous.

How come I can say those things and still don't blame Japan? Well, we were the ones who let Japan step on us. We should not let that happen again.

We made it possible for them to do such evil things. We should never let it happen again. We should make sure that we are the conquerors. No, it does not mean that we should do wicked things to Japan if we are the conquerors.

I sighed, exasperated.

The Japanese thought only of themselves. They wanted to see Korea perish in order for them to live better but I still think it was our fault. If only we had been powerful enough, Japan could not have done what they did to us. We were the losers. They killed us. They took young men and women by force. They stepped on us. No, it does not mean that we should step on weak ones; we should not do that. You keep pushing me to say that Japan was wrong but I still say they did it for their country and we let it happen to us because we were not powerful enough.

Pause.

Well, we should never let it happen again. Never. The young generation should be mindful of education, be strong and let no one do what Japan did to us. We should not be defeated, not by Japan, not by America. By no one. None. Of course, I wish I had gone to school. My mother didn't send me to school. We were born in bad times. We couldn't be educated but now Korea is in a strong position. No excuse now for the young people not minding to learning and being responsible for keeping our country strong.

> *My head as well as my heart seemed to jerk around. I had a million words that I wanted to push down her throat. How could she defend Japan after all they had done to her. Pain and anger mixed like snow and rain, heaving inside, I counted ten, twenty. I knew that I had to return. She was right; it would take a few years to truly hear her story, to understand what happened to her and how she feels. Collecting my things, I managed to smile. She went outside with me, stood in front of her apartment building and watched me walk to the bus stop. Every time I looked back, she was still there.*
>
> *A week passed and I called her. She greeted me on the phone in a voice full of relief and delight. "Since you left, I have regretted that I did not ask how I could reach you. I've waited and waited until my neck would stretch. Come right away. Only, don't eat stupid noodles. I am getting my rice started right away." As I approached her apartment building, she was waiting for me on the street, her body small and vulnerable.*
>
> *"I am so glad to see you. After I talked to you last time, I felt as if something that had been causing indigestion for*

years had disappeared. I felt relieved to let it out. Today, though, I just wanted to see you. I don't often see people who seem to be genuinely concerned. I felt sad to see you go last time. More than that, I want us to have a meal together. I felt so bad that I didn't feed you before." With her chatting away, we rode the elevator to the 7th floor and entered her clean apartment. I could smell lunch cooking.

"We will have lunch right away." She set her table in the sitting room and started placing a variety of dishes on it. She took a big glass jar from her refrigerator, took out a half head of Chinese cabbage, dripping with red pepper juice. She carefully laid it on a butcher block, cut it into small sizes fit for the mouth, and stacked them in a special bowl with the delicacy of a flower arrangement. "You know, this is Kimjang Kimchi. Do you remember how we used to put these in great big earthen wares and bury them during the winter time?" "Of course, I do."

As I looked at her kimchi, my mouth watered and my mind raced back to the scenes of "kimchi making" for the winter, kimchang. This pickled cabbage, or more to the point, rotten cabbages and turnips, is as essential to Koreans as rice. The garlicky juice of Kimchi is in the blood of every Korean — that's what makes the Korean soul spicy, daring and undaunted. Just as the cabbage harvest is completed and barely before the winter frost, every household in Korea concentrated on making enough kimchi to store for winter. Relatives and neighbors scheduled their kimchi making "operation" in close consultation with each other so that plenty of helping hands were available for each family.

In our household, my maternal grandmother supervised kimchang. My mother, a couple of neighbors, relatives, and our maids worked methodically under her command. They cut each head of cabbage into half with a surgeon's precision. Smaller ones often remained uncut. Divided, the cabbage heart revealed layers of tender leaves, shorter inside gradually becoming larger. The first order of the operation is to sprinkle just the right amount of salt, not too much, not too little, between each cabbage leaf and carefully stack them up until they become tender.

When the cabbage is just tender enough, the women wash it carefully. And one by one, the seasoning mixture goes between each leaf. Crushed red pepper, garlic and gin-

ger roots, chopped or sometimes thinly sliced scallions cut diagonally, at just the right angle, and a whole host of other things go into the seasoning. The more things thrown in, the fancier the mixture. Sometimes, pear slices and chestnuts go in, even oysters and squid! I was always a little saddened to see the heart of a cabbage, such a delicate mixture of ivory and light yellow becoming mercilessly spiced up with hot red pepper and garlic.

The cabbage goes into huge earthen ware. When each earthen pot was filled, the women put a stone on top, closed it, and buried it under ground, Come winter, the family is armored with kimchi.

"You know, we no longer have the excitement of the fall kimchang. Most people, especially in Seoul, don't bother making it; they buy it at the stores and put it in the refrigerator. Do you make your kimchi in America?" "No, I am afraid not. Most of time, I go without kimchi but whenever I crave it, I buy it at a Korean grocery store." "What a pity. I still make all my kimchi. Whenever my Japanese friends come, I give them my kimchi. They are crazy about it. There is this Japanese who would like me to come to Japan and open a Korean restaurant with him." "Why don't you?" "No, I am too old. I have worked all my life until every bone in my body feels like it is crushing."

We ate lunch together, with Grandma Bae describing every dish on the table, especially about two more variations of kimchi. "Now, at least, I don't have to worry about starving. The monthly help we get from the government is not nearly enough but I make do." "Even without that, I can't see you starve. You are so capable. I bet you can still do gut (shamanistic ritual) and make some money if you have to." "But I don't want to. I told you about 'shinbyong,' the spirit sent illness when I looked like a stick . . ."

She stopped eating, with her eyes travelling far into her past. "All my family ghosts, especially my mother's ghost could not rest in peace. That's why it entered my body. I told you about it, didn't I?" I was afraid to chew the food in my mouth lest I break the silence. "I told you that when I returned from China, I couldn't find my mother. Well, I could have found her if I had wanted to. Actually, on her deathbed, she sent for me but I didn't go see her. I didn't want to see her . . ." I racked my brains but there was simply no grace-

ful way to take out my recorder but what if she stops . . . "I will tell you why I never looked up my mother. I had no 'chung'[57] for her . . . It's okay if you want to take out your recorder."

Did I tell you how beautiful my mother was? She could have put any of the actresses on TV into shame, if she were properly dressed and all that. I told you there were three girls in our family. My father grew some tobacco among other things. One evening, he went to the back of the house where he hung tobacco to dry. He wanted to pick some to smoke. There he found a man hiding near the toilet. My father grabbed him and asked, "Why are you here? Are you here to steal people or money?" My father had gone nuts; he accused my mother of screwing around. He dragged my mother around the yard, threatened to kill her with a kitchen knife . . . Then, my father reported the man to the police as a thief. The story spread through the entire village like a wild fire. My parents decided that they could no longer live there. They could not keep their face.

They packed a few things and left the village with two of my older sisters walking in front of them and I on my mother's back. We stopped at a small village, rented an outer room and decided to live there. The oldest sister was sent to an uncle's house. Both my father and mother did day labor, snatching whatever work they could find in order to make a living. One night, I could overhear a fierce fight. They were yelling and screaming. Then, my mother asked for a divorce and just left. So there were two of us with my father.

My father rolled up worn out quilts and a few other things, and put them on his A frame. He then put me on top of the things, and with the loaded A frame on his back, walked toward our village. My sister trudged along beside us. I remember my father climbing up a snow covered hill, so much snow. We walked like that all day without food. I cried, asking for food. I was so hungry. But where could he find food? He found some red berries from snow covered trees but we could not eat them. We finally reached my uncle's house. They were all asleep but we continued calling until my aunt came to the door. In the middle of the night, she cooked some rice and fed us.

It was impossible for all three of us to stay at my uncle's house. So my father left the two of us with my uncle's family and went away to work as a live-in servant. I can't tell you how much my uncle and aunt hated us; they could not stand the sight of us. They barely fed us. So I went around the yard and picked up grain and put it in my mouth. No one bothered to comb my hair. No one gave me any change of clothes. My body and hair were nests for lice. One night my father tiptoed into the dark barn where we slept. He lifted me gently, put a straw mat underneath, hugged me tightly to his chest and wept. But he left before dawn, leaving us there. That was when I was about four or five years old.

One day, my mother appeared, looking for us. Her belly was huge; she must have been pregnant. Seeing us—we were quite a sight— she just crouched on the ground and wailed. She took both of us with her. So the three of us went looking for my father. We went to the same village where we had been before and tried to make a living there again. In the meantime, my sister, who had been with me at my uncle's house, died when she was 12 and a baby boy was born.

When the boy was about five and I about nine, he started getting sick often. So my mother frequently went to the temple in order to appease the gods. The various shamans told her that it was our fate that we would not live long: I would die at the age of 15 and my brother even before that. So my mother took both of us to a temple. There was a monk. Whenever my mother was not around, he would just beat me for no reason at all. About a year after we arrived there, my brother died. So I was the only one left. My mother would leave me with the monk and go out.

She visited homes to tell people's fortunes. I begged her to take me with her but she wouldn't. If I begged more, clutching to her skirt, she would hit my hand hard and kick me. And as soon as she disappeared, the monk would beat me. Why did the monk beat me? Thinking back, they had a thing going between them. So he simply didn't want me around. It was simply unbearable . . . So sometimes I would just sneak out, follow my mother. Whenever I thought she might see me, I would quickly hide myself. I would linger around the village, making sure that I did not lose sight of my mother. Between my mother and the monk, I hardly knew whom to ask for help; when he whipped me, I went to my mother and begged her to stop him and vice versa, but neither cared if I lived or died. They also fought with each other like a cat and a dog. I finally went crazy.

Then, my mother stripped me naked, put a sign on my back that said I had gone mad because of the evil spirit. They both beat me to chase away the evil spirit. My body was covered with blood and bruises. So I no longer cared about anything. I didn't care if she went out or stayed. Nothing mattered.

My mother started a business selling simple food and alcoholic beverages, mostly Korean rice wine. That's when the Japanese policeman came and I was sent to China. I told you that story. I told you that I had a baby girl. She was an exact copy of him. I saw her face before they took her away. When I was in China, a woman who had known about the baby told me that the baby died shortly after she was given to a couple who worked for the Japanese. No, I didn't think of her. I don't know why but I didn't think of her at all.

I went to China when I was 17 and came back to Korea when I was 25. I was gone for 8 years but the last year I was just waiting. When I returned to the village, my mother wasn't there. People told me where I could find her but I didn't try. I had no desire to see her, none whatsoever. All those dreadful things she had done to me when I was small and helpless — I remembered every bit of it and it haunted me. The images were so vivid, so real. I shivered. How could any mother do such things? When I was small, I thought I could not live without my mother but as I grew, I realized that what she had done were not motherly things! When I was in China, I didn't think of her one bit.

While I was away, my father died. And you remember that I had an older sister who had been sent to my uncle's house? I have a feeling that she was subjected to the same fate with me but I had no way of finding her. She just disappeared. Do I think that my mother slept around? Yes. When I was little, I had no idea but as I grew older I could put things together. About that man behind the out house — I was too little to understand those things then and I didn't want to believe anything like that about my mother but I do believe he and my mother had a thing going already and that my father was right. I know usually people tell stories about men, husbands sleeping around but not women. My mother's case was exactly opposite. And I bet my mother was not the only one. You would be surprised to know what actually happens to people. Your books tell you only half truths, if that.

You know, my mother was very pretty. Her beauty was second to none. She could sing and she was so good with sewing. She married my father at the age of 13. She had to serve five mothers-in-law. My grandfather did not have sons. So he got one wife after another but none of them bore him a son. My father was not his son; he was adopted.

I feel sad for my father. Even when I was old enough, I could not offer him a bowl of warm rice. After my mother ditched him, my father got himself another wife and had a son and a daughter. Then, he became sick. His wife left him taking a four year old son and a baby girl. He died alone, totally alone. I did find where he was buried. I visited his grave but I wouldn't go see my mother even on her death bed.

Of course, it pained me not to go see my mother! You have no idea how much my mother pleaded, begged me to come to see her but I didn't go. When she was dying, she sent for me. She sent a paid messenger but I wouldn't go. How is it possible that I wouldn't go? Well, how is it possible that I would go? What she did with that dreadful monk and what she did to my father, I could not face her.

I had no one but my dying mother but I still wouldn't go. Family affairs—it is the most difficult thing. . .You know, even after they are long dead, my folks didn't leave me alone. That's why their ghosts entered my body and made me sick. You remember my telling you about the spirit sent sickness. My family members, my grandfather, mother, sister and the kid brother, even after their deaths, didn't leave me alone. Each ghost entered my body one by one and told me about their piled-up sorrow, pain and suffering . . .

I told you about my mother's ghost entering me and crying. "Oh, my daughter, oh, my daughter, you have gone through so much." The ghosts of my sister who died at the age of 12 as well as my kid brother entered. When my sister came, she cried asking for food and my brother, when he entered, I played like a little boy. Those things happen during *gut* but afterwards I was just like I had been before. No sign of any of those spirits. Then, once in a while, I become crazy again. Even in the middle of cooking, I found myself chanting. The neighbors would hear my chants and come. The ghosts would take me over completely; I was no longer myself. Then, I would tell people's fortunes one by one.

Roughly once a month, I had to climb up the mountain. It wasn't my wish, you know, I was instructed by the spirit inside of me. I had to bathe myself in cold water, sometimes breaking the ice and changing into new clothes. Even in the freezing winter, I did not feel at all cold when I bathed in icy water. I also had to offer food. Sometimes, I had to sit alone in the deep mountain until I could utter words.

When I first received the spirits, I was told that a big fortune would come to me. After that, I was able to obtain a small house and my luck changed. Everything I touched worked out. It was magic played by the gods. For a while, I was able to earn quite a bit of money by telling people's fortunes. My predictions turned out accurate. At the same time, the orders the spirits gave me were not easy to obey. So when I didn't listen and did not act as instructed, I lost all that money almost instantly.

How could I lose money so fast? Of course, I could. You'd be surprised how fast money can go. For instance, I played with money. You know the Korean *kei* system, don't you? The system where a group of people put certain amount of money each month and individuals in turn take the collected sum. The sooner your turn comes, the more money you have to put in. Once the person who collected the whole thing just disappeared. There were other ways people cheated. You wouldn't know how inventive people can be with their cheating. There are a thousand ways of losing money. You'd be surprised.

The spirits gave me the money and took it away because I disobeyed them. No doubt about it. After I became penniless again, I rented a room. But I wasn't myself. I was crazy. I roamed around the mountains, everywhere. I begged and begged for a clean spirit. Then, I went to see a fortuneteller nearby. I was told to do *gut*, you know the shamanistic ritual. So I was restored.

> She told me again how she lived with an older woman, her adopted mother, how they performed "gut" together, how she kept all the money, how she met her husband and went to his house and discovered she had been cheated. The story was the same, amazingly the same.

While I was going through awful lot after I came back from China, I rarely felt desire for men. No, not really. I told you that there were lots of men who wanted me but, me, I had no time, no energy to think of men. All my nerves were concentrated on my daily survival — how to put food in my mouth and where to sleep. . . If I did have feelings, I didn't feel them. Besides, if you do not do that "thing," you sort of forget about it. Even between a husband and wife, if you don't do that, you forget. The more you do that, the more the desire. At least that was true for me.

You remember my telling you about my husband's obsession with sex, don't you? He attacked me every possible chance. He wanted to do it all night after an incredibly hard day's work. I would be falling asleep with bone melting exhaustion but he still wanted that. If I refused during the night, the next day was rough. Sometimes, he would just throw the breakfast table. The house became like a war zone. That's not all. He would abuse me, beat me. You have no idea how he beat me if I refused sex with him.

You might think it was another kind of comfort woman life. With the Japanese, though, I never knew what sex was. They did it so fast, bang, bang, as I told you. I had no feelings. I didn't know what an orgasm was. It was with my husband that I experienced it. Because we are both women and I feel I can trust you, I can say all kinds of things to you. I've never spoken like this before.

As much as I protested, I must have liked it, you know, hooked to the taste of sex. That's how I endured all those years. I must have had a love/hate relationship with my husband. Mostly sexual attraction. With the Japanese, I had no such feelings. There was absolutely nothing. How can you feel anything with all those soldiers who stood in line and stuck that thing inside you. Impossible. No time to feel. Many officers came too. They were mostly old, with so much gray hair. Most would not even talk. They gave me simple orders about what they wanted. Sometimes, they came dead drunk and then they would abuse me.

She paused. More to come, I was sure. I waited in silence.

There was this soldier. His name was Ishikawa. He would sometimes break military rules to see me. Many times, he was caught and punished. He brought me all kinds of things, soap, candies, anything he could put his hands on. He was absolutely crazy about me. I believe he really loved me. Back then, I didn't know. I felt something for him but I said nothing to him. I didn't say I liked him. Now? I would hug him close to me, kiss him and tell him that I love him. I would do that now, but not back then.

So it was only after I was forty that I lived with this man and tasted what sex was, but I could not get married. Sure, I lived with my husband but you could hardly call that getting married. I didn't even have a new pair of rubber shoes, let alone a wedding![58] I couldn't tell him about my past; I just lived with him and he taught me what sex was. After he died, I felt a sexual urge from time to time but it wasn't strong enough to subject myself to another man who would make me a slave. I couldn't take that risk.

You keep telling me I look beautiful even now. Well, I don't know about that but I know that I could find a man who would take me in, but no way. I wouldn't do that for anything. It is my fate that I would slave for men. Why would I subject myself to take care of some old man at my age?

Yes, I wish I had money but not for me; it is for my stepchildren. They could all use help, especially the oldest son. He doesn't have a steady job and their livelihood depends on his wife's income. She works as a day maid and cooks for different families. I told you that the vitamin you brought the last time, I gave it to her because she is always exhausted. She needs it more than I do.

For myself, I would like to have enough money to buy a small piece of land in the countryside. If I die here, the government would take care of my funeral and bury me. Actually, I did see the government burial ground for us because one of the grandmas died last year. You know, Koreans are particular about the location of their graves since it will influence the fate of their children. This burial ground for us is a very good place, surrounded by mountains like a wall scroll and the light shines on it. But they don't bury comfort women; they cremate us and put our ashes in a box, bury that and mark it with a small stone with our name carved on it. So it's no use that the place is good since they burn the body. So I don't want to die here. I would like to move to the countryside and be buried there. I want to claim a small spot in this vast universe for my body, somewhere quiet and peaceful, away from the throngs of people.

I do believe that everything in life is acting out according to the fate we are born with. I told you that I had to go through all that struggle because of my previous sins. Yes, you might say that Japan was merely an instrument to carry out my tragic fate. I can't really blame Japan and I don't.

Then, with her voice a pitch higher.

If only Korea were a stronger country, Japan could not have taken all those women! It was our fate that we were born as Koreans. Everything is fate, your *karma*. How can I sit around and attribute everything to fate? I should try to make it better? How? If you could, it is not fate. Do I go to church? I think I was at church three times but I quit. It is so damn far and I don't know how to get around Seoul by myself. Besides, I am not really interested in the church. I can deal with God sitting right here in my room. After all, I still have spirit in me.

You want me tell your fortune? When is your birthday? I have to know your lunar calendar birthday. Otherwise I can't tell your fortune. Ah, you are a June tiger. It is written all over you that you were not born to wear a skirt, cook, clean or take care of a household. You were born to do greater things. A June tiger, strength and spirit surging and ready to conquer the world.

Actually, it would have been better if you were born a man; you are not a typical woman. So don't act like a woman. This is good proof of that. What you are doing, this is not the work of a woman; it is man's work.

I know, I know that you don't think it is just man's work. Of course, it is man's work. What woman would go around the way you are? Your American husband, he is also a tiger, you say. Two tigers. You two are really good together. You care for each other deeply with so much affection but you are both stubborn. You would not easily give in. If one of you touched a core of something essential and got angry, it will be very difficult to be normal again. You are both stubborn. As long as you know that, you are a good match.

> *Boy, is she on target! I remembered the time, one time, in the heat of a discussion, I told Don, my husband, that he was a racist. I nearly lost him. I can get by calling him an asshole but not a racist!*

Sure, I sometimes feel ashamed of my past. I know it wasn't my fault. No matter, shame is shame. All those things, they were so dreadful that I feel like washing out my mouth with soap every time I talk about them. They were simply unimaginable things; so unspeakable, so dreadful, so shameful . . .

> *Her body shook violently, and her jaws were clamped.*

I know I shouldn't blame myself for what happened, but I do feel dirty, ashamed. Even now, I see some of those soldiers in my dreams. Maybe, it is their ghosts who follow me around. So many of them. Then, the smell, the stink. It was terrible. And it was so cold even with a charcoal fire going.

In the middle of it all, I rarely thought of my mother. I told you. When I was little, I thought I could not live without her but as I grew older, all I felt was rage towering over me. For what she had done to my father, how she had carried on with that monk. I didn't ever want to see her. No desire. Absolutely none. I felt so violated by her. I did think of my father, though, with much tender affection and sympathy. The images of my father putting the straw mat under my little body in the middle of the night, carrying me on his A frame and walking over the valleys, sobbing his heart out, hugging me . . . those stayed with me.

Whenever I think of all those things, how could I not blame my mother? After all, she ditched us, didn't she? And so many cruel things that monk of hers did to me. Sometimes, I would sit by the stream and wash edible plants I had picked. If the monk happened to pass by and see me, he would kick the basket into the water. I would rush to salvage it and get all wet. I could not tell my mother about that because I was afraid of their fighting. My mother and that monk, carrying on in secret. I was obviously a burden to them. You know, that terrible monk outlived my mother. She died long before he did.

You want me to tell you more about the Japanese soldier who fell in love with me? Once, he took off his undershirt, drew a Japanese flag on it and then wrote his name and mine. Then, he inscribed it, "I will never forget you even if I die." You know what he wrote that with? With his own blood. The sight of the blood frightened me. When I told him that I didn't like it, he put his head down like a criminal and cried.

I also had an officer, a very old one, who wanted to have me to himself. When he was transferred, he told a friend of his to take good care of me. Whenever the soldier saw me with that officer, he was so jealous. He would have killed the officer if he could have. When he was able to come to my room, he would not do anything; he would just sit there and talk; or sing. Could he sing. If I were with other soldiers, he peeked into the room. That gave me the creeps.

No, I didn't sing with him. I can't sing. These days, when I watch television, and see all those young people making out, I wish I could have done those things but for me, no way. Lots of officers liked me. There was this officer, really old. His face was so full of wrinkles, big and small. He would not go to other women. He would come to me, only me. He would come to my room dead drunk and give me such a hard time all night. He didn't talk; he just wanted me to do all kinds of weird things. Even now, the thought of him makes me shudder.

Ishikawa is the one who comes to my thoughts even now. The one who wrote on his shirt with his blood. There were times when he made me detest him but his persistence moved my heart. He broke the rules many times because he could not help himself. He wanted to see me so much. So many times, he was punished. Sometimes, he would be kicked and thrown into the mud. His uniform would become muddy. I washed it, ironed it and put it back on him. Sometimes, if I saw an officer coming, I would hide him.

He asked me to marry him when the war was over. I remember telling him that I would not because I did not want to be treated as *Chosenjin* (Japanese used this term for Korean somewhat like a nigger). The Japanese would look down on me because I was not a Japanese. In any case, at that time, I had no thoughts of marriage. None. For one thing, I was afraid of being cheated. There was no way for me to tell if they had other women back home.

I was pregnant only once. I told you about that. After that, never again. I didn't want to. Do I regret that I don't have a child of my own? What's the use of having a child? Look at my fate. I was afraid mostly for myself. What could I have done with the baby? I was born with a fate that brings misfortune. Besides, I already had six stepchildren.

When I was in China in the military, I never thought it possible that I would live long enough to come back. Not one moment. The only wish I had was for Japan to win the war. I prayed for Japan's victory. Nothing else. No. I had no feelings for Korea. My *chung* for Korea had long been taken away from me. Whenever a Japanese airplane came, I felt so much exhilaration. What did Korea ever do for me? No Korean man ever loved me. I am still in favor of the Japanese. I think of Ishikawa more than my husband. I still like the Japanese in my heart. The only thing I wouldn't like —being looked down as *Chosenjin.*

It was with the Japanese that I experienced love. From the start, it was the Japanese who trained me, instructed me and showed me feelings. I never had such experiences with Koreans. I like the Japanese. Even now, if there were a good Japanese and conditions are right, I would marry him, not a Korean. If I find a Japanese who could take pity on me and give me some peace and rest for my remaining days, I would live with him.

I feel no *chung* for Koreans, I told you that. I was loyal to *Dennohaikai.* I saved all my pennies and contributed to the cause of the Emperor. I wanted Japan to win. You can't imagine how I felt when I saw a Japanese officer captured by the Chinese, tied and tortured. It broke my heart.

I confess, I had to work hard to control my urge to grab her shoulders and shake her.

I understand that others would feel differently and think it strange. . . . But I still like the Japanese. I don't blame them. It was the times in which they lived and in which Korea was too powerless to defend itself that made it possible for them to take away women. I only think about powerless Korea and the times in which those things happened. I feel so much more for the Japanese. Can you tell me why?

"Are you asking me to explain? You tell me. . ."

If I am puzzled myself why I feel this way, I surely can't help you understand. Maybe because Korea gave me nothing other than the accident of my birth. From the start, it was the Japanese who got me pregnant, tore away a baby girl from me and when I went to China, they literally stepped on me. But there were good people even among them. There were some for whom I felt *chung.* So much that I can't forget. I am being honest. I still think of some of them. If I knew where to find them, I would try to get in touch with them.

They were kind to me. They stole a blanket when I was cold. You should have seen our rooms. It was not like a Korean room in which you could get heat from underneath. It was so cold. No bed, either. Then, they would make a bed for me. When the mosquitos bothered me, they would somehow get hold of a scent to drive the mosquitos away. The small things they did for me, they were the ones who tied me to them with human warmth. When I was hungry, they stole food for me. You must understand that the soldiers didn't do those things for all the women. They did them for me, though.

*Her eyes held memories and a private smile appeared on her
lips.*

What I felt was human warmth, sympathy that bonded human beings together. You know, they were human beings. I remember the holidays when they made sticky, sweet rice Japanese cake. They stole those for me. I would fry them and eat them with soy sauce. It tasted so good. You should know that not all Japanese are bad. Even among them, there were good men. Believe me there were a plenty of bad ones but . . . The image of Ishikawa is still so vivid, it is still alive in me. My feelings were all mixed, detest, sympathy, and warmth. He was persistent, beaten so much and so often by the officers because of me but he wouldn't give up.

When Japan was defeated, I was sad. Not only that, I was mad that Japan had been defeated. I couldn't understand how Japan could lose! I had expected no less than Japan's victory. I had firmly believed they would win. Thinking back, I was totally converted to be a loyal Japanese. It never occurred to me that they would lose. I believed that they had to win! After all that, I don't blame Japan. Even now, if there were two men proposing, one Korean and the other Japanese, I would rather marry the Japanese.

I smothered sigh and clasped my hands together over my heart.

No reasons. No conditions, either. I was totally converted. My whole body and spirit were saturated with the spirit of Japan, maybe just like the communists. You think about what I had to go through on this Korean soil. Is there anything I could feel for it, I could care for? Suffering, toil and slaving. . . I had not known any good Korean. The reason why I could endure all that hardship with that husband of mine, is partly because I did not know any better Korean men.

Another thing. I don't like being a burden to others. I like to be on my own. The only thing I blame is my fate. It was my fate that I was born of such parents, especially my mother. The way my mother made me work . . . there isn't a thing I did not put my hands on. I did everything conceivable and inconceivable.

*She cited again all the hardships she had to go through with
her mother, then with her husband almost <u>verbatim</u>.*

I can tell you still want to know the reasons for my feelings about the Japanese. Don't ask me the reasons. Can't you just accept some things without knowing the reasons? I had *chung* for the Japanese but not for the Koreans. Ture, I did have some feelings for my husband. He was handsome, learned, and proud. So I felt proud to be with him. He had no money but he himself was so presentable. And of course, I tasted what real sex was like with him. But I don't think it was love. I am frank about this. Most of the time, I just accepted him as part of my fate. He didn't buy me a pair of rubber shoes, not one dress. That's not all. Would you believe that he had other women? He would bother me at night but during the daytime, while I was doing bone crushing hard work, he would do that thing with other women.

That far away look again . . .

Think of that blanket. You have no idea what he risked stealing that blanket. How can I forget the touch of that worn out army blanket he wrapped around me? Never. Not until I die and after I die. . . At the time, I had serious indigestion problems. He even improvised a heating pad for me whenever I felt sick. Of course, he brought medicine whenever he could. He was so tender, so gentle, so caring. . . How can I forget that? To Ishikawa, I was a person. I could not forget that blanket. How could I? That was Ishikawa. After he was sent back to Japan, he wrote me once but I never replied. He was persistent. Would I marry him now? If anybody, yes. What did Korea ever give me? Starting with my own mother . . .

I can't forget those individuals who showed me human tenderness, made me feel like a human being. How could I? Even now, in Japan, if I see men with gray hair, I think about those people back in China. I remember the nice things they did for me. For instance, that Japanese officer who came to me, only to me, he took me out just once to show me around. I remember that. No one had done that for me. I can't forget that. I don't know anything about Korea. Do you think I know how to get around in Seoul? I know nothing, just the unspeakable hardships.

Did I feel power when I was a shaman? When the spirit entered my body, I knew nothing. I was no longer there. In any case, I would not want to be a shaman. Do you know why? There is no recognition for shamans in our society. Only contempt. Many think of it as a lowly position. But you can't deny the existence of ghosts. They do exist. When people die, their souls travel around, the lost souls are in limbo. They couldn't go to heaven or hell. Strayed souls and mountain gods. You have to mind the mountain gods. They are powerful.

The life of a shaman, that's also a part of my sad fate. It is tough to be a shaman. It is like living under a wicked mother-in-law. You know the ghost orders me around and I have to obey no matter how difficult. These days, those ghosts of my mother, sister and brother largely leave me alone but not completely. They still chase me especially in my dreams. I feel no affection for those to whom I have blood ties.

There is no one to whom I feel tied. I am totally alone, just alone in this whole wide world. Totally alone. I am not lying. Whenever I think about this,

I stand in the storm of grief and tremble . . .
    Do you understand?

> *It wasn't really a question; she wanted to make sure that I under-stood.*[59]

Postscript

Ever since I met Grandma Bae in 1995, I was often invaded by the image of a woman following a man to be her husband, through the fields and valleys, deeper into the mountains in Kang Won Province, unaware of the fate awaiting her. Frequently, her voice rang in my ears, "What wedding!? He didn't buy me a pair of rubber shoes, not one dress!"

In 1997, I went to see her with my film crew. Inside a now familiar apartment building where she lives, I had the security guard dial her number. At the sound of "hello," a voice rang out, "I am on my way down. Stay put. I can't wait to see you." She didn't bother to find out who I was. After my call that morning, she must have been glued to the phone. Almost a year since I saw her last, she was the same. We hugged over many "aigo"s, a Korean phrase, an expression of both joy and sorrow. Only then did I notice a woman, shorter than Grandma Bae, standing behind her. "Oh, I brought a friend of mine to meet you, Grandma Hwang Koom Ja. You know, she also went. No need to ask what she meant.

When we stepped out of the elevator, the smell of soy bean soup welcomed us. "I prepared lunch for you all. You must eat before you do anything. Nothing good will come from an empty stomach," she declared firmly as we entered her apartment. The two grandmas started putting out little plates and bowls on the table which had been set in the mid-dle of the room. Charles, my director of photography, leaned against the wall and, responding to my worried look, said, "The sight of food makes me feel nauseated. I ate too much last night. Now sitting on the floor, leaning his back against the wall, Charles said, "A little rest will cure me. Just go ahead and eat. I'll be alright."

The food Charles missed! Two women would not join us, too busy making sure that every plate and bowl was re-filled. Grandma Koom Ja, her face shadowed with worry, surprised us. "You sick?" she asked Charles. "You speak English?" I exclaimed. "A little." She went to Charles, put both her hands on his shoulders and began massaging. "His muscles are tight," she explained in Korean, then to Charles, "Relax. Let your body rest in my hands." In Korean again, "From his eyes, I can see that he is a man of gentle soul. You know, I like these people (she means Black people)," now with her eyes sweeping from Charles to Willie who was busy enjoying the soup, "They know suffering. They would under-stand us." Here I had been secretly worried how they would receive African-Americans. I was almost in tears. Then, Grandma Bae sat by Charles, a needle with a long thread in her hand. "Ask him if I could go to work on him. I need to twitch his finger tip to get bad blood out and I will do some-thing for him that should help his sickness." "Of course," I said to myself, remembering her story about being a shaman when she returned from China. "Charles, Grandma Bae would like to help you. Will you trust yourself to her?" "Of course," is all Charles said with smile. Charles did not eat food with us but after the table was cleared, he did film them, looking remarkably better, as they told wrenching sto-ries.

I asked her again why she wanted to see Japan win the war. "We went there with the Japanese. We were the same with the Japanese. I knew nothing about Korea and Japan. I was too young and ignorant. I was blindly on the side of Japan. I am being honest. I am not lying. I was happy to see the Chinese lose and happy to see the Japanese win. I had no idea that the Japanese and Americans would fight each other. When the Chinese and Japanese fought, I believed that we could live only if Japan won. We had been thor-oughly contaminated by Japan." Then, I couldn't help but ask if she still rather marry a Japanese than a Korean. "I like Japanese because it was to Japanese that I first gave my feelings." Her tone, this time, was more cautious.

While I sat with camera rolling but unable to ask the next question, Grandma Bae volunteered. "when I was about eight or nine, the monk-you remember my mother's lover I told you about—he would tell me to come in, take off my clothes—whenever my mother was not there—you know, he would make me naked and do that thing and then I would bleed. He tried to do that thing whenever my mother was gone. So

96

whenever my mother was going out, I would follow her, crying. I yelled to my mother that he was trying to kill me. Then, my mother would throw stones so that I couldn't follow her."

My chest felt tight as if a thousand knots were tied around. What right did I have to yell at her for liking the Japanese? A Korean monk, her mother's lover, molested her and her mother didn't care for her enough to see what was going on. Or did she see it and ignore it?"

Grandma Bae wanted to give me a jar of home made kimchi to take back to my husband. That, I could not take but I did accept a black polyester blouse with a glittering zipper which she had bought for me as soon as I phoned from the States. That filled me with sorrow.

Whenever I think of her, which is often, I bow to her with my heart overflowing with shame and sadness that I had dared to think I understood this grandma and yelled at her. How can anyone come close to understanding this grandma? In the end, I believe she told me about her mother's monk lover to console me.

Chapter 5

REVIVED PAST

Silence Broken

Comfort women were not discussed openly in Korea or elsewhere until recently. Many attribute this to the women themselves, too ashamed of their pasts and too fearful of society's condemnation.

There is some truth in that. But not all women felt ashamed; many tried to reveal their experiences only to be ignored or stifled. Grandma Chung Seo Woon, a graceful woman, who speaks in even tones raised her voice one octave when I asked if she felt ashamed of her past. "No way! Why should I be ashamed? When I returned home, I told everything openly to all my friends and neighbors. Those who think it is shameful, I consider strange. Why is it our shame? Those who dragged us and treated us like slaves, as sex slaves, the Japanese government, they should feel shame, not us. Why us?" This grandma had told me about her first encounter with a Japanese officer, "At night, an officer came to my room. He ordered me to take off my clothes. I had heard that for some Japanese women (she was referring to Japanese prostitues)—they think nothing of putting on and taking off clothes. But for Korean women, we even avoided wearing short sleeve tops. How was it possible for me to take off my clothes and show my naked body to a strange man? You know that in those days, to Korean women, chastity was more precious than life itself, don't you?" She valued chastity but it had nothing to do with "the shame" often cited as a reason for silence.

The reasons for the long silence dwell with the governments and people of Japan as well as Korea, and the Allied Forces.

The Japanese government long advanced the view that the Emperor was all powerful and that any military act or policy could be justified in his name. That was the official memory under which the truth about its colonial domination or about the Asia/Pacific War was either suppressed or rationalized.[60] The Japanese wanted to push the military comfort women issue out of their memory, private and official. To that end, they destroyed most of the evidence and are unwilling to reveal what remains even today. Professor Yoshimi

98

Yoshiaki, a history professor at Chuo University told me in his cramped office, "The Japanese government burned public documents during the two week period between its surrender and the arrival of the U.S. Army of occupation. During that period, they burned most documents they had, because those documents might have worked against them in a court-martial. Since they could not recognize which documents would be used for trials, they burned everything published by government offices—especially documents about the Army and the police."

Attorney Takagi Ken'ichi, the chief counsel representing the former comfort women and other victims of the War who are suing the Japanese government, characterizes the Japanese people as "those who avoid confronting the past," but notes that the former soldiers who talk about the past, "boast how they had killed Chinese and what they had done to the comfort women but rarely do they look at it as regrettable history that should not be repeated."[61] Professor Yoshimi Yoshiaki echoes this observation, "In Japan, talk about the issue of 'military comfort women' was circulated secretly as a juicy story for a while after the war, but the issue was never taken up as a problem of human rights violations."[62] If they boast of their bravery, they also stress their suffering. Yoshimi says, "I have lived here all my life, and I know that Japan only talks about half of its history, the half where Japan is victimized."[63]

Neither the Korean people nor the government helped break the silence. Most of their families shut their ears, rarely giving these women a chance to talk to them, let alone to others. The family honor as well as keeping their faces were matters of far greater importance than the justice and pain of their sisters and daughters. I visited a former comfort woman living in the United States. She could not talk to me, she said, because her brother and sister threatened that they would send her back to Korea if she ever made her story public.

The violation of the chastity of these women was a matter of male as well as national pride. Some men felt dishonored by the violation of their (Korean) women by the colonizer and others ignored it as a non-issue. Some simply did not want to recall their colonial past. Further, the government has not considered it important enough to warrant attention in face of pressing economic issues and has been unwilling to alienate Japan, a crucial economic partner. The government neglected the issue in negotiating the 1965 Treaty with Japan which settled damages of the war and colonialism. In a society that still exploits women workers and embraces male dominated customs and laws, it is hardly surprising.

All in all, the political climate was not conducive to paying much attention to these appalling human rights violations. There were more important issues at hand such as the Cold War. Immediately after World War II, the Allied powers compiled extensive evidence about these women but took no steps, political or legal. Largely because the United States was eager to use Japan in the Cold War struggle with the Soviet Union, most Japanese war crimes were either swept under the rug or bargained away. The issue was ignored at the International Military Tribunal of the Far East (Tokyo Tribunal) and was not revived in the Peace Treaty of San Francisco in 1951.

Ironically, it was Japanese men who helped Korean women discover and expose this issue. The Republic of Korea in the 1970's experienced a thriving prostitution business around American military bases and among Japanese men. Japanese men flocked to Korea to enjoy sex easily and cheaply followed by fabulous dinners of Korean delicacies and with so much liquor that it could "break the table legs," as the Korean saying goes. This phenomenon earned the name, "sex tourism."

Because it involved a high percentage of Japanese men, Korean women, activists and scholars — many of them Christians—linked the thriving sex tourism with the buried past of Korean women sex slaves. Calling it a "new *Jungshindae*," these women recognized the importance of exposing the comfort women issue, at first not so much in its own right but as a political weapon against Japanese sex tours.

These women, under the auspices of a variety of organizations, urged their government to confront the issue. Sadly, however, the Korean government promoted sex tourism in order to obtain much needed foreign currency. Specific talks between the two governments came neither easily nor rapidly. During South Korean President Chun Doo Hwan's visit to Japan in 1984, the first friendly visit by a Korean head of the state, Japan's Emperor Hirohito, ruler of Korea from 1925 until 1945, said at a televised state banquet, "It is regrettable that there was an unfortunate past between us for a period in this century."

In May 1990, on the occasion of President Roh Tae Woo's official visit to Japan, three Korean women's organizations submitted a list of demands that they said should be presented to the Japanese government: admit the crime; apologize; and compensate the victims. During that visit, the new Emperor Akihito was still reserved but Prime Minister Kaifu Toshiki expressed apologies for the sufferings inflicted by Japan during the colonial period. Roh took this as a sign of progress and turned his energies to economic concerns.

Korean women persisted. In 1988, the Korean Church Women United, in conjunction with other women's groups, launched several activities, including: a survey of military sexual slavery; an International Conference on "Women and Tourism," where a historical connection between the sex tours and comfort women was discussed; and issuing public letters to both the Japanese and Korean governments urging them to disclose the truth about the comfort women. Also in 1988, pioneer researcher, Professor Yun Chong-Ok, accompanied by two members of the Korean Church Woman United, set out to investigate the issue first hand.

Outrage about sex tours spread beyond Korean women. Other Asian women joined and, as early as 1977, formed the Asian Women's Association to protest Japanese sex tours; and the protest spread to Japan, the Philippines, Taiwan, Thailand and North Korea.[64] In Korea, heightened efforts brought birth to "The Korean Council for the Women Drafted for Military Sexual Slavery by Japan"—*Jungshindae Daechaek Wewon Hoe* (Hereafter, the Korean Council). A coalition of 18 women's organizations dedicated to exposing the truth about the comfort women and other issues related to Japanese colonialism in Korea, this historic formation was achieved under the leadership of Professor Yun on November 16, 1990. A similar coalition was formed in Japan.

The Japanese government resisted acknowledgment every step of the way, advancing three points: 1) the comfort houses and women were privately run businesses without government involvement; 2) the women were not recruited against their will; and 3) the 1965 "normalization" agreement between Japan and the Republic of Korea officially resolved all issues related to the war.

In August 1991, a crucial event gave impetus to the movement; the first public testimony by a former comfort woman, Kim Hak Soon.[65] I went to see her in 1995 in Seoul. "What prompted me to come out publicly were the lies by Japan. In 1991, I learned in the television news and in the newspapers that the Japanese government kept denying its involvement in drafting comfort women and administering the comfort stations. They kept saying Koreans sent these women to make money; that Japan had nothing to do with it; that Koreans did it to make money. It hurt my insides, heart and mind. I said to myself, 'Why doesn't someone stop them? Someone has to stop the lies.' After all those cruel things they did to the Koreans, they still lie. I couldn't bear it. How could they tell such lies? Finally, I had to declare that I was a living witness." She did in August 1991.

In December 1991, Kim Hak Soon along with two other former comfort women sued the Japanese government in a Tokyo district court. Of the three, only Grandma Kim revealed her name. Since then, many other comfort women joined the suit, beginning with six Korean comfort women in April 1992. The Korean Council, joined by groups in Japan, Philippines, Taiwan, Hong Kong, Thailand, and Indonesia, have engaged in a number of activities including: installing a hotline in Seoul for victims, relatives, former recruiters and others to come forward; and the "Wednesday Demonstrations." The longest running weekly demonstration in South Korea, a noon time gathering in front of the Japanese Embassy in Seoul, began on January 8, 1992 and continues.[66]

When Japanese Prime Minister Miyazawa Kiichi arrived in Seoul on the

16th of January 1992, he flew into a storm of demonstrations by Koreans demanding that the Japanese Government apologize and compensate for tens of thousands of Korean women whom Japan had forced to become sex slaves. On January 17th, in a speech to South Korea's National Assembly, Miyazawa made a carefully worded statement: "Recently, the issue of 'comfort women' in the service of the Imperial Japanese Army has come into light. I cannot help feeling acutely distressed over this, and I express my sincerest apology."[67]

This did not come easily. During the few weeks prior to Miyazawa's official visit to Seoul primarily to discuss economic issues, two crucial events had taken place. First, in December 1991, Yoshimi Yoshiaki discovered documents that made it impossible for the Japanese Government to deny its involvement in the comfort women system. He explained to me on camera in April 1997, pointing to a document. "Let me introduce the first material I found in December 1991. One document stated that the Japanese government approved governmental involvement with the comfort women system. The document was issued by the Japanese Army. On March 4, 1938, it stated that war broke out in China and that the Army had started to establish comfort facilities. The army chose purveyors and sent them to Japan, Korea, and Taiwan to recruit women. This document is a notice addressed to the chief of staff at the Japanese Army in China—North and Mid Region. The notice said that an expeditionary army should control the recruitment of comfort women to avoid problems, the purveyors working with military and civilian police." Second, prompted by Yoshimi's discovery, the Japanese Government admitted on the 13th of January 1992 that the Japanese Army forced tens of thousands of Korean women to have sex with Japanese soldiers

Two Japanese, Miyazawa and Yoshimi, the prime minister and the professor, prompted American newspapers in January 1992 to print stories about the comfort women. 1992 was a crucial year for the comfort women issue, cutting across boundaries of nationality, race and ethnicity, especially among Asian women. This movement of women in Asia extended to men and around the world. In addition to pressuring the Japanese and Korean governments, they engaged in fact finding efforts. Scholars, legal experts and activists from around the world put this issue in the wider context of a variety of war crimes. Soon the Japan Federation of Bar Associations (JFBA), an independent organization of Japanese practicing attorneys, and the Korean Bar Association became devoted supporters. Further, the comfort women issue attracted Koreans abroad: support groups were born among Korean American communities in New York, Los Angeles, Washington, D.C., Chicago, Hawaii, and Toronto.

In February 1992, the Korean Council petitioned the United Nations Commission on Human Rights to urge Japan to investigate the issue properly, reveal Japan's war time wrongdoings, and compensate the survivors. Since then, the issue of sexual slavery has caught on with an impressive array of

Non Governmental Organizations (NGO) around the world, exploring the issue in the context of contemporary forms of slavery, trafficking in women and forced labor. The efforts of individuals and organizations of the international community culminated in August 1993 when the Sub-Commission on Prevention of Discrimination and Protection of Minorities resolved that a special rapporteur be appointed to study systematic rape, sexual slavery and similar practices, marking the first UN investigation of Japanese war crimes.[68]

Pressed by the irrefutable facts persistently dug up bit by bit, no matter how deeply they had been hidden; the sorrow and fury expressed by the victims; and the moral outrage expressed by the advocacy groups, the Japanese Government responded, issuing on August 4, 1993 a special report, officially admitting the direct involvement of the military. It acknowledged the military establishment and operation of the comfort stations. Further, when discussing recruitment, the report states that: the "administrative/military personnel took part directly; even the private recruiters acted "at the request of the military; and that such means as "coaxing and coercion" were used.[69]

The Japanese government issued a number of public apologies, some to specific countries, including South and North Korea and the Philippines, during United Nations sessions. Japan has apologized. Prime Ministers Miyazawa Kiichi, Murayama Tomichi, Foreign Minister Watanabe Michio and others apologized in public, a long journey from the initial denials of any coercion or official involvement. However, these apologies are what non-Japanese journalists call "diluted apologies" and my grandmas call "meaningless" since the expressions ranged from "remorse (*hansei*)," "deep reflection," "aggression like acts," and "acts of aggression." No expressions like "crime" and "war of aggression" have been used.[70]

Additionally, in September 1994, the Japanese Prime Minister announced the "Murayama Plan," which evolved into a proposal to establish a governmental foundation with over 1 billion dollars (U.S.) from the government and a non-governmental foundation with funds donated by private citizens and organizations. Both funds are called "Asian Peace and Friendship Fund for Women." There is a catch, however. Only civilian funds may be used for direct payments to the victims; government funds would promote Asian peace and friendship.

The apologies and the "Murayama Plan" do not mean an admission of guilt in any legal sense. The long-kept silence was broken but the struggle to bring justice is on-going. No movements are more significant than the actions of the women themselves. It is only fitting to end this account with the words of the women.

Grandma Chung Seo Woon responds to this plan: "10 *won*, 100 *won*, *1000 won*, it doesn't matter. If the Japanese government compensates us legally, that money I will accept. Instead of legal reparation, they offer us private money. Unthinkable. What happened to us is bad enough. Why should we become prostitutes? If we receive private funds, we become prostitutes. I want to die as a daughter of Korea."

I went back to see Grandma Kim Hak Soon a few months after I initially met her. I asked if she would tell me her experiences since she went public in August 1991. "As you know, I have been to Japan many times to give testimonies. I've been amazed by how the Japanese people, especially the young ones, are unaware of what their country did. They don't know the aggressive war history at all. On the other hand, every single one of them knows about the atomic bombs dropped on Hiroshima and Nagasaki. That's the only thing they have been taught; that Japan was a victim, not the victimizer. So everywhere I went, I told them, 'It is your obligation to know about your past. I want the Japanese young people to know about what happened.' For that matter, it is same with Korean young people. They don't know about any of this either. I stressed, every chance I got, the importance for young people to know about the past horror so that it won't be repeated. It is important to leave as accurate a history as possible.

"As far as I could tell, for the past four years since I told the world about my past, Japan has not really changed in any fundamental sense." "But what about the fact that the Japanese government apologized?" I asked. "What apologies? If they did apologize, they did it bit by bit whenever they were cornered and had no place to hide. They hardly make any straightforward statement about anything. They always say, 'It appears . . .'"

"I am fed up with their lies. I tell them, 'You would be amazed how good it would feel to tell the truth, to get the truth out of your chest. Try that and that's the only human thing to do.' That's what I say in the Japanese courts as well. They seem to be in the perpetual habit of saying one thing and even before I have a chance to turn around, they say quite another. I also tell them, 'You should learn how to keep promises. A promise is something you say and keep.'

"The most impressive or most unforgettable thing — the prayer meeting with a fast in Japan. We did it last year (1994). We all sat around in front of the Japanese Diet. Lots of Japanese including Japanese students came and joined us. The majority of Japanese of our generation simply avoided us. But there was one Japanese man, about seventy years of age who came and said, holding my hand, 'I know you are telling the truth. I know all about it because I was an army doctor in China.' Then, he sat beside me. So there are some good Japanese people.

"But it's a different story for the government. The government must come clean and admit their guilt, both legal and moral. It is nonsense for the Japanese to talk about civilian funds.

"Sometimes, I feel more discouraged with my own people, the Koreans.

From left to the right
Song Shin Do, a former comfort woman living in Japan, Hwang Koom Ja, Bae Jok Gan, former comfort women in Seoul, Korea.
Chung Seo Woon, a former comfort woman in Jin Hae, Korea, Hwang Keum Ju, a former comfort woman whose testimony I translated in 1992.
Ha Gun Ja, Hong Kang Lim, former comfort women whom I met in Wuhan, China.
Park Oak Yeun, a former comfort woman whom I met in Sharing Home, Seoul, Korea.

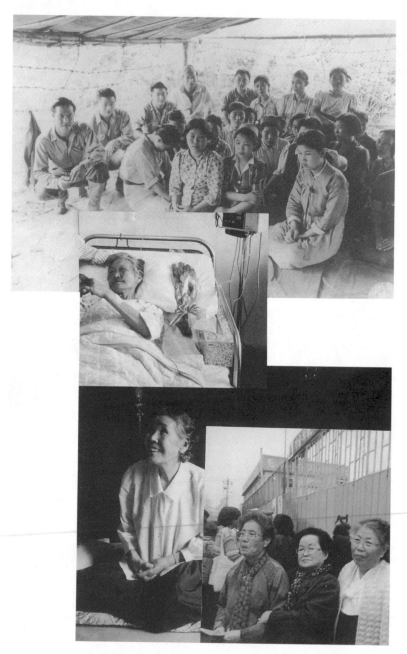

Capt. Won-loy Chan, Sgts. Howard Furumoto, Grant Hirabayashi, and Robert Honda with Korean comfort women, Myitkyina, Burma, August 1944. Courtesy of Grant Hirabayashi.
Chung Soo Jae, a former comfort woman who was brought to Seoul by Elder Kim Won Dong.
Kim Hak Soon, a former comfort woman who became the first public witness.
Chung Seo Woon, Bae Jok Gan, Hwang Keum Ju at Wednesday noon demonstration 1998.

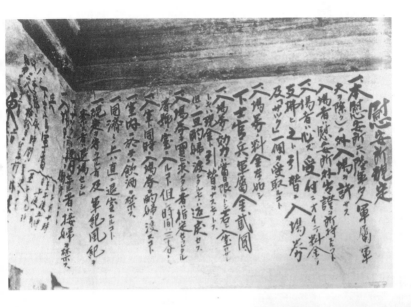

Regulations posted at a Japanese military-run comfort station near Shanghai, 1938.
Draftees to Jungshindae (voluntarily committing body corps) some of whom were forcibly sent to comfort houses.
Soldiers lining up at a comfort station in Hankow, China.

Ikeda Masae, a former elementary school teacher in Seoul, Korea.
Professor Yun Chong-Ok, pioneer researcher and activist.
Professor Yoshimi Yoshiaki, History, Chuo University, Japan.

Kawakubo Toshio, a former Japanese soldier.

Tokuda Masanori, a former Japanese soldier.

Yun Doo Ri, a former comfort woman living in Ulsan, Korea. Dai Sil Kim-Gibson.

Wednesday noon demonstrations in front of the Japanese Embassy in Seoul, Korea.
The longest running weekly demostration in South Korea, it began on January 8, 1992 and
continues.

The film crew.

As you might guess, quite a few people recognize my face. I would see Korean women in their sixties and fifties. They would say, 'Did you get some money from Japan?' They ask not because they are concerned about it; they are cynical — they think we are out to collect money, that that's the only thing we are after. You should see their tone and expression. Whenever that happens, I truly wonder if they are human beings, let alone Koreans who share the same history. So many Koreans are so selfish; the only thing they think about is their own welfare. You know our history is full of factional strife. I believe that still continues. If we don't watch out, Japan will snatch our country again in no time at all.

"Of course, I am grateful to those who have worked hard on our behalf but I must tell you that sometimes they forget the real thing, the victims. They mean well but sometimes they are immersed in their own self-righteous cause."

Legal Hide and Seek

In April 1996, the Special Rapporteur of the United Nations on violence against women, Radhika Coomaraswamy, submitted a report on the comfort women to the fifty-second session of the U.N. Commission on Human Rights. Despite the Japanese government's protest, the report was officially recognized by the UN Commission on April 19, 1996 (E/CN.4/1996/53/Add.1). Concluding that "the practice of 'comfort women' should be considered a clear case of sexual slavery and a slavery-like practice in accordance with the approach adopted by relevant international human rights bodies and mechanisms," she recommended that the government of Japan accept legal responsibility for violating its obligations under international law; pay compensation to individual victims; and "identify and punish, as far as possible, perpetrators involved in the recruitment and institutionalization of comfort stations." This was a dramatic development.

In response, expressing serious reservations about the legal arguments, the Japanese government denied that under international law Japanese actions were crimes of slavery, crimes against humanity and war crimes; and disputed the individual victims' right to compensation, claiming that the San Francisco Treaty of 1951 and the bilateral treaty between Japan and Korea in 1965 had resolved this issue. Further, Japan should be allowed, the government argues, to claim the statute of limitations in dealing with the legal issues, including prosecution of offenders.

Despite mounting opposition in the world community, including many Japanese citizens, the Japanese government's position on legal liability remains unchanged. In response, another report by Special Rapporteur Gay J. McDougall was submitted to the UN Commission on Human Rights in June 1998 (E/CN.4/Sub.2/1998/13). Calling Japan's actions of sexual slavery, "the most egregious international crimes of slavery, crimes against humanity and war crimes," McDougall concluded that "the Japanese government remains liable for grave violations of human rights and humanitarian law, violations that amount in their totality to crimes against humanity." She recommended that the United Nations High Commissioner for Human Rights establish mechanisms for criminal prosecutions, and for individual legal compensation. She recognized that the Japanese government "has taken some steps to apologize and atone" but stresses that "anything less than full and unqualified acceptance by the Government of Japan of legal liability and the consequences that flow from such liability is wholly inadequate."

Crimes against Humanity

To date Japan refuses to admit that the actions related to the sexual slavery are crimes against humanity, arguing that the concept of "gross violations of human rights and fundamental freedoms" is vague as a legal concept and requires further study. (E/CN.4/Sub.2/1994/7Add.1)[71] Further, the government points to the Tokyo Tribunal of 1946 where the Allies did not find anyone guilty of crimes dealing with comfort women. Thus, what Japan did to these women cannot be crimes against humanity.

There is nothing vague about Japan's acts; they were "enslavement," "deportation," "other inhumane acts," and "persecutions on political or racial grounds," as defined in the Nuremberg Charter and adopted at the Tokyo Tribunal.[72] Japan committed crimes against humanity under international law by violating international treaties and customary international law. The Hague Convention of 1907 "Regarding the Laws and Customs of Land Warfare" dealt with civilians in occupied territories, and identified the need for the "respect for the lives of the persons," and to protect "family honor and rights" (Article 46).[73] Japan's treatment of comfort women is a direct violation of customary international law. Further, in international law, especially in relation to armed conflicts, rape has been condemned as a form of torture. At Nuremberg, all forms of torture were denounced.

The case of the comfort women would certainly be considered slavery and forced labor—acts which received strong international condemnation long before World War II, going as far back as 1815 Declaration Relative to the Universal Abolition of the Slave Trade. At the beginning of the 20th century, all nations were under the obligation to prohibit the slave trade under customary international law. The 1926 Slavery Convention of the League of Nations defines slavery and the slavery trade in Article 1 as follows: "Slavery is the status or condition of a person over whom any or all the powers attaching to the right of ownership are exercised. The slave trade includes all acts involved in the capture, acquisition or disposal of a person with the intent to reduce him to slavery . . . , and, in general, every act of trade or transport in slaves." In March 1996, at the 83rd session of the International Labour Conference, the Committee of Experts on the Application of Conventions and Recommendations concluded that the acts committed against the comfort women were "sexual slavery in violation of the ILO's Convention No. 29, namely, 'the Forced Labor Convention,' which Japan ratified in 1932."

Traffic in women and children was included in customary international law even before slavery was prohibited under international law. In the latter half of the 18th century in Europe, women and children were kidnapped, frequently for the purpose of prostitution. As a result, in 1910, the International Convention for the Suppression of Traffic in Women and Children for the Purposes of Forced Prostitution was convened. In 1925, Japan became a party to this convention with an expressed reservation about the article defining minors as those under age 21. Japan's prostitution regulation set the minimum age at 18.

As for the Tokyo Tribunal, no judgment was ever rendered on this issue; it was simply never brought forth and properly adjudicated. After Japan signed the Instrument of Surrender on September 2, 1945, the United States, directing and dominating the occupation of Japan, spearheaded the Far Eastern war crimes operation. General Douglas MacArthur was appointed Supreme Commander of the Allied Powers (SCAP). The International Military Tribunal for the Far East (IMTFE), the so-called Tokyo Tribunal, was born on January 19, 1946 with the explicit purpose of insuring "the just and prompt trial and the punishment of the major war criminals in the Far East" (Article I of the Charter of the IMTFE).[74] It was prompt; the trial was completed November 12, 1948. Whether it was "just" is another issue.

Twenty eight civilian and military leaders of the Japanese government were indicted on 55 counts. Seven military officers were sentenced to death by hanging, sixteen to life-sentences, one to twenty years and one to seven years imprisonment.[75] The predominant charges were waging wars of aggression, Class A crimes, "Crimes Against Peace." When it came to the cases of gross human rights violations, the B and C class war crimes,[76] the Tribunal concentrated on Western victims, and no justice was meted out to the crimes committed against Asians, especially comfort women. Based on their own documents, it is clear that the Allies knew about the comfort women; they repatriated many and conducted studies about them.[77] Direct documentation of the Korean comfort women appears in a report attached to U.S. Army Forces Ladia-Burma Theater, prepared by the United States Office of the War Information, Psychological Warfare Team. I interviewed a Japanese American, former U.S.Sgt. Grant Hirabayashi, who interrogated Korean comfort women in Burma immediately after the fall of Myitkyina on August 3, 1944.[78]

Despite this omission, General MacArthur stated, "I can find nothing of technical commission or omission in the incidents of the trial itself of sufficient import to warrant any intervention in the judgments which have been rendered. No human decision is infallible but I can conceive of no judicial process where greater safeguard was made to evolve justice . . . I pray that an Omnipotent Providence may use this tragic expiation as a symbol to summon all persons of good will to a realization of the utter futility of war . . ." Further, they made deals. The United States Army helped cover up the biological warfare program conducted by Unit 731 and made a deal to grant immunity from war crimes prosecution to the doctors in exchange for their data. This most revolting experiment, far removed from actual combat, was ignored during the Tokyo Tribunal.[79]

While those responsible for the crimes committed against Asians were not prosecuted, the Allies convicted a total of 178 Taiwanese and 148 Koreans of Class B or C crimes at trials in Singapore, Yokohama, Rabaul, Manila and elsewhere. Twenty nine Taiwanese and twenty three Koreans died in prison.[80] Some of the best educated people in Korea were mobilized to serve in the Japanese military, given the status of para-military personnel with the rank of noncommissioned officer, but their actual status was worse or as bad as that of a common soldier. Countless Koreans were taken to POW camps in Southeast Asia by Japan and forced to work as prison guards.

"No one could imagine anything worse than a Japanese guard until Korean guards began turning up," writes Gavan. "Tens of thousands of Korean men were drafted into the Japanese Army as service troops. Three or four thousand wound up as prison camp guards in Southeast Asia." If Korean guards proved worse than the Japanese, in part at least, it was because they received unspeakable treatment themselves from the Japanese. "Japanese guards treated Korean guards no better than prisoners," explains Gavan, "like another breed of mongrel dog to kick. One Korean who learned a bit of English in the camps used to say on the quiet, 'Japan no pucking good.' The prisoners christened him George Pucking, and he preferred that name over the Japanese name he hated."[81] The prisoners knew the names and the faces of the Korean guards. That's why so many of them were convicted of Class B and C war crimes. These Koreans, people of a colony, were punished again by the Allies for the work they did, forced by the colonizer.

It is clear that a major factor in the Allied decision to terminate the war trials in 1948 was for a greater cause, Cold War strategy. They were eager to rapidly demilitarize and democratize Japan and to restore political and economic stability to East Asia. The United States was anxious to fill the Pacific power vacuum, and to forestall potential Soviet aggression. When war broke out in Korea in June 1950, the United States had already made Japan a useful ally. That war made the United States even more convinced that an early peace with Japan was imperative.

The tribunals conducted by the Allied Forces, especially the Tokyo

Tribunal, while not designed to "set standards of international morality," as General MacArthur stated, clearly failed to meet basic standards of racial and gender justice, that is, if Asians are to be included in what General MacArthur called "all persons of good will." At a minimum, the Tribunal made a serious mistake of omission or opportunistic behavior. The Tokyo Tribunal did not call Emperor Hirohito, who under the Meiji Constitution bore ultimate responsibility for the war, into account for Japan's war of aggression. The Tribunal did not even summon him as a witness. This was most likely a calculated political decision in the best interests of the Allied powers.

Individual Rights to Compensation

Japan argues that individual victims have no right to compensation (the word, "compensation" is often used to distinguish from "reparations" which is traditionally referred to as collective claims by states, and to define it as individual rights to claim damages, including injustices inflicted). They maintain that the San Francisco Treaty and the Japan-Korea Treaty of 1965 preclude individuals from bringing claims, and that individual rights cannot be claimed under international law unless recognized by treaties.

That is not the case with the two treaties. In San Francisco, fifty two nations met with Japan and signed the Treaty of Peace on September 8, 1951. The Treaty terminated the occupation, dissolved the office of Supreme Commander for the Allied Powers, ended the war between Japan and the Allied powers and recognized the sovereignty of the Japanese people.

The Treaty acknowledged that "Japan should pay reparations to the Allied Powers for the damage and suffering caused by it during the war," simultaneously recognizing that "the resources of Japan are not presently sufficient, if it is to remain a viable economy, to make complete reparation for all such damage and suffering and at the same time meet its other obligations" (Article 14).[82] The Allied powers attended to their own damages, and waived reparations from Japan but ignored other victims in the Asia-Pacific theater.

The Allied powers bent over backwards to accommodate the interests of Japan, but not those of the former Japanese colonies. The nations that were inflicted with the worst damage—China, Korea, both North and South, and Mongolia—were not invited to the negotiation table. The Democratic People's Republic of Korea cited its guerrilla activities in China to contend that the country was in a state of war with Japan and should be a party to the Treaty. It was to no avail. Hence, because of its former status as a Japanese colony, Korea could not be regarded as a sovereign belligerent on either side. The treaty, however, did restore Korean sovereignty and provided for a legal settlement of claims, which eventually became the basis for the 1965 Treaty. The government of the Philippines, which was a party to the Treaty, did not approve the above waiver by the Allied Powers and did not ratify the San Francisco Treaty until 1956.

Japan steadily relies on the San Francisco waiver and maintains that all claims have been settled. The Allied Powers demonstrated remarkably little interest in seeing justice done to peoples of Asian origin and they acknowledged that Japan was unable to provide reparations at the time of the Treaty but there is no clear evidence that the right of individuals to seek compensation was waived and that Japan was released from obligations.

The 1965 Treaty between Japan and Korea was a political rather than a legal settlement, the primary objective being the establishment of future economic ties. Japanese funds provided under this treaty were described as the "Independence Congratulation Fund." The total funds consisted of $300 million in grants, $200 million in soft loans, and an undertaking to obtain private credit in the order of $300 million.

From the early 1950's, negotiations between Japan and Korea were troubled. Japan and Korea did not see eye to eye about the colonial administration of Korea by Japan. At the third negotiating session, a Japanese representative, Kubota Keichiro, suggested that Korea's autonomy prior to Japan's agreement at the San Francisco Peace Treaty was a violation of international law[83] and that Japan did much good for Korea through its colonial rule.[84] The talks were broken off in October 1953.

The United States intervened, deeming it necessary to improve relations between Japan and Korea in the interest of unity against the Soviet Union and the People's Republic of China. The United States pressed for re-opening of the Japan-Korea talks and, in 1961, Japan recanted the statement by Kubota. The resulting Treaty of 1965 created a Japan-U.S.-South Korean tripartite system in Northeast Asia. On June 22, 1965, the Minister of Foreign Affairs of the Republic of Korea, Lee Dong Won, and the Japanese Foreign Minister, Shiina Etsusaburo, exchanged documents. Japan recognized the Republic of Korea (ROK) as the "sole legal" government in Korea as defined by the U.N. South Koreans made claims for debts, such as unpaid wages and savings held in Japan. Japan demanded that the claimants present justifiable legal grounds and compile extensive documentation. Koreans were in a difficult position to meet this demand; the country was in a state of chaos due to the Pacific and Korean wars. Further, there were a number of unclear legal aspects arising from the Japanese sovereignty over Korea from 1910 to 1945, e.g., the 1905 Treaty between Japan and Korea and the 1910 Annexation of Korea to Japan. South Koreans could not conduct an exhaustive and speedy search for evidence of claims. And Japan rejected all claims having to do with reparations.

The Koreans engaged in the negotiations did not take up the comfort women issue. Given the male chauvinism that runs deep in Korean society, it is not likely that the negotiators would have considered these issues sufficiently important to be on the political agenda, already fraught with obstacles. As for the United States, the rights of these women was a non issue. And Japan maintains that all claims were settled at the 1965 Treaty. Special Rapporteur, McDougall, thinks otherwise. She writes, ". . .it is an economic treaty that resolves 'property" claims between the countries and does not address human rights issues. There is no reference in the treaty to 'comfort women,' rape, sexual slavery, or any other atrocities committed by the Japanese against Korean civilians." The funds provided by Japan under the Settlement Agreement were intended only for economic restoration; it was not intended to address the atrocities committed against individuals and the "claims" that were settled in the 1965 do not exclude the rights to individual compensation.

McDougall further points out, "Agreements concluded by Japan with some of the Allied Powers refer to individual redress, unlike those agreements concluded with Korea and the Philippines, which refer only to State claims for redress," and cites as cases in point the Greece-Japan Agreement, the United-Kingdom-Japan Agreement, and the Canada-Japan Agreement. Cearly, Japan made explicit apologies and agreed to pay personal injury compensation with Western powers but not with Asians.

Finally, the Japanese government refutes the applicability of international law to individuals. The individual is not a subject of international law, it argues, and there are no international procedures available for individuals to exercise their rights. Much of the human rights question is "a matter of the domestic policy of each state, including the 'right to reparations'." And each state has a different legal system to protect human rights, which makes "genuine international applicability" of any standard difficult.[85] The Japanese government states, "As for the obligation to pay compensation to individuals, it is the established rule that an individual cannot be a subject of rights or duties in international law unless his or her right is expressively provided in a treaty and the procedure for exercising the right is guaranteed under international law as well."[86]

Many find this argument without merit. Again, both Special Rapporteurs argue that international human rights instruments are examples of individual rights recognized by international law and cite the Universal Declaration of Human Rights as further evidence that the individual is often the subject of international law and entitled to its protection.

Prosecution and Punishment of the Perpetrators

Special Rapporteur McDougall stresses the importance of prosecuting those responsible for implementing the comfort women system and recommends that "the United Nations High Commissioner for Human Rights should work for the prosecution in Japan, and in other jurisdictions, of those responsible for the atrocities that have now been clearly linked to the actions of the Japanese military in establishing Japanese rape camps."[87]

The former comfort women and others argue that in order to bring full legal justice, the persons responsible for the system should be prosecuted. Without this, the struggle will merely become a question of monetary compensation at the expense of the human rights issue. For this reason, the Korean Council for the Women Drafted for Sexual Slavery by Japan filed a "Complaint" in the Tokyo District Prosecutor's Office on February 7, 1994. They brought charges "against the defendants for committing War Crimes and Crimes against Humanity and firmly requests the Public Prosecutor of the Tokyo District in Japan to investigate the charges and to punish the defendants accordingly." They want not only apologies but also penalties. McDougall urges that the Japanese government act as a matter of urgency on this complaint and seek to bring charges against any surviving individuals responsible for this crime.

The demands for prosecution are growing stronger. The Fifth Solidarity Forum of Asian Women on Military Sexual Slavery was held in Seoul, Korea in April 1998, with participants from the Phillipines, Indonesia, Taiwan, Japan, South Korea and America (including myself). The three day conference, defining the case of comfort women as "an unprecedented case of systematic sexual slavery, forced upon by the Japanese government on women during wartime," declared that the successful resolution of this issue will mark a most significant event in combatting the continuing human rights violations of women worldwide, and resolved "to make more forceful efforts to prosecute those responsible for the crimes and to uncover relevant documents to establish truth about the matter."

Japan objects, resorting to legal technicalities. "It is true that some of the international humanitarian treaties drafted after the Second World War, including the Geneva Conventions (1949) and the Optional Protocol I thereto (1977) require States to take domestic measures to punish violators of certain human rights, and that most of the States in the world have acceded to the Geneva Conventions. But this does not prove the general applicability of such requirements." They claim that without "common understanding of what activities constitute 'crimes under international law,' it is not possible to punish, *nulla poena sine lege,* no punishment without law. The current definitions about what activities warrant punishment are too "vague."[88]

Then, there is the statute of limitations. Japan duly acknowledges that "The Convention on the Non-Applicability of Statutory Limitations to War Crimes and Crimes Against Humanity" was adopted by the United Nations General Assembly in 1968, came into effect in 1970, and has since been ratified by 36 states." However, the Japanese government maintains that it is not a universally recognized principle. Japan did not ratify it![89]

Japan, then, expounds the wisdom of not making exceptions in applying the statutory limitation on the grounds that: 1) in civil cases, it is a mandatory provision for the stability of society; 2) in criminal cases, "the necessity of punishment declines and the effective value of punishment is extinguished as the social impact of the crime declines over time; and 3) there is increasing difficulty in proving a suspect's guilt with the passage of time, due to the "scattering of evidence." They maintain that, as time passes, the victim's feelings and the public demand for retribution against the offender gradually fade. Further, they worry about the "possibility of wrong judgment," if too much time has passed.[90]

There is, however, a consensus about Japan's responses in the legal community including McDougall, Theo von Boven, Radhika Coomaraswamy, and former Special Rapporteurs of the UN Commission on Human Rights. First, they agree that "gross violations of humanity" is not a vague legal concept, at least by the judgments at Nuremberg; any disinterested person can clearly see that the offenses committed against the comfort women constituted a gross violation of humanity. Nothing but legal hide and seek. This becomes even more apparent when compared with Germany's postwar policies and practices. Germany has paid billions of dollars in direct compensation to its World War II victims. German industries that utilized forced or slave labor have also made reparations recently. For instance, in the June 12, 1988 issue of the *Los Angeles Times*, it was announced that Daimler-Benz agreed to pay $11.7 million to the survivors of some 46,000 laborers. To date, the Federal Republic of Germany has paid over $55 billion in reparations to Israel and to individual victims. Clearly, Germany considers compensation a matter of national honor and an expression of its commitment to principles of international law. Japan should do no less.

Second, it is generally agreed that the time bar should be removed in the case of the comfort women, primarily on the general principle that claims relating to reparations for gross human rights violations should not be subject to a statute of limitations at all. In cases of the comfort women, evidence is by no means stale; it is compelling. Most of the evidence only came forth recently largely because Japan itself has been withholding much of it. It is absurd for Japan to claim a time bar when it controlled much of the evidence. Above all, on the basis of all the victims I interviewed, I saw no sign of fading feelings. They have only begun to express their pain. They still have nightmares; the imperial soldiers are still invading them in a variety of forms.

All in all, the obstacles to rendering the justice due to these women, i.e., legal compensation to individuals and punishment of the perpetrators, seem almost insurmountable. Even if Japan's legal objections could be removed and legal recourse could be found to deal with the prosecution of the perpetrators, there is the problem of finding defendants. Because the crime was committed so long ago, it is a difficult, if not impossible task to find the criminals. Many of them are, of course, dead. The best known defendant who was ultimately responsible is dead — Emperor Hirohito! In all forty four years of his post-war reign in Japan, the Emperor never discussed the war with his own people, the Emperor whom the war-time generation had been taught to worship as a living god, and in whose name so many innocent people died. Of course, we remember that the Tokyo Tribunal did not charge him.

As long as Japan hides behind legal technicalities and interpretations, forever keen on procedures and interpretations guided by political interests, legal arguments may continue long after all these women are dead and buried. These women are old, frail and lonely. Some suggest that the current Japanese proposal for private funds, as a joint project between the government and citizens, is based on an admission of moral guilt, not legal. However, in this case, if one truly admits moral guilt, there is ample room for interpretation that would directly point to legal guilt. Law as a system is fundamentally based on notions of right and wrong, on basic moral concepts of human worth and relationships. Japan, in attempting to separate morality from law, backed itself into a corner with legal arguments that are technical and hollow. The proposed solution, designed to avoid admitting legal guilt is, itself, a sign of immorality, a lack of true contrition. It is clearly a political effort to mollify critics and to avoid government acknowledgment which might lead to law suits.[91]

I asked Grandma Song Shin Do what she hoped to get from the lawsuit. "Justice and money," she said. "You know, the Japanese dragged and killed Koreans like dogs. That's not all. They killed Chinese like flies. They can't just get away with that. But the words of apologies are not enough, no matter how many words and how many times they say them. Their words are meaningless anyway; they don't say what they mean and mean what they say. I want money."

"What would you do with the money?" "All those Japanese who were involved in the war, the veterans and such, they live on government pensions. And the pension for them is a sign of pride. But the Koreans? They are not treated the same way, no matter how much we did for the war effort. I had to fight like hell to receive some help from the government. It is not the same as a pension; it is welfare, which is not nearly enough to live on. Even then they do everything to make the welfare recipients feel shame for that help. We are constantly looked down upon.

"It is important for me to be independent. Even now, I get up at 4 o'clock every morning and do whatever work I can to earn money for my living. I want the compensation so that I can live the remaining days of my life with my head held high. More than that, I want to pay back all those who helped me with my lawsuit. I am grateful for their help but I want to pay them back.

And of course, I will give money to those who need and deserve it. I have no attachment to money but it is something I can put to good use.

"Greed is no good. I knew nothing about the war and all that but I know this: the Japanese were blind with greed and that's why they lost the war. They are still greedy because they are not returning things that rightfully belong to others. I am not begging for money. I demand my money. Justice demands that they return my money."

I asked Grandma Kim Hak Soon, the first public witness, what she thought about all this. "I want a real apology from Japan. You know, the Japanese are very keen about treaties and signatures. They are in the perpetual habit of citing treaties, documents, or the lack of documents, in order to refute our demands and protests. So I want the same thing. A thousand apologies uttered by their mouths are useless. As I told you, they say one thing and change the story even before you turn around.

"I want the Japanese to give us a signed document in which they acknowledge that Japanese colonialism was wrong, not even legal, strictly speaking. What they did to us was simply wrong, a crime, no matter how you look at it— legally, politically or simply humanly. I want them to give such a document signed by the Emperor of Japan to our government. I don't want it for myself. I want them to give it to our government."

Chapter 6

I WANT TO BUY A HOUSE FOR MY SON
Park Oak Yeun

Morning

Whack, Whack, Whack
Tender whip twitching the cow's tail
Chasing after darkness
Dark, dark, darkness growing deeper
Then light dawning.

The morning of this village
As green as a cow's rump
Fattened by grass.

The villagers eating bean porridge
Made the summer grow
Watering it with their sweat
Drops of their sweat wetting
Each leaf of grass.

This morning without wrinkles
In and out
Suck the air deeply
Again and again.

In June of 1995, I went to Korea to talk with former comfort women. Even before I set foot on Korean soil, researchers had warned me that those grandmas would be extremely reluctant to talk. I was further warned that some might expect compensation for their stories since many Japanese journalists offer them money. I was told all this again on the morning after my arrival in Korea when I visited a group of researchers in a tiny office. I was taken by an overwhelming sense of anxiety, my mood darkening by the minute. The long

116

flight and the sleepless first night in Korea didn't help me either. I stifled a sigh behind a big yawn, and said," Well, the sooner I find out for myself, the better. Would you kindly direct me to where I can meet some of these women?"

Out in the crowded street, I caught a cab and handed the driver a map drawn by one of the women. "I will take you as close as possible to the place but you will have to do the final searching. The house is probably tucked away in a narrow street," warned the driver as he moved into traffic. Another warning. Sure enough, soon I found myself walking up a narrow street, squinting my eyes to read the numbers on the houses.

I stood in front of a traditional Korean house. Like a bird taking flight, the corners of the black tile roof curved skyward. The solid wooden door was locked. I carefully pressed the doorbell. No response. A couple more tries and finally a voice called out, "who is it?" and I heard simultaneous footsteps. Off to my side, I saw a courtyard with a clothesline from one end to the other. Socks, underwear, and towels were gently dancing in the wind. The Korea I had left some thirty years ago suddenly re-materialized before my eyes. I was home. "Please do come in," a tiny woman with a lovely oval face smiled at me as she led me across the courtyard to a wooden floored veranda, called daechung-maru, designed to be a room where everyone in the family, regardless of sex or age could meet. A space turned into a living room, furnished with a television set, a couch, and a couple of chairs. Several other women greeted me.

"Please sit down," said one of the women. "You probably heard about the living arrangement here. There are seven of us here in a group home called, "Sharing Home," run by a Buddhist temple nearby. "I come from America where I have lived for the past thirty some years. I was hoping to talk to you . . . ." They looked at each other and the same woman, smothering a sigh, said, "We are kind of tired of talking but we will be happy to answer any questions you might have for a little while." I felt their polite gaze. "Well, I can understand why you are tired of talking. To tell you the truth, I am also tired today. Maybe I can just sit here with you on this nice floor and rest a while. The house is wonderful." "Sure, stay as long as you like."

We made small talk. Mostly the grandmas asked me about

the United States. Slowly but steadily the tension eased and soon we were laughing and gossiping like old chums at a long-delayed reunion. At first, they didn't believe I was nearly fifty seven. They grew increasingly less dubious of my claim to have been born in Korea while Japan ruled the country. "Your Korean is excellent. Are you sure you speak English?" asked the cutest grandma, giggling. Then, another woman nick-named "loudmouth" began worrying out loud about what they should have for dinner. "I have an idea," I said. "Let's order in some Chinese food. My treat. I had wanted to bring you something all along but couldn't decide what." It did not take lots of arm twisting to have my wish granted. We sat on the floor around a low, round table and ate long noodles, cutting them with our teeth as we noisily pulled them into our mouths, vigorous and satisfying. It was a jolly evening. After supper, I bid them farewell knowing that I would be welcome again.

I spent about four days at "Sharing Home," and took any comments that were thrown in while we laughed and watched television together. Before I turned on my tape recorder for individual conversations, I told them, "I am not rich. I don't have much money. Even if I had money, though, I don't believe in paying for interviews." With this under-standing, we did talk but all was not well. They all started out with their age when they were taken by the Japanese, ready to move on quickly to where they went, and how it all started, etc. A formula had been firmly established in their talks with previous interviewers. They were convinced that they knew what I was after. They were experienced; they would provide me with the information I needed.

A host of people had come and gone ahead of me. Even while I was there, the grandmas were entertaining a non-stop flow of Japanese journalists and activists, greeting many, clearly not first-time visitors, with genuine warmth. My complex feelings intensified as I sat watching the Japanese visitors bantering with such easy grace. Finally, when the grandmas and the visitors began conversing in Japanese, the language they had learned bit by bit while serving the Japanese soldiers as sex slaves, I reached the end of my tether. A volcanic feeling erupted in my body.

I shoved my feet into shoes and paced around the court-yard trying to figure out why my emotions were spiking. They were innocent young Japanese who wanted to correct the wrongs committed by their country and their ancestors. Maybe I was mad because I felt they were buying the tragedy Japan created and making "formula" people out of these grandmas . . . "Damn." I said as I paced the courtyard, knowing full well that I might be a tad too emotional and unfair.

Of all grandmas in the Sharing Home, one drew my attention effortlessly, just being herself. Everyone called her "elder sister." Whenever she laughed, I could see her gums, no teeth but one in the middle and the wrinkles on her face were pronounced. Yet, her face could light up with the mischievousness of a toddler trying to pool the wool over her mother's eyes. Like my own grandmother had, she wore her hair neatly divided in the middle, pulled back, formed in a round bun anchored with a silver pin. She wore a pair of pants, covering her waist and hips like a balloon, narrowing as they went down to her ankles and the blouse was a modified version of a Korean dress top. She could be Calvin Klein's newest model. The clothes were in complete harmony with her body. There was no way that I could stop the affection welling up within me for this cute grandma. I was hooked.

She approached me as I restlessly stalked the courtyard. "Would you like to come to my room and talk?" she asked, touching me gingerly on my shoulder. "Would I?" We went to a small room, most of it covered with a pink quilt, as thick as an American mattress. I tried to find enough floor space to sit down with my large shoulder bag but she wouldn't have it. "Please sit on the quilt. You should not put your butt on the bare floor. It's not good for you."

"You want to hear about that experience, don't you?" Eventually, yes but now I would love to know everything about your childhood. So start as far back as you can remember. Thus, she began.

My father had three girls, only girls, no sons. My hometown is Ahn Sung, southern Cholla Province. My oldest sister passed away not long ago. She was 80. She was very alert. My younger sister, three years younger than I, is also very sharp. I am the only one who seems to be losing my memory. I forget things instantly. I would be thinking something, and as soon as I turn around, I'd forgotten.

My mother was short but really pretty with her lips gathering just the right thickness in the middle, with delicate lines. Those lips of my mother, they were beautiful and sensuous. Actually, all the women in our family are beautiful. I am the only exception. So my older sister used to lament, "Why is it that the ugliest one always brings the most heartaches to the family?" My two sisters were married and lived in the neighborhood. I was the only one who resisted marriage. That's why I was taken to Japan.

This was not the case in the story I read in Forcibly Drafted Korean Military Comfort Women. I made a mental note to deal with it later.

My mother was an old-fashioned woman, but her ideas about education were progressive. She bugged us to go to school. So both of my sisters completed elementary school, I remember learning *Izzi, Ni, San, Shi (one, two, three, four)* from a Japanese teacher, but I was never interested in school. In the morning, I would leave the house with a bookbag but I didn't go to school. I went to the mountains and played there all day. At the time other children walked back from school, I would join them and arrive home about the time they did. A few times, my mother saw mud on the back of my underclothes. She told me to quit school. A sensation as light as dancing steps swirled inside of my body, tinkling me with joy. You can't imagine the trouble I gave my mother!

I loved playing with friends, aimlessly walking around and exploring places. Whenever I got angry, I climbed a tree. Whenever a matchmaker appeared, I insisted that I would never marry even if I had to die. I was a tomboy but you know what? I was best at sewing and ironing . . . all kinds of household chores.

My grandfather was rather well-to-do. I had three aunts and an uncle. They were well versed in Chinese characters. I was told that they all lived in the same house for a while but when my mother had her first daughter, my father was given some land and he moved out. My mother was a real homemaker. There was hardly anything she couldn't do. You name anything and she could do it. She could weave, sew and work in the fields like no one else could. Our life was happy and warm.

We did not grow up feeling hungry until the Japanese took away all of our rice and things. I remember the Japanese coming to our village and giving us smallpox shots. They picked a house with a large yard and ordered us to line up. They told us to go through one door and come out through another after the shot. There was this remote relative of ours—he came out through the same door. A Japanese man caught him, kicked him hard, saying, "*Bagayaro* (you idiot)." He was flung to the other end of the yard and he landed hard. You should have seen his face, so full of pain and humiliation. The power the Japanese people had — the way they ordered us around — I was in fear and awe. Those Japanese took all of our harvest and left us nothing.

We used to peel the bark from pine trees, boil the inside layers and eat it.[92] We ate other tree roots as well. You had to eat something. The Japanese snatched all of our crops. They said that food had to be sent to the battle fronts. They didn't stop with things; they took people, Korean people, to meet manpower needs. They drummed in us constantly that Japan had to win the war. I didn't know exactly why the Japanese were in our country and didn't ask direct questions about it. I do remember, though, my mother once bringing home some beautiful dress material and my asking her where she got it. "At a Japanese dress shop," she said. I remember those Japanese people lived far better than we ever could. They dressed and ate better. There was a Japanese policeman in our village office. He routinely arrested Koreans for no reason at all and beat them. For any slight resistance or protest, he would put water inside their nostrils and kick them around.

I remember my father's shame one day. He used to wear a white *durumaki* (traditional Korean overcoat) and have his hair rolled up all the way to the top of his head, you know we called it "*sangtu*." One day, he came home—I couldn't believe what I saw— his hair was cut short and black ink was sprinkled all over his white coat. Who do you think did that? The Japanese had cut his hair and spread the ink! The black ink was to tell my father not to wear the white overcoat any longer. My father could not bear to look at himself. He felt so ashamed of his looks that he stayed home for days.

When we had nothing to eat, my parents went to the mountains to dig up edible plants. They usually left at dawn. One morning, I insisted that I go with them. The walk was long and exhaustive. I was so tired that my nose bled and I got sick. I had to stay in bed for two days. Because of the lack of proper food in my stomach, my feet frequently swelled. I remember once when I was sitting under a tree, my mother came and held my hand and cried. "I am sick to my stomach that you might not be able to live a normal, long life. You have such a frail body." Well, my mother was wrong since I am still alive after all that I had to go through. The ship I was on wrecked twice, you know, and I am still alive.

Pause, with her eyes travelling far . . .

My father was a man of few words. My mother, she was so thoughtful, so attentive, always with so much affection. When she looked at me, or held my hand, her feelings went right through my body. I lived at home until I was nineteen. The president of our neighborhood association reported to the Japanese officials that an unmarried woman was in our house. That's me. One day a Japanese official came and told me to come with him. My father said "no" firmly but he was insistent. He said that I would get a well paying job. There were some other girls in our village who went with me. We were at an inn in Seoul. The next day, they gave us each a blue dress and a pair of shoes. Then we went to the Seoul Train Station, joined by many other girls and went back south, to Pusan. There we got on a huge ship. There were horses and cows on the ship and even a small theater. The ship was full of Japanese soldiers. The ship pulled into Shimonoseki and we rested there for one day.

Then, we had no idea where our ship was headed. There were some Japanese women on the ship. They told us to observe those women carefully and learn. I noticed that after a bath, they put body powder all over. Some of those Japanese women, whenever they felt sick, were given shots. I had no idea what it was but later learned that it was opium. Their bodies were full of needle marks. They were prostitutes. I got to know some of them. They tried to teach me to smoke cigarettes and all kinds of bad stuff like that.

They had told us that we would be on the ship for fifteen days but we were there for forty days when it finally pulled into some harbor. I guess it took as long as it did, because it was tricky to avoid the mountains in the water and other obstacles. More than anything else, though, I remember how difficult it was to avoid the heavy bombing. Darkness surrounded us when our ship pulled in but we were happy to see the long voyage coming to an end. I can still see huge flames going up. I was excited as if they were splendid fireworks but they were countless shootings from below and above. American planes flew over our ship to bomb. It was a battlefield. Death was all around us but we emerged alive.

After things calmed down, we got off the ship. It was pitch dark. I knew nothing; I had no idea what was happening. They took us to a large, two story house. My two friends, Akiko and Yoshiko (the Japanese names of my two friends) and I each took a room on the second floor. We had no supper but someone brought us a ripe papaya. We didn't know what it was but we devoured it. I later learned that the place was Rabaul.

At this point, I had to leave because I was already late for a dinner appointment with an old friend and there was no way to cancel it. I should have known better; I should not have made any plans . . . Silently cursing, I said, "Grandma, I am afraid I have to leave now but I will be back tomorrow." "But tomorrow is Wednesday. We will be all going to the Japanese Embassy for our Wednesday noon demonstration. You know about this demonstration, don't you?" "I know and I am planning to join you but couldn't I come back here with you after that?" I was pleading. "Of course, you can but I can't promise that I will talk to you. The demonstration usually wipes me out. I might have to take a nap."

The next day, I went to the Japanese Embassy a little before noon and found the grandmas from the Sharing Home already there. After the demonstration, we had lunch together. One of the women was feeling ill. I stopped a cab

*for her and offered to stop another taxi so that all of us could
ride taxis but three grandmas said they would rather take a
bus. "It is just as convenient and sometimes it is faster."*

*They urged me to ride the taxi with the sick grandma
and a couple of others. When we arrived home, everyone
was getting ready to take a nap. I decided that there was no
point in hanging around that day. On my way to the subway
station, I met the three grandmas who had just gotten off the
bus, one of them my grandma Oak Yeun. "Where are you
going?" she asked, grabbing my hand. "I thought I should
leave today because everyone seems to be so exhausted."
"But you are already here. It would be a shame for you to
waste an afternoon. Walk back with me and we can talk. If I
am too tired, we can rest together." It did not take much per-
suasion. Again, I was invited to her room and she offered me
a small bottle. "Drink this. This is supposed to renew your
energy." "What about you?" "Not to worry. I have another
one. I keep some of these in my room." She was already
drinking hers and I followed suit but didn't like the taste. It
was mediciney but to get the grandma going, I would drink
it. "Where was I yesterday?" she asked me. "You had just
finished eating one third of a papaya." "That's right. You
have a good memory."*

That was all the supper we had that night. The next morning, They told
us to go downstairs. A Chinese man with gray hair greeted us warmly and
gave us cooked rice. Nothing else. It was difficult to swallow the plain rice
but we forced it down simply to fill our empty stomachs. Then, they told us
that from that time on, we had to learn some basic Japanese words and phras-
es such as "good morning," "good evening," and "please come in." They said
we had to use them and be polite to the customers. The three of us whispered
to each other. You can imagine how puzzled we were. We had no idea about
what was happening. We had been led to believe that we would be going to
work in a hospital.

At first, an officer came to my room. Another Japanese officer, named
Nakamura came in with Hanako. So the four of us, though we could not communicate freely, giggled and tried to have a good time. After a while,
Nakamura held Hanako's hand and left. The officer lifted me up, put me down
on top of the bed, pulled me close to him and hugged me so hard that I felt
crushed. Frightened, I started to cry. What I felt was not exactly fear; I just
felt I had lost my mind, that my soul had left my body. Eventually, though, he
did that thing, you know. I felt a sharp pain but I was so ashamed that I could
not even talk about it to friends. That officer came to me all the time I was

there. He went to no one else but me.

Rabaul was an island, you know. The water was so salty that whenever it rained, we gathered rainwater and used it to cook rice and to do laundry. When it did not rain, the soldiers supplied water. Many times we were told that the ship carrying the food had been bombed and that we had no food. There was no way for us to escape; there was no place we could go. We would have needed an airplane or a ship. Besides, our place was always guarded by military policemen or soldiers. I never did go outside the place by myself. They told us that if we went outside, we would be raped by the black people on the island.

> *Imagine the Japanese warning these women about being raped by the blacks on the island! I did not know if I should cry or laugh. She told me this as if it were the most natural thing. Talk about absurdity . . . I managed to keep my mouth shut.*

From our place, I could watch smoke, the size of a huge house, coming from a round mountain top. I was curious about that and itching to see it up close. This Japanese officer who came to see me was a lieutenant and an army doctor. For three and a half years while he was in Rabaul, he came to see me often and tried to prevent other soldiers from coming to me. One day, I asked Lieutenant Abe if he could take me to the smoky mountain. He came in a military car driven by a soldier and told me to get in. When I looked at it, the mountain appeared to be just around the corner but it was far away. On the way, I saw all those palm trees and banana trees and the pebbles underneath were so clean. You know, there were no seasons on this island. It was always summer.

I was about twenty-two and he was roughly fifty. He had a wife, son and mother in Tokyo. He said that after the war, we would live in Tokyo together but told me never to tell anyone where I worked. About a three and half years later, he came, gave me his wrist watch and sat there looking sad. He said nothing but a friend who accompanied him told me that they were being transferred to New Guinea. After he left, there was no one to protect me. Lots of soldiers came and lined up. One day, all of a sudden, his friend, Nakamura, appeared. I grabbed him and asked why my lieutenant hadn't come. Avoiding my eyes, he told me that he had been hit by a bullet on the battlefield and died. My soul went out of my body again.

You want to know if I was in love with him? Well, I wasn't sure. First, I think it was just affection but later I think I loved him. I believe I would have married him if he had asked me to. No, I didn't care that he was a Japanese. At that time, we all believed that Japan had to win the war. If it occurred to us America might or should win, maybe we, Koreans, would have protested against the Japanese. I believe many Koreans obeyed the Japanese orders because they thought Japan's victory was their means for survival as well.

No, I didn't hate the Japanese. Lots of former comfort women tell stories about how they were beaten and tortured but not me. Looking back, I realize that many women who had already been prostitutes got drunk and often fought like dogs with one another. So the owner (manager) had to deal with them harshly, frequently slapping them and whatnot. But you know, I didn't drink. I couldn't sing. I just laughed. So nobody hurt me. In fact, our owner, or you might call him manager, whom we called "Japanese father," was very nice to me. Whenever there were air raids, he took me with him to a hiding place and we waited together until everything quieted down.

Many soldiers were also kind to me. They told me that if it were in their power, they would send me home. They said we were a part of the Imperial war effort and that they appreciated my efforts to comfort them. Sometimes, they even gave us some money in addition to what they were required to pay. But do you know what? We even gave that money to our Japanese father. I was stupid or naive beyond belief.

Save money? We were not supposed to keep our own money. I didn't have any money. About three years after I arrived in Rabaul, I went outside my room and stood just watching the sky in the direction I thought my home might be. A soldier was passing through the gate and dropped something. I went and picked it up. It was his wallet. I found lots of money inside. The next day, I gave it to a military policeman. The soldier came running and took his wallet. He gave me half of the money in the wallet. It was a huge sum. Even then, I gave it to the manager. The deal was, at least that's what they told us, that the manager had to subtract all our expenses including the ticket for the ship to get there, food and clothing. Whatever money was left, he would keep at the post office and give it to us when we were ready to go home.

I returned home in December 1944 and was twenty seven. When I returned, my parents were still alive. I told them that I had worked as a nurse in Japan. I was confident that I could live alone without ever getting married. But for some reason, lots of men, especially Japanese men, came to our yard in the evenings and tried to flirt with me. I think they had guessed about my past and treated me accordingly. My father finally told me that I had to leave home.

Then, I met this nice man from a good family, actually of noble stock. He had a wife and two sons. He was a village clerk in charge of food rations. He had been unhappy with his wife for some time. She was sloppy and careless. She didn't even know how to prepare nice meals for her husband's frequent guests. So I became his second wife, you know, the concubine. My mother-in-law had three sons and three daughters. My sisters-in-law were awfully nice to me. They said that I was a dream come true to their brother. The whole family was nice to my own parents. What's more, the first wife was grateful to me. She was grateful that her husband was satisfied.

You know, because of my past, I didn't think I could have children. The first month after I became his wife, I became pregnant. I had a son! I couldn't believe it. All of us became a happy family. Even the two sons by his first wife were nice to me. They all graduated from college and now one is principal of a senior high school and the other principal of a junior high school. Even now, they invite me to live with them. I can't be sure if they know about my past. I believe that they are unaware. That's why I never do television interviews. Some of my relatives have high positions.

"But your story is written up in a book with your picture."

I doubt if they would read a book like that. But television is a different story. Why did I come here to live? I was sick of being alone at home all day. You know, they all go to work in the morning and my grandchildren go to school. The two sons by the first wife were able to go to college but my own son, Kwang Mann, is a high school dropout. My husband died before our son could finish high school. He is now married and has two sons. He works somewhere . . .

> *Something told me that she was picking and choosing for her story, sometimes making things up. Strangely, instead of feeling resentful, I was more and more drawn to her and determined to get to the bottom of the things in time . . .*

I am not sure if my son knows about this place. I told him that I was with one of our relatives. My grandsons always ask me why I don't come home. I am not as worried about their knowing as I feel ashamed of myself.

I told you that my husband died before our son could finish high school. When he died, he had so much debt, most of it incurred for his other two sons' education. After his death, I came to Seoul and worked as a maid for ten years. I did that to send my son, Kwang Mann, to school. When I came to Seoul, my youngest daughter was only three years old. I left her with her father's first wife and came to Seoul for my son.

After I came to Seoul, my son walked miles and miles, looking for me. One day, I was told that someone was at the door asking about me. I had no idea who could be visiting me but I went and found a young man, dark with sunburn and skinny. I didn't recognize him at first but it was my son! I went to see a relative of mine who was a policeman. I begged him to help. "My son is here and I don't know where to send him. Can you please do something for him?" "Please don't worry. I will see what I can do." He found a job for him at a Chinese restaurant. I could not believe what was happening to us — I was a maid and my son worked in a Chinese restaurant. I was burning inside. I quit and decided to sell vegetables but I was lucky if I didn't lose money, let alone earn anything. I lived on the food my son brought from the restaurant.

As if that weren't bad enough, there was lots of communist agitation in Seoul at that time; demonstrations and frequent reports about deaths. I decided we had to leave Seoul and go to the countryside. My son didn't want to because someone told him that he might have a chance for a good job. There was no way, though, I could leave him in Seoul alone. He was eighteen at the time and I was worried that he might be beaten to death somewhere. So I dragged him with me.

We were back to where we had lived, but with no food and no housing. We rented a small room and lived on rice that friends brought here and there. In a little while, I was able to get my hands on a small piece of land where we could grow sweet potatoes. In the meantime, my son gathered logs in the mountains and built a cottage for us by the river. Once in a while, the sons of my husband's first wife sent some money without telling their wives. You know, even now, they would not mind taking out their own liver for me but the wives are something else. In any case, they had their share of trouble. They had to cope with the huge debt their father had left. Even when I left home to be a maid, I could have married a man with some money. Once in a while, I regret that I didn't because if I had, I could buy a house for my son.

When I married this man, at first I was a little worried about my past. But I was more worried that I might not be able to have children but when I had a son, all was well with me. Thanks to my friend, Lieutenant Abe, I was free of venereal disease. You remember my telling you about him, don't you? You know he was a doctor. He watched over me. I didn't have to be inspected like the other women because Lieutenant Abe gave me a private inspection. He was really crazy about me. Had he not died, we might have lived together.

I had no idea why Japan was fighting. There was an awful lot of bombing but I had no idea why they were fighting. My friend, Abe, didn't talk about the war. The only time he said anything at all was when he was going away. He told me that he had to go away because of the war. Anyway, even when he talked about our living together, I always thought of home. I wanted to return to Korea and live with my parents. I just thought about living with them and I never wanted to get married.

It was winter when I came home. I remember the snow. But did I tell you about the shipwreck the first time I was to come back to Korea? Our manager gave each of us a bank book and told us to tie it around our waists. He said we could get our money at any post office. We got on a huge ship and were at sea for about a week. One morning after breakfast, we saw huge waves of water rushing into the ship. I believe our ship was bombed. We had been instructed always to wear life preservers but I had taken it off because of the unbearable heat. The gushing water was so powerful that it divided the stomach of one of the women and she was swept away with her stomach open. You see, she was pregnant. Such a terrible sight!

Our ship was divided in half. A friend of mine, a man, and I were desperately trying to untie one of the boats but I was also swept away by the water. I tried hard to lie on the water floating but I was moving away from people. One of the soldiers spotted me and threw a rope, shouting orders to grab the rope. Then he pulled the rope toward him. The two of us were far away from others who did not seem to see us. I took off my white underpants and waved, then finally, a boat came and some people tried to help me in but I had no energy and my legs were trembling so hard that I was thrown into the water again. A soldier saved me again and finally pulled me into the boat. You should have seen me. What a horrible sight. Blood was everywhere in the boat. Some lost legs, others arms. After a while, we were taken back to Rabaul. We couldn't go anywhere. I had so many wounds. You can still see traces of them.

We went right back to the same house. No money, no rice. Nothing. Of fifty women, only fifteen survived the wreck. The old manager also died. A small, Japanese grandfather became our manager and we called him "father." We were again stuck there for a while.[93] Toward the end of that period, there were so many air attacks we hardly had time to smoke a cigarette. Again, we were put on a ship with countless soldiers, thousands and thousands of them. The ship was bombed again and of the fifteen women, only four of us survived. They sent two of my wounded friends to a hospital in Shimonoseki. I went to Pusan with my friend, Hanako. When we arrived in Pusan, we had no money. I don't remember how I managed it but I got on a bus and went back to my parents home. I appeared in a thin dress. My father and mother couldn't believe their eyes. They wrapped me in warm clothes and made me drink warm water. I told them that I had worked as a nurse in Japan. They asked no questions, especially not, "How come you have no money if you were a nurse?" They just felt sad for me and did everything possible to make me feel good.

These days when I think about the past, my husband comes to my mind more than anything. He has been dead a long time but I still blame him for the enormous debt he left behind. I don't understand why he had to borrow so much money to send his sons to school. Even they don't seem to appreciate what he did. They blame their father for irresponsible management. They forget that much of that debt was because of them, especially their wives. No sign of appreciation.

I should have looked for a rich man after he died. Had I done that I could have bought a house for my son long ago. You know, he and his family live in a rented room. My only wish is to buy a house for my son. If I could do that now, I could close my eyes in peace. I am responsible for what he is now. I did not give what he should have had when he was growing up. If I had thought a little, I could have done what many other second wives do, that is, hide the man's money but I was a stupid idiot. So I ruined my son's life.

I usually tell people that my son works at a bank. Even though he is a high school dropout, he has a remarkably good brain. He is really smart. I'll tell you what he really does. He is a cleaning man at a hotel. How can I ever be forgiven for making my son do such a thing? The hardships he had to endure, you can't imagine. I told you that he built a small house all by himself. He lugged all that lumber on an A frame on his back. For a while, I went to Pusan and worked in a hospital as a maid. During that time, my son lived on potatoes and was forced to sell that house. I was told that he and my mother wept together when that happened. There was no way they could survive in that tiny rural village. So they decided to sell the house and move to Dae Jun, a large city.

I am just obsessed with my son, loaded with guilty feelings. I don't blame Japan as much as the man who took me there. Even after that horrible period of my life, if only I had been smart enough I could have taken better care of my son.

She paused a little, soaking up the air.

Of course, I am not without anger about Japan. I ended up staying in Rabaul longer than my contract and . . .

You know, at the time, I didn't know what was going on between Japan and Korea. Now what I know is this: the Koreans let Japan do that to us. We were the ones who were stupid enough to let Japan mess around. I know no more than that. Even now, unless we are strong, Japan will mess us all over again.

She excused herself, telling me to stretch my legs and relax. Alone in her tiny room, I struggled with my own confused feelings. For the first contract, whatever the length, she does not blame Japan. What does this mean? In her mind, she was not a totally innocent prey of Japan; she wants to take some responsibility. She blames the man who took her there but not Japan . . . She was back on her quilt, sitting with her legs folded and smiling, looking like a little Bodhisattva.

When I literally tore away my three year old girl (*actually two according to our way of counting*) and left home to be a maid in Seoul, my breasts were as large as this. (*She put her hands on her breast, making a big lump*). You know, that baby girl grew to be a beautiful woman and she is so good to me. My conscience is full of shame. All these dresses and things you see around here, she bought them for me. My older daughter is not as well off as the younger one. She and her family can take care of themselves but she does not have enough. But my younger daughter lives in a city called Muju which looks almost like Seoul. They own a four story building.

My daughter finished high school in Pusan. She did that all on her own. I could not give her a penny. She worked her way through high school. You should see her. She is incredibly smart and beautiful. She is not like me; she is really pretty. She calls me frequently. (*Lifting a beautiful silk blouse*) You see, this one, she sent this to me on Mother's Day not long ago. I always tell her that I have more than enough to wear but she always says, "Don't worry, mother. Whatever you can't or don't want to wear, I will take them back later." But she had her share of hardship. She married an only son and her mother-in-law was a witch. While the witch was alive, my daughter's life was a living hell. You know all those wicked stories they tell about cruel mothers-in-law. In my daughter's case, it was worse. But her mother-in-law died last year. She is at last free of the wicked mother-in-law.

> *Grandma Oak Yeun giggled, like a little girl in a fairy tale, relieved from the fear of a witch. It was hard to link this woman with her horrendous past. She was still a tomboy, ready to slide down the slopes of the mountain.*

Free at last, what did my daughter do? She moved to Dae Jun for her children's education. She has a son and a daughter. You know my grandson is a scholarship student. He is just like his mother, so smart. I have five grandchildren altogether; my older daughter has a girl and my son has two boys. Whenever I have something, I hide it for my two grandsons, you know, my son's boys. Once my second daughter sent me a box of fancy apples. I wanted to hide them but could not think of any place. I put them in the washing machine. My granddaughter complained, "Grandma, you only think of those boys!" "So what," I said, "after I die, who is going to bury me and cut the grass on my grave? You?" "Of course, I can do it." "No . . . the grandsons will do it. You will be married off to another family!"

I know, I know, girls are grandchildren, too, but I can't help it. I am biased toward my two grandsons, you know my son's boys. I told this to a friend of mine. She said the same thing as you. "Grandchildren are grandchildren. They are the same and should be treated the same." I know this with my head but still I can't help favoring my grandsons! It is unconscionable. I might be punished for this.

No, I don't believe in God. My daughter-in-law goes to a Buddhist Temple. Whatever I believe or don't believe, I am obsessed with only one thing! Every night, before I fall asleep, I pray, "Oh, God, wherever you are and whoever you are, please listen to my prayer. Please protect my son." That's all.

> *Outside of her room, a small bird landed in the court yard. I felt a strange warmth gushing through me. I am the fifth*

child, and the first daughter of a Korean family of eight children, six sons and two daughters. I am married to an American whose great grandparents come from Scotland via Ireland. I thought of my own widowed mother when she lived with us for several months. Her eyes sparkled with one call from any of her sons, while a thousand things I did for her passed without the slightest sign of recognition, I often felt. That was just expected from a dutiful daughter. The confusion, resentment I felt.

"I am sure God listens to your prayers," I told her and gathered my things. "Please get some rest. I would like to come back, though. May I?" She held my hand and said, "Of course, come back any time." I closed the large, wooden door quietly behind me, fearful that I might disturb other grandmas still taking naps.

About ten days later, I went back to the Sharing Home. The house was in disarray, especially the daechung-maru with paintings spread all over. A couple of grandmas were packing their paintings under the instructions of their art teacher. They were going to a southern city, called Dae Gu, for an exhibition of their works. A Japanese filmmaker was there, accompanied by a Korean translator. He was videotaping the grandmas' activities. He asked me why I was there. For some reason, the taste in my mouth was sour and I wanted to get the hell out of there but grandma Oak Yeun appeared, with her eyes glittering like rippling water in the sun, and held my hand. "Aigo, you are here. When did you come?" "A while ago. Your door was closed and I was fearful that you might not be here." "I closed my door because I did not like all this commotion. They will be leaving soon. So just hang around and the house will be ours." All was well with me again.

Back to the daechung-maru, Grandma Oak Yeun invited me to sit down on a cushion. "You must not put your butt on a bare floor." "Grandma, the other day when we talked, you told me that you had not been married when you were taken away from home. According to the story in the Korean oral history book, you were married at the time. I am confused. Tell me which is true."

Well, now I understand better what we are trying to achieve, I can sort out what is important to tell, and what isn't. I didn't think my marriage added anything to our case. So in the beginning, I told the interviewers about it but now I kind of skip it. Besides, it is difficult for me to talk about my husbands.

"Husbands?"

Yes, husbands. I was married twice.

She looked into my eyes. I sat still, feeling aghast.

You know, when everyone is around, I become self conscious. We are sick of hearing each other's stories. The others tell me that I should just tell a few things, not go into a gory detail. Today, you can sleep over and we can talk our hearts out. There is no one but us.

You better believe me that I was really not interested in getting married. My mother wouldn't have it, though. One day my mother and my aunt went to check out a man. They nagged me to marry him. I said, "No way!" My father did not interfere. He kept silent but my mother and aunt were something else. I was eighteen years old and he was maybe nineteen. We determined the wedding date and invited the groom to come to our house. You know, it was a customary thing for the groom to come, get married and live in the bride's house for a while before the bride returned to the groom's house. But he was reluctant to come. "He must be a stupid idiot," I thought to myself.

On my wedding day, I wore a persian blue skirt and yellow top, you know, the traditional Korean costume. I did not put on the bridal hat until I arrived at his house. I rode a palanquin. The groom wore the traditional Korean costume, the whole bit including the wedding hat. After we bowed to each other, for the first time I stole a glance at him. Yuck, what an ugly face. It was a face that I didn't want to look at twice. I was so angry that my chest felt like bursting. I knew, then, that I could not live with him even if I had to die. I never, ever wanted to look at him. The first night, we did nothing. We just went to sleep.

What made my mother and aunt settle on him, you might ask? When they went to his house, they saw all this rice spread on a straw mat in the yard. At that time, the first thing they ever thought about was food, whether they would have enough to live on. The two women were impressed. But you know what? This is what kills me even till this day. My mother-in-law cheated. It wasn't all rice, only on the surface. Underneath was husk. It didn't take long for me to find that out. My mother-in-law was not a bad person, though. When I went there, she was about thirty two. Such a young woman still. After I was married to that family, she herself bore a baby girl. My father-in-law was also a good man. They were both crazy about me. Wherever I went, grown-ups liked me.

132

We made straw sacks for rice and sold them at the market. The year I married, rice farming in the region was in deep trouble. Mobs of locusts invaded all the rice paddies but for some reason, the locusts did not invade our little field. We were the only family that had a good rice harvest that year. They said I was the one who brought luck to the family. After selling straw sacks, once in a while my father-in-law would buy some sweets at the market. He would never give them to his own children until I came back from the field. After supper, he divided them evenly and gave exactly the same share to all of us. I think he liked me better than his own children.

My mother-in-law was very talented at sewing, she could really sew. In fact, there was almost nothing she couldn't do with her hands. She made me lots of clothes and my mother had also given me quite a few things. However, because I couldn't stand my husband, I had no interest in clothing. I couldn't care less about my looks.

In April, we started planting rice. The women got up before dawn, prepared breakfast and carried it in huge baskets to the fields to feed the men. One day, after my mother-in-law left with the food basket on her head, I decided to run away. I packed a few things in a basket and started walking. As I passed by my parents' house, my maternal grandmother saw me. She yelled at me, chasing me, "Where are you going?" As I sped up, a truck passed. I lifted my hand in a hurry. I had to get away before my grandmother grabbed me. It stopped and I hopped into the front seat. We sat in complete silence. He stopped at a police station and told me to get off. He must have known that I was running away.

A policeman took me inside the station. He interrogated me; who my parents were, husband, in-laws, even my uncle's name and address. All the while, I insisted that I had to be released in a hurry since I was on my way to see my sick father. "My father is dying and he would like to see me before he closes his eyes. Why are you detaining me?" Finally, he let me go.

I had no idea where I was going. I walked faster and faster. Feeling out of breath, I sat by a well, held water in my palms and drank it. On the street, another truck stopped for me. There were two men, a driver and his assistant. The young assistant got off the truck and invited me to get in. As I hesitated, he simply helped me to hop in and asked where I was headed. I vaguely remembered the name of the town, Guh Chang, where my uncle was supposed to live. The truck climbed up a big hill where a distant town came into sight and stopped. "Now you can get off and walk," said the assistant. I had some money. I tried to offer him some but he refused. I just threw a coin and walked away, but he threw it back to the street.

I passed a house and saw a woman sitting on an open veranda. Suddenly, hunger made me dizzy. The world spinned in front of me and my feet would not move. I asked the woman where I could buy myself some food. She invited me in, saying that there was no place where I could buy food. Soon, she brought me some food. As I was devouring it, another woman appeared and asked in a low voice, "Who is that young woman?" "She says she is going to Guh Chang," replied the woman. "How come?" "This is a case of the white fence within the black fence." I never forgot that expression. No doubt, it was their secret signal, meaning that I was a "runaway." I tried to pay her for the food but she refused. I thanked her profusely and left.

I was worried sick about where I could spend the night. Then, I saw three women walking ahead of me on the street. I ran after them. "Do you know where I could find an inn around here," I asked. One of the women told me that her mother sold wine not far away in a small cottage and told me to go there and sleep. I was afraid that drunkards might harm me if I went there. Another woman understood my hesitation and took me to her mother's house. Once inside, I just fell asleep. When I woke up, the sun had been up for a long time. As I tried to stand up, my nose bled like crazy. I found a well and washed myself. Everyone was out to work but the mother took pity on me and offered breakfast. I was too nervous to swallow any food.

Again, I was on the street, walking. I came across a grandpa who was walking beside an oxen pulled cart full of wood. I asked him for directions to Guh Chang. He said, "You asked the right man. I am going there to sell wood." The old man helped me find my uncle's house. While I was exchanging greetings with my uncle, the old man just left. Till this day, I regret that I let him go without a meal and a bowl of rice wine.[94] It was two years after I had been married off. I lived five months with my uncle's family.

All the while I was there, they tried to persuade me to return to my husband but I was firm. I simply couldn't go back to him. Then, they said I should find another husband. Lots of people tried to do matchmaking. They found a well-to-do widower and strongly urged me to marry him. My aunt was reluctant because she had been told that he had a crazy temper. However, they could not find an ideal candidate for me. My welcome was wearing thin in my uncle's house and I didn't have much choice at all. I married him.

What happened to my first husband? Well, after I ran away, the entire household went upside down. Of course, the first place my in-laws went was my parents' home. They accused my father and mother of hiding me somewhere. My mother became sick. She never recovered from that until she died. When I think of all the trouble I caused my mother . . .

Soon after I married the rich man, I became pregnant and bore a beautiful baby boy, a son! But we constantly fought, if not in the house, outside somewhere. He was a wife beater. How he beat me, I can't describe. He kicked me, slapped me around, threw me against the wall, yelled and pulled my hair. I often thought about shaving my hair like a monk. It was a living hell; I could not bear it anymore and threatened to leave him. So this second husband of mine, it was he who sold me to the place where they sold off women. It was from there that a Japanese man came and took me to Seoul, where I was shipped to Japan with fifty other women.

When I was in Rabaul for seven years,[95] the one and only thing I thought of day and night was my boy, my baby whom my husband had kept when he sold me off. He was such a handsome, cute baby. How could I forget him? He was the only one I ever cared for all this time. That's why I was desperate to return to Korea.

Of course, the first thing I wanted to do when I returned home was see my son but my mother was adamant: I shouldn't and couldn't go. Then she told me the story. After I went away, my mother wanted so badly to see her grandson. She went to see him on foot. When she finally arrived at his house, she found her grandson playing in the yard. He was alone. She tiptoed to him and asked, "Where is your mom?" "She just went out," replied the boy. He meant his step-mother. So she learned that he had remarried. She asked neighbors and learned that he still abused his wife. In fact, it was so bad that the new wife did shave her hair and always wore a scarf.

When I lived with my third husband, you know the one whom I married after I returned from Rabaul, my mother-in-law, mother of my first husband, came to me, hugged me and pleaded that I come back to her house. Once, I ran into my first husband. He just stood there like a piece of wood and then walked away. I was surprised that he didn't slap me; if I had been he, that's what I would have done. Later his mother told me that upon seeing me, his legs shook so violently and his heart beat so strongly that he became absolutely petrified. He just went home.

So I never did go see my son born between me and the husband who sold me. I couldn't. My mother convinced me that his father would beat me to death if he ever saw me. When I was in Rabaul, my one and only wish was to return and live with my son. At that time, it was difficult for a woman to live alone. I wanted to live with my son. That was the only thing I ever wanted. You know, human nature is a strange thing. As I married again and had other children — you know I bore seven of them but only three survived — my desire for my very first boy gradually dimmed and life went on. When you think about it, that's one of the things that makes life sad. But the boy came to see me when he was sixteen. He had completed junior high school. His stepmother did not treat him properly. So he decided to look for his real mother.

When he came, I couldn't tell if I was happy to see him. I guess I was ambivalent at best. Most of all, I think what I felt was shame. He didn't stay long with us. He was seventeen when he left us. He got a job selling things on the train. Eventually, he met a nice man who liked him a lot and wanted him to be his son-in-law. He is a happily married man now with a good wife and a son. He owns two houses. For a while, he was in the lumber business. He used to pass by where I lived in a truck loaded with lumber. He would stop by to see me. He never came empty handed. He brought lots of beef which was always expensive. He bought me gold rings and things. He has always been in touch with me. He and his wife are very good to me. When I was at the bottom, struggling with three children, he would come and say to me, "Your life is so bad. Even the dogs live better than you. Why don't you come and live with me?" But I couldn't go and wouldn't go. I had to take care of my three children.

Now my obsession is my son from the third marriage. There is nothing more I want than buying him a house before I die. If that is realized, I can close my eyes and drop dead without a shred of regret. If only I had been able to get him more education, he would not be a cleaning man at a hotel. His sons are very good students, which gives me some consolation. Whenever I see them, I tell them how important it is that they study hard. There are some women, even some here, who don't hesitate to spend money whenever they get hold of it but not me. I can't spend a penny. I save every bit for my son, to buy him a house.

Sometimes I wish I had died during the shipwreck I told you about. If I had died, I would not have brought my children into this world and given them such hardship. The adversities I put them through, you can't imagine. I can't take one bit of credit for what they are now, especially the youngest one. I did nothing for her except bring her into this cruel world. Then, look at me, I take her kindness for granted and think of only my son. I know I am crazy but I can't help it. He is the worst off of the three children.

You know, I don't blame Japan as much as I blame my third husband who left so much debt behind to educate his sons with his first wife, making it impossible for me to help my own son get a college education. He was born with smart brain. If only he could have been educated . . .

What about my second husband? Do I blame him? I tell you, he is not worthy to be blamed. To blame him means I think about him. I try to wipe him out of my life, my memory, everything. Besides, my fortune teller told me that what happened was my fate. He once told me that I was to cross deep blue water. And I blocked away my memories about the Japanese. I only think about my son. I pray day and night for my son, for his health, a long happy life, abundant blessings and a house.

All this talk about compensation. I am no longer hopeful that it will happen before I die. Before I blame the Japanese, I blame my President (Mr. Kim Young Sam). I think he should fight on our behalf but he does nothing. Actually, lots of Japanese were very kind. They took pity on us; they felt sad for us. I heard lots of testimony about brutalities, cruel acts but that was not the case in my experience. Well, if some of the women got drunk and went crazy, the soldiers beat them . . .

You know Koreans sing a lot. When we were there, lots of my friends sang when they were homesick, sad or drunk. I don't sing, not that I don't want to but because I cannot carry a tune. Instead of singing, I laugh. I laughed then and I still laugh.

When I turned the recorder off, she invited me to spend the night. I packed my things, without taking my eyes from her.

Let me tell you something. There is someone in this house who has two sons. She will not report about her sons because that might lessen her chances of getting money from the Japanese. You know, I would never do that. There is a Korean saying that if you deny the existence of a living person, a great harm will fall upon that person. I will never do anything that could possibly harm my son, not for all the money the Japanese might give me, not for the whole world.

I sat around with her and spent a couple of hours chatting about anything, everything. I found myself urging repeatedly that she never abandon her hope of being compensated. "I know you will be able to buy a house for your son." It was my prayer for her. As I started putting on my shoes, she grabbed me, making me sit down close to her. "Write down your address," she produced a small notebook underneath her pillow. "Well, I will have to write it in English." "Don't you worry. My grandsons read English," her eyes aglow with pride. Then, she ordered me to write down their names. "You never know. They might go to America to study like you did." "You are right. If they ever come to the United States, please have them call me."

She came to the door with me and opened it. A small flock of sparrows sat on the edge of the roof. We stood for a while and I started walking down the narrow street. When I looked back, she was still there by the door, waving. Her prayer would be the same tonight, I thought to myself. I trudged through the street, with no tears in my eyes but my heart strangely moved by this tomboy grandma and her son.

Postscript

The few times I have been back to Seoul since then, I tried to reach her without success. Then, in 1997 I called the Sharing Home which had been re-located (that is, the grandmas were moved into a newly built house on the outskirts of Seoul), and learned that she was visiting her son in

*Dae Jun. They told me that Grandma Oak Yeun was at her
son's house nursing her grandson who broke his leg. My
first reaction? I was excited. Imagine filming this grandma
tending her grandson's broken leg! What visual power it
would have! Even then I could not just appear at her
doorstep. My greed as a filmmaker aside, I knew better; I
needed to get her permission especially since she was with
her son. I was headed south to see another grandma in a van
with my crew. Dae Jun was on the way. I don't know how
many times I dialed her number before I could hear her
voice. When I presented my case, she was reluctant.
Actually, all that warmth she had shown me during my previous visits was absent in her voice. Selfishly, I felt hurt. It
took me a couple of minutes to understand that she would be
guarded at her son's house. She agreed to ask her son if I
could come.*

*When I called back a few days later on my way back to
Seoul, she gave me directions to her son's place. As we
arrived, she was waiting for us outside. She greeted me
politely. Inside, we were introduced to her son, his wife and
two grandsons. The older one was, however, just on his way
out with his girl friend. I couldn't compete with that.*

*It was a rented place with two bed rooms and a small
kitchen. Grandma Oak Yeun shared the room with her
grandsons. The younger one, In Kyu, a handsome boy about
13, sat on his bed, with his broken leg stretched inside a cast
and his grandma by his side. In Kyu told me that he had
some idea about what happened to his grandma a long time
ago—it had something to do with the Japanese soldiers.
"But as far as I am concerned, all I want now is to see my
grandma enjoy a long life in good health." Her son, Kwang
Mann, I could tell, was a proud young man. Asked how he
learned about his mother's past, he said, "About four or five
years ago. My mother didn't say anything but letters kept
coming. Then, some visitors came from Seoul. At that time
my mother was living with us. So I put one and two together and guessed." "What was my response? I couldn't blame
my mother but I did blame the Korean politicians at that
time. Of course, the Japanese should be held responsible but
before we blame them, we should blame our own politicians.
They were responsible for losing our country to Japan in the
first place." "I did feel a little bit of shame at first but I got*

over it. My mother didn't volunteer to do that. Those bas-
tards in power, they are the ones to be blamed." His wife, an
alert good looking woman, jumped in. "Women at that time,
they didn't know much and they didn't have power. They
were victims. Even at the sound of 'Japan', though, my heart
jumps. What they did was inhuman. However, I agree with
my husband, quite apart from Japan, it is our government
that should resolve this issue."

I could not get anything out of Grandma Oak Yeun.
Most of what she said was incoherent. Clearly, she found it
difficult to talk about it in the presence of her family; she
was almost a different person. In the end, the only thing she
said with clarity and force was: "I want to buy a house for
my son." Asked if she still prayed for her son, she said, her
face radiant with overflowing affection, "It is not just when
I go to sleep but always."

As we were gathering our equipment, the son said, "You
have our permission to use our interview if it is shown in the
States but not in Korea." "Why?" It was In Kyu who
answered, "We have to worry about people's perceptions.
Sometimes, it doesn't matter whether they are right or
wrong. People's perceptions don't change easily. They stick
to old ideas and assumptions." The father, grandma, mother
all beamed with pride. They obviously think he is so smart.
And he was to me.

I told In Kyu to look me up if he comes to America some-
day and gave him some money to buy books. And I know he
will buy books. As I was putting my feet inside the van to
leave, Grandma Oak Yeun came and squeezed my hand.

Chapter 7

I ASKED MY BABY GIRL TO DO ME A FAVOR, TO DIE
A Mother-Daughter Story

Spring

Spring flowing in my veins,
Dol, Dol, like a brook

On a hill near the brook
Forsythia, azalea, yellow flowers of the cabbage

I blossom like wild grass
After enduring three winters.

Delightful skylark,
Soar up from any paddy in the field

Bluestone sky
Growing high
Bit by bit away from the eyes. . .

I met a feisty grandma at the home of another former com-fort woman, Grandma X.[96] She had just stopped by to see her friend. Her wrinkled face was somewhat red and her eyes were not exactly focused, which made me wonder if she had had a couple of drinks. Grandma X introduced us. "Would you be willing to talk to me?" I asked. "Sure." Her manner was decisive and direct. A no nonsense grandma, I could tell. "You want me to start from the time when I was drafted, don't you? I was seventeen . . . " She didn't wait for my answer. She, too, believed that she knew what I wanted to know.

I was born in Pyong Yang, now the capital of North Korea. My mother died when I was seven and so my grandmother brought me up. My grandmother had five sons and my father was the oldest. So I was like her youngest

140

daughter rather than a grandchild. When I was old enough, I got a job in a cigarette factory. One day when I came home from work, grandma told me, "You must get married and you can't be fussy about the man either. If not, the Japanese will take you away to work somewhere." "Grandma, don't talk like that. Everyone will die one day. What difference will it make if I die here or elsewhere? Let me go to work in a textile factory and earn some money so that you can live better. I will be gone for three years. You must stay alive until I return." Our family farmed but we barely had enough to put food in our mouths; I wanted to do something about it. That's how I left home.

You know, in those days, cotton was precious. In Manchuria, I made four cotton quilts, two mattresses and two covers. I also bought some clothes for my nephews and nieces and sent them home. Three days later, on the 16th of August, I learned that Korea had become independent. I learned that in Manchuria. I never knew if they received what I had sent. We have been unable to communicate since then. I have no idea what happened to my family, if some of them are still alive or what. Most probably, most of them are gone, especially my father and grandma. Most unlikely that they would be alive.

I was seventeen when I went and was twenty when we became independent. Exactly three years. That's all.

"But you never said a word about what happened during those three years," I protested.

Well, what is there to tell? We were on a ship for fifteen days. I think we passed Shanghai and Nanjing. There were two other girls from my village and many others. What had my father said? He urged me to get married and not to go but I insisted, because I had been told that we would earn lots of money. Had I known what was waiting for us, I would not have gone for all the money in the world. But I believed strongly that I would be working in a textile factory.

We were taken directly to the front.[97] They built temporary barracks, long rows of them. I was like a captured country chicken; didn't know what to do or where I was. I just followed them. I just started to receive soldiers. Soon I was infected with venereal disease. A woman, with a white top, a black skirt and a cap on her head, treated me and told me to go right back and receive the soldiers.

We had no way out. It wasn't just one or two who committed suicide. Life was unbearable. I didn't know then but looking back, it could have been iodine and cotton they used when they just cut there and put in some kind of white powder. What human being could have endured that? The pain was beyond belief. I don't know how many times I contemplated killing myself but then independence came.

When we got on a ship, Chinese came on board and searched everywhere including the innermost parts of our bodies. Why? They were looking for money, gold, anything. So this time it was the Chinese who ripped us apart and took everything away from us. A naked body, that's the only thing I had, nothing else.

The ship pulled into Pusan harbor. Not a moment of peace on the ship, either. There were lots of opium addicts who screamed, yelled and crawled in desperation. They travelled between life and death. When we arrived in Pusan, we were lined up and each of us was given some money, I don't remember exactly how much it was but it was supposed to be enough to buy tickets to go home.[98] Had I been educated and better informed, I could have gone back home in north but I knew nothing. So I just stayed around and have been stuck here in south Korea ever since.

As I wandered, I met a kind woman, about two years older than I. Not a soul to help and not knowing what to do, I asked her to be my adopted mother and to register me as such.[99] You wouldn't believe what I had to go through. I was sold many times over to drinking joints, you know places where they sold hard drinks and things.[100] Many took money and ran away. Then, the man I hooked up with was beaten by the communists until he passed out and died. Since then, I haven't wanted another man, determined to live alone. So that's what I did, all these years since I was twenty when I came back from China.[101]

Oh, yes, I have a daughter. She lives in an apartment complex called Chil Sung (*Seven Star*). Let's see, she is about forty now. She has two sons. I don't want or expect that she take care of me. I am very stubborn. I hate to depend on others even if it's my own flesh and blood. I want to be on my own until the bitter end. Maybe she can come to my deathbed but until then, I am going to stick it out on my own. Some women who are in the same situation, you know, the former comfort women, they could not pay their rent for many months. Not I. I grab any work.

What it was like to raise my baby girl alone? How can I tell you about it? I can't! When she was just a bundle of blood, I had to carry her on my back, doing everything, anything, to make a living. For a while I sold earthenware for kimchi, red pepper bean paste, etc. You know how heavy they are. I had to carry the whole bunch of them in a huge basket on my head. My arms were stretched to hold it, and the baby girl on my back was scratching and pulling. She constantly cried for food. I didn't even have a free hand to hit her. I walked miles and miles on country roads, crushed from the top and pulled at the back. As I heard the baby crying, I cursed . . . "why don't you do me a favor. I can't kill you. Just die for me, the one and only favor you can do for me." That's not all. I sold apples, baskets, barley rolls, you name it. The things I did, only the sky and earth would know.

Do you know that baby grew up to be a beautiful woman, happily married and tries to take care of me. But as long as I can move around, I do not want to burden her. She often says to me, "Mother, I sometimes don't know why I call you 'mama.' When I think of all the things you did and said to me, it's a miracle that I am still alive. I must have been born with a long life line." Sometimes words just pour out of her mouth when she recalls our past, blaming me and anger growing by the minute. But what can I say? What she says is all true. I just sit and let her talk.

A long pause, silent breathing heavy on all of us in the room, herself, Grandma X and myself.

She was blessed with a kind husband. He is a good man. No, no, they didn't court each other on their own, nothing like a love affair. My daughter was careful. She used to say, "I am not going to do anything rash that would give the slightest opening for gossip. It is hard enough to be a widow's daughter. People watch you." She did not marry until she was twenty seven but she married as a virgin. Someone did matchmaking for them. My son-in-law is a teacher. You would not recognize my daughter from the looks of me. She is not anything like me. She is a good looking woman and she is good to me. There is no one who does not like my daughter. Everyone thinks she is great. They sing praises of her until the spit is all dried out.

No, no. I never talk about my past with my daughter. I never told her until I learned about registering. When I talked to her, she jumped, "No way, mother, how can you even think about it?" But someone close to both of us argued, "Look, there is nothing to be ashamed of. She didn't knowingly plunge into it. She didn't do anything wrong." My daughter reluctantly agreed to reporting but until this day, my son-in-law does not know about it. My daughter is adamant about keeping it from him. I protested, "Why? Why are you so afraid? I didn't do it on my own. They inflicted it on me. They are the ones who should be ashamed." But she would not give in. Anyway, no reason for me to tell him. No matter whose fault it was, it is nothing to be proud of. So I keep my mouth shut.

Then, she gave some money to Grandma X, "Here, the money I owe you. I picked up some work today and earned this. I planted spring onions all day." "Oh, my, my, I didn't expect it but since I don't have a cent left, I am glad to have it back." Grandma X was happy. The two grandmas started talking about work they could pick up, and about demonstrations in front of the Japanese Embassy every Wednesday noon. Though the demonstration lasts less than an hour, it is an all day affair. It takes them forever just to get there, transferring buses. I knew that my ration for talk for this day was over. I did ask, though, causally, for her daughter's phone

143

number before saying good night.

The next morning I called her daughter, introduced myself and asked if I could come and talk to her. She was reluctant and shy but I gently prodded." "You don't have to reveal your identity." She gave me directions. She lived in a huge complex with dozens of apartment buildings. Her apartment door was open when I got there and thriving plants were on the balcony. She even had a crown of thorns just like mine at home in Washington. I stood there feeling homesick. "You must be the one coming to see me. Please come in." I saw this gorgeous woman; her beauty far exceeded my expectations. Suddenly, I felt sweaty and dirty in front of this graceful woman. She pointed to a seat where I could feel the breeze from a fan. She sat down, facing me.

"I wouldn't know how and where to start. My life was so full of hardship . . . I find it incredible that I am alive today. I don't know if I can tell. I never talked about my past to anyone. Not even to my husband. I told him bits and pieces but it was impossible to tell him the whole thing. My past has been buried deep in my chest all this time. It was unthinkable that I could talk about it." "Until you try, you will never know if you can tell or not," I said. A moment or two passed by in silence. Then I heard her sigh, followed by an almost inaudible groan. "It is clear that your mother is very proud of you," I tried to break the silence. "I guess she is. Sometimes I wonder, though, if she has the right to claim me when I think of all the things that she did and said to me. You know she used to tell me to die for her and for my sake." Now she was animated, despite herself. "Your mother told me," I responded.

With a firm promise that I would not reveal her identify, she agreed to talk. The minute I pulled out my recorder, though, she asked, "Why do you have to record it?" "I have to. If I don't, how could I remember what you tell me? There is no way I would remember every bit of your story." She nodded, hesitation hovering all over her face.

Symptomatic of my life, I don't even know exactly how old I am. According to my mother, I am forty one but according to my father's papers, I am forty two. My mother insists that she is right. "How dare you doubt my ability to remember when I brought you into this world. After all, I am the one who carried you around nine months in my belly," my mother maintains.

I don't know where to start. My mother was twenty nine when I was born.

She was born in northern Korea and had no papers, but she found a way to register in a village called Dang Jin in Choong Chung Province. She met a kind woman, only two years older, and asked her to adopt her. So, legally this woman is my mother's mother but I call her aunt because she is more like her sister.

It was this aunt who arranged for my mother to meet this nice man, a government official. He was a good looking man, tall, with distinctive features. My understanding is that they lived together for a while. After my mother became pregnant with me, she heard a rumor that my father had a wife and children. So my mother said to him, "Why would I set fire in someone's flower garden? I would have no part of it. As long as I didn't know about it, it wasn't a sin but now I can no longer live with you." Then, she set out to verify the rumor. Everything was true; he had a wife, children, daughters-in-law, the whole bit.

So my mother took off and started to sell earthenware, you know the jars for kimchi and red bean sauce. My father put me in his family registry but he died when I was in elementary school. He was a well known calligrapher as well. Everybody respected him. He was well versed in Chinese literature and he even wrote some prose and poetry. Everyone in town asked him to help whenever they needed written documents, for weddings, funerals, you name it.

My father proposed that he raise me with the rest of his children but my mother wouldn't have it. I can't tell you how many times my mother told how she pinched my dangling legs and cursed me when she carried the earthenware on her head. She said I cried all the time. "How you cried and cried . . . " says my mother, sighing.

After a while, my mother married a widower with daughters, no sons. Can you imagine what it was like for me? I was nobody in the family, only someone to be pushed around or ignored. I shared neither father nor mother with my step-father's daughters. They treated me rough, I mean really rough.

My mother gave birth to twin sons. She was ecstatic about the birth of sons but alas, her husband became sick. Now I know that what he had was stomach cancer but at that time, we were told that it was a stomach ailment. So my mother did *gut,* you know the shamanistic rituals, to cure his disease. Sometimes, it lasted for five days. What little they had, they had to sell to cover the expenses of those rituals but he did not live long enough to see their sons' first birthday.[102]

After her husband's death, my mother was once again left to do everything. From her looks now, you might not believe it but when my mother was young, she was very beautiful. Imagine my mother taller with her back straight and erect, her face without wrinkles. So many people told me how my mother was quite a woman. Whenever she had a chance to put on decent

Korean costumes, she carried herself with such grace and finesse. With the sleeve curve of the Korean dress top and the long skirt, my mother looked like an angel with wings, ready to fly. Moreover, she could apparently sing. People called her Pyong Yang *Kisaeng*. You know Pyong Yang was famous for producing trained artisans to entertain men. There were schools where women received training for such.

Left alone with twin sons and myself, she had to find ways to feed us. There was hardly anything she did not put her hands on. She worked in the rice paddies, potato and vegetable fields, you name it. All kinds of things, rough and tough things. No matter what she did, it was difficult to sustain a daily living. What to eat was a daily worry. There was a pottery factory in our village, actually a small operation run by a few families. She bought pottery wholesale and carried it around. She often went to small islands in the vicinity. When I was old enough, I sometimes went with her. I was always out of breath trying to catch up with her. Even as a little girl, I knew how incredibly difficult it was for my mother to sell those. Imagine carrying those heavy things on top of her small head.

Who took care of the twin brothers? Well, I don't know whether I should go into it or not. It has never been told to anyone. I don't know if it is because of the sins we committed in our previous lives . . . Those two kids were both epileptic. My mother would be out selling things and I would be at home with my twin brothers, my epileptic brothers. It was before I entered elementary school; I was only a small girl but it all fell on my shoulders to look after them. I would cook for them. Sometimes I would be alone with them at night. During the night, if they suffered a seizure, I didn't know what was happening. I desperately clung to them, trying to hold them close to my chest, crying . . .

> *Her voice dwindled and she sat immobile, leaving unshed tears in her eyes. I looked away resisting my desire to touch her hand or shoulder. I decided it best to leave her alone to cope; she was such a proud woman. Each moment felt like eternity . . . wanting to cross the line between us and do something . . . I held still.*

You know, now I understand that epilepsy has something to do with nerve disorder, but at the time I thought it was a form of liver disease. Because it is called *Kangil* in Korean and because *Kan* in Korean means liver. So I would desperately massage where I thought the liver was . . . You see, people think women like my mother were victims but their children were also victims. Think about what I had to go through . . . And now I wonder if my brothers' disease had something to do with her past . . .

> *She finally broke down and put both of her hands on her cheeks. Relieved, I handed her a piece of kleenex in silence.*

They were six or seven years old and I must have been about nine or so. Anyway, at that time, I was in elementary school. My mother was cheated by some man. She gave all her savings to a man who talked about making a great profit on some business ventures. When he didn't come back with the money, my mother went to Pusan to look for him. She was gone for two months or so. The younger of the two missed my mother like crazy. Whenever he saw the postman, he would hang onto him and ask, "Is my mother back? Is she back? Do you know when she will be back?" He would follow him around as if the postman held the key to his mother's return.

One day, I went to school in the morning and his brother was also off to school. Of the two, the older one was sent to school but not he. I guess his sickness was more severe. While I was at school, a neighbor woman came running to look for me. She said, "Let's go home. Your brother is dead." We both ran. The well where I got our water was not close by. You had to walk a while to reach it. I saw lots of neighbors carrying water from the well to our house. They were cleaning my brother.

I learned all this from people. That day he was left alone. He went to our cousin's vegetable garden and asked for some lettuce. "I want to get ready for my sister when she comes home," he said. After putting the lettuce leaves in the kitchen, he went to the outhouse. Do you know what the outhouse looked like in the countryside? Of course, it was always outside and there were two pieces of lumber with a hole in between.

A female relative of ours was tilling the field that day and had to use it. When she got there, she found two legs sticking in air. She found my brother between the two lumber pieces with his head inside. When I reached him, my neighbors were cleaning him up. We had no telephone then. I don't know how people got in touch with my mother. Maybe they sent a telegram. While my other brother and I were waiting for my mother, we were both so scared that we could not stay in our house. We locked it up and stayed with our cousin.

One night, dark and quiet, so quiet that you could almost hear the water drop, I heard wailing from a distance. It was my mother. She asked where her son was buried but we didn't tell her. Why? Because I was afraid that she would drink herself to death at his gravesite. For sure, every single day, we would have to drag her down from the mountain where my brother was buried. As expected, after his death, I believe my mother lost all desire for life. She drank heavily. In the evenings, all kinds of neighbors assembled at our house because we had no male in the house and my mother was hospitable and fun. So they came to visit each other at our house, both male and female.

At that time, I didn't have the slightest inkling about my mother's past with the Japanese. One night, while I was trying to go to sleep, I heard my mother talking with a woman who asked her how she happened to come from northern Korea. The woman must have been her close friend. I heard her confide in that woman. "When I was seventeen, I went off to work in a Japanese factory but that was not what I did. By the end of the war, there was a Japanese man who wanted me to go back to Japan but I could not go with him. I had to go see my grandmother before she passed away. I could not die in peace if I didn't see my grandma's face once again. I wouldn't be able to close my eyes on my deathbed." Her real intention was to go back to North Korea, her hometown but she was stuck here.

Under those circumstances, my mother had no real interest in life. She drank day in and out. She would sit with her eyes staring into blank space and say, "I don't want to go on living. I want to die. Why can't I just drop dead?" Even as a girl, I detested my mother drinking like that. Sometimes, I felt ashamed of her. She wasn't like other mothers. I do understand her so much better now, but at the time, all I could think about was why she wasn't like other mothers.

Now, looking back as a happily married wife and mother, I have a better understanding. For instance, I have something to live for. Even the mild praise I receive from my husband for the food I prepare gives me comfort. For my mother I now understand that everyday was a pure struggle for survival, all the burden of raising us on her fragile shoulders, not to speak of the unspeakable pain life wrought her. At the same time, it wasn't easy for me, either. My mother was gone most of the time, trying to earn money and I was left alone with my brother. I cooked for him and did everything. I played his mother and I was only a girl. I never did have a normal girl's life. If that wasn't the impact of a mother with no normal life, what was it?

You know, I told no one about this, but sometimes I threw stones when I saw my mother drinking with people. I never hit her directly and of course, I did it hiding. I couldn't stand the sight of my mother getting drunk, especially with men. I hated to see my mother even in the presence of men, let alone drinking with them. My entire body burned with shame. When she was really drunk, she would verbally abuse me. "Why don't you go live with your own father? What business do you have here?" I was also so frail. Whenever there was a strong wind, I literally had to grab something, a tree trunk, anything within my reach. Otherwise, I would be blown away. So each time my real father saw me, he encouraged me to concentrate on my studies. He said I was not fit to do heavy physical work like my mother. He told me that he would see to my college education. He also pleaded with my mother that I be entrusted to his care but my mother — no way. She would say, "she came out of my own belly, didn't she? She and I will live and die together." My father was a real scholar, widely respected but he, too, passed away when I was in the sixth grade.

Did I want to go live with my father? My mother repeated day and night how he had cheated her and she cursed him all the time. So consciously and unconsciously, I must have been brainwashed by her. So I came to dislike him. At the same time, my mother was so full of contradictions. At a special season of the year, like new year's day, my mother would send me to my father's house in worn out clothes. I don't know why she did that. I guess to make him feel guilty or to have me come back in new outfit, I am not sure. I know one thing, though. I hated going to see him like that. What child would want to visit her father in clothes with so many patches?

Once I was in his house, the difference was like day and night. Such a contrast with ours! Everything in that household was prim and proper. They would always set the table for my father and myself so that we could enjoy each other's company. Everyone treated me well with impeccable manners. I was impressed by all the books he had in his room. And his first wife was a woman of virtue. She was kind to me as well. You see, she had no girls and so it must have been a real pleasure for her to have me around. But after my father passed away, the contacts stopped.

It is only about three years ago that we started to see my father's families. One of my nephews called us here in Seoul. I was glad to hear from him. Since then, my husband and I visited my father's house a few times. Strangely enough, he feels more at home there than in the house I had built in another town for my mother. He enjoys all the traces of my father's scholarship, calligraphies and books he had. They also welcome us wholeheartedly. Even my mother has softened her feelings. We gave a huge party for my mother's seventieth birthday. People from my father's side came and bowed her a deep bow, the real respect. My mother's frozen stubborn heart thawed a little. So I believe the two families are now reconciled.

Yes, I know I made a big jump in my story. I was a child and then suddenly I talked about my husband, didn't I? It was hard but I managed to finish elementary school. My teacher encouraged me to go to middle school (*junior high*). I was too ashamed to tell her that we were too poor for me to continue schooling. I simply told her that I didn't feel like going . . . When I came home after graduation, my mother hugged me in our rented room and said, "Don't you think you should go to middle school?" "Mom, you know we can't afford it. We should figure out how to make a living . . . not how to go to school. Can you imagine how I felt?

> *She choked . . .* [103]

There was a porcelain factory in our region. I asked one of the neighbors, an employee of that factory, to look into the job situation there. He told me to bring appropriate papers, my birth certificate and the family registration. I don't remember the year but I do remember the date, January 4th. The snow was knee deep and I had to go to an office over the mountain in order to get the required documents. It was no use telling my mother since she spent her days smoking and drinking. I ventured to go by myself but I was scared. I asked a neighborhood boy to go with me. He was only a little boy. We had to walk about eight kilometers. On the way, with our feet constantly in the snow, the boy started to cry. I had to carry him on my back. Still his presence helped me. When I finally reached the office, there was a man sitting by a stove. When I explained what I needed, he said, "Don't you have a mother, somebody who could have helped you? How could two kids like you come alone on this horrible winter day?" He sat both of us by the stove and told us to warm our frozen bodies. When I returned home, my mother was blowing her cigarette smoke, drunk.

So I got a job in that factory. I was probably fourteen or fifteen years old. I rented a small room but I still had to walk four kilometers each way. Most days, I had to walk home in the dark. There was this bridge which I had to cross over. Whenever I was on it, a chill went down my spine making me pour out cold sweat. I had heard so many stories about the communist soldiers killing people and throwing the dead bodies over the bridge during the Korean War. I often felt as if something was pulling my legs down. It was spooky. When the fear paralyzed me, I waited under a big tree until a car went by. Then, guided by the head lights, I would run as fast as I could . . . On those nights, when I reached home, my body would be soaked in sweat.

Remember, I wasn't living at home while I worked at this factory. You would think that I would have felt liberated, relieved to be away from my mother. Strangely though, the only thing I thought about was my mother — when I went to the bathroom, when I ate, especially if it was something tasty or rare. You name it, whatever I did, I thought of my mother. She haunted me; I could not shake my thoughts of her away. I never wasted a cent; saved everything and each month, gave my pay to my mother. I worked like that for several years.

My mother, the way she drank, you would think that she would squander my hard earned money but she never did that. She was sober and responsible when handling money or anything that had to do with our survival. With all the money I gave her, we bought some land to grow rice. Then, someone told me that I could work in a textile factory in Seoul. It would be a better paying job. I was so determined to earn money; that was the only way I could make something for our family. So I came to Seoul. It was a small textile factory. I worked the night shift. One winter morning, after work, I was washing my face. I wore thin slippers. As I turned around, the bottom of the slipper was frozen to the ground and caused my body to spin and fall. I broke my arm. They sent me home, telling that I should treat my arm and come back healed.

My brother had finished elementary school and worked cutting stone from a mountain, such heavy labor. On the first day of my return, my mother was kind and caring but after a few days, she started nagging, "No one should sit

150

around idle." I felt so hurt that sometimes I locked the door and just cried my heart out half a day. "What kind of mother is she? I am not sitting around lazy. I have a broken arm . . ." There was no way that I could stay home long. I had to figure out a way to get out. At the time, I could not fathom my mother's behavior . . . Thinking back, maybe it was her way of pushing me into hard reality, to face it, to be strong . . . a different way of expressing her concern. . . I am sure it wasn't out of hatred of any sort. Don't you agree?

I simply nodded and she went on.

I had a neighbor, a man. He was always kind to me and treated me as if I were his adopted daughter. He told me that he had been on the train coming back from Seoul and struck up a conversation with a gentle old man. The old man ran a business in front of the train station in Chun Ahn[104] and was looking for a reliable clerk. He had a series of bad experiences filling this position. "Jobs are hard to come by but a good worker is even harder to get," he sighed. He added, "I would prefer a woman but to be truthful, if she is good looking, it would be a bonus." My neighbor jumped at this opportunity and told him about me and promised to be in touch.

It was 1974. The neighbor came and told me about his encounter with the old man. He said I needed to be good at the abacus, among other things. I never learned how to use it in my elementary school days. I rushed to another neighbor who gave me a few lessons and then I went to Chun Ahn. The store was large with all kinds of sporting equipment, fishing tools, and a variety of clothing. Actually, it was a small department store, designed to accommodate people's needs in one place. I met the old man, the store owner (*she refers to him as grandpa*) who greeted me warmly. He handed me a large abacus and told me to add up the numbers he called out. All my nerves stuck out like pine needles but I concentrated. The total was accurate. With a smile and his hand on my shoulder, grandpa told me, "The job is yours. Good luck."

As I worked there, I occasionally came across some money, sometimes a bill and at other times loose change. Whenever I found some, I could hear my heart beat harder. I would go to grandpa and say, "Grandpa, I don't know where this money comes from. Some customer must have left inadvertently. I thought you should see to that they get the money back." Those incidents were repeated. Later, I learned that I had been tested. I became the apple of his eye.

Soon I became to be known as a woman who walks straight, only gazing frontward, and a competent woman with good manners. You would be surprised how many customers were male, eligible males who came and freely spent money buying fishing tools, sporting goods, etc. Many of them wanted to take me out. Some tempted me with substantial gifts, sometimes even cash. Every time that happened, I would report it to grandpa.

Part of me always saw my mother as a negative example; I swore that I would never be like her. I have always admonished my brother that our behavior should never cause others to point fingers at us. I was armed like a stone wall. In that frame of mind, so determined and so stubborn, no man could tempt me. I wouldn't even have a cup of tea with men. I had this idea that a small thing like that would lead to something catastrophic. The men even had a bet going around. "Whoever succeeds in taking the woman at Moon Hwa Sang (*the name of the store*) wins a large amount of money." I don't know how much they bet.

The grandpa came to call me his granddaughter. I worked there for six years. Every month, I sent money to my mother. Thus, we built a house with three bedrooms and a tile roof. I furnished the house carefully; I picked each piece of furniture in Chun Ahn. Whenever I bought furniture, I thought of my brother and his disease. I hoped that an impeccably furnished house would increase his chances of getting a good wife. I was very close to my brother. He used to tell me, "When I grow my own rice, I wouldn't send it to you. I would personally carry it to you on my A frame." So in my mother's neighborhood, there is a saying "Be like Young Ja (*fictitious name*)." I was a role model.

You have no idea how many times people tried to match me with men. Grandpa encouraged me to study Chinese characters and English in my spare time. He used to say, "Knowledge is power. You must teach yourself as much as you can." No one knew that I only went to elementary school. They all believed that I had completed at least high school. So all the men who wanted to meet me were college graduates. In the end, it became nearly impossible to refuse meeting men altogether. I agreed to meet quite a few candidates in the presence of matchmakers. When I finally decided to marry my husband, a boy in grandpa's family told my husband, "Do you know that you are one out of 37?" He had been counting!

How did I meet my husband? My husband's sister lived in Chun Ahn and was a good friend of a daughter-in-law of the family I worked for. She was frequently in and out of the house. Naturally, she heard about me and saw me. She always wanted to make me her sister-in-law. She had five brothers. "Which one of them should I match with this woman?" was her worry. One day she came into the store and asked if I would be willing to meet her brother. First, we went to a fortune teller and asked if we were a good match. She said, "if you marry this man, you will give birth to sons, the family fortune will increase and you will have a happy, blessed life."

We finally arranged a meeting. My husband was not a tall man. Actually he was rather short. He was hesitant to meet me in a public place like a tea room or restaurant. "I am not one of your dashing men, you know. I have no confidence that she would be attracted to me. No public display," he told his

152

sister. So we met in his sister's house. As he came in, I felt my heart sinking. He was indeed short and there was not much to look at. . . I said, "Well, I am worried that the store needs me. I must go back." But he surprised me. He did not give in easily. He wasn't rude or arrogant but quite gentle. "Do you know that every meeting is not just an accident. Wouldn't you at least like to explore if we might have anything more than a fleeting moment together?" I sat back and we talked. I began to feel good about him.

He went back to Seoul and I continued to work at the store. His sister, however, never lost interest. She was persistent. I think partly because she was impressed to see me do things for the grandma of the house, the wife of the store owner. She had had a stroke and was paralyzed. Her own daughter-in-law was unwilling to clean up her messes. I believed that things in life go around. My turn to get old would inevitably come and who will be kind to me when I need help? I would wear gloves and clean up her mess. My husband's sister thought it most unusual that a so-called modern young woman could be like me.

Finally, I invited his sister and others in the family to our house in the countryside, you know the house we built. I will never forget it, October 26, 1979, the day President Park Chung Hee passed away. I was a flower lover then as I am now. I did all kinds of flower arrangements; chrysanthemums were in full bloom and there were all kinds of beautiful autumn flowers. My future mother-in-law was impressed. "Oh, my, I had no idea that you liked flowers. I am crazy about them myself." I believe their expectations for our house were low. So it took them by surprise, I could tell.

Do you know what my mother did? She looked over the fence without being seen and saw this man walking toward our house. He was not only short but his hair. . . He was just out of serving in the army. His hair was cut still like a soldier's. Naturally, his looks were anything but smashing. My mother was bowled over. She yelled, "After so many men, how did you manage to pick him? He looks like a short piece of shit!" She had taken her best Korean costume out of a chest but she threw it back in.

Even while his family was there, my mother just poured out what was on her mind. I can't remember everything she said but it was quite something. Believe me, it was incredible, the things she said. But you know what? This kind of relationship is a strange thing. I believe that it is in your fate. Every human meeting is not just an accident but how a man and a woman are paired, it is mysterious, maybe beyond our own doing. My husband later told me that my mother amused him rather than making him angry. He admired her frank and feisty character and couldn't wait to have such a mother-in-law. He thought it would be fun! He also thought that her daughter must be okay if she was anything like her mother. Talking about irony. . . I don't exactly know how I persuaded my mother but she finally agreed.

She laughed, almost a lustrous laughter and I was happy to share her laughter.

I was married on the 30th of March; on the 24th of June of that year my brother died. He complained of stomach pain. My mother told him to rest and went out to buy some groceries to cook him special food, something soothing. Upon her return, she found him dead. When the news arrived, I was still a bride. It was awkward but I had to get some money from my husband's family and go to my mother.

Again, left all alone in the countryside, my mother became ill. She had some kind of a gastrointestinal disease, caused by the years of hardship, frustration and bottled up anger. It used to come and go. In those times and where my mother was, people did not go to a doctor; they just coped with disease. So we didn't even know exactly what my mother had. It was at my husband's insistence that my mother was brought to Seoul. We took her to a doctor who told us that we discovered it barely before it turned into stomach cancer. My husband also arranged for an operation and treatment.

She brought out the most delicate and delicious sushi and invited me to eat. As we ate, she expressed the anxiety she felt about her husband finding out about our talk. I assured her that I would keep it confidential. "You know, my only regret is that I could not show off to the world how beautiful you are," I said.

These days my mother laments that she cannot read. "I go to all these demonstrations and meetings and they give me things to read. I wish I could read. It is like being blind with good pair of eyes. I wish my father and grandmother had sent me to school!" Sometimes when I feel low, I become snide, "Mom, who are you to say things like that to me? You are not fit to say such things to me. Look what you did to me. I wished you had sent me to school no matter what." Then, my feisty mother lowers her voice in true contrition and says, "You know I do regret that. I am truly sorry." Then, she cries and I join in. We often cry together on the phone.

I can manage most things without difficulty and fit into my husband's family and friends. I only wish I had more education for my sons. I would be so thrilled if I could help them do homework.

"Why don't you study now? I am sure you can find plenty of adult education courses. It's not too late. Look at you, you are still young."

I hate sitting around at home like a typical wife. So I put my hands on many things, flower arrangements, hair styling, you name it. I want to improve myself in whatever way I can. I have this desire to study English but I found it most challenging. Maybe one's head is not geared to mastering a foreign language after a certain age.

> *"I know. The younger one is, the easier it is for one to study a foreign language. I know it is a struggle for you. But try. Learning English is not just a matter of studying another language. Knowing a foreign language means your world becomes that much wider, broader . . . Language is never just a language; through it you get much more. By entering an alien world, you understand your world much better. By entering a different world and coming back, you might find something that had been always there but couldn't see. English is a good tool to learn about the western world which, in turn, will help you understand your own world better." I abruptly stopped. I couldn't believe that I was lecturing this woman on multiculturalism.*

I can see that. You know, my husband is considerate but too protective for my own good. If I told him that I want to learn English, he would gently brush me away. "Why? There are a plenty of other things you can enjoy without learning English." If my sons come to me with questions about their homework, he would promptly tell them, "Please don't bother your mother. She is busy enough. Besides, when she had you boys, she had a caesarian. Ever since her ability to remember diminished a little, caused by the anesthetic. So he makes up stories for me. His intentions are good. He wants to protect me.

> *Protective or patronizing? It wasn't easy but I kept my mouth shut.*

I could not bring myself to ask if he drank when I met him, though I was most concerned about that. You know my obsession about drinking. But he does not drink or smoke. I feel lucky. Everyone in my husband's family is crazy about me, especially my mother-in-law. She likes my cooking. When she comes here to visit us, she does not want to leave. My husband is very content and proud of me. She says no other woman could have fit in as well as I did. Since our marriage, our property multiplied. I often think that that fortuneteller was right.

My mother still sings old songs whenever she becomes blue thinking about her past. As for me, I believe I was fortunate to meet my husband. I don't think about my past. Even now, if I see my mother drinking with her friends, I feel like throwing up, I feel so upset. It's almost like a sickness on my part but I can't help it. When I was little, I protested to my mother often, "Why are you like this? Why can't you be a mother just like any other?" But it was no use.

We sold our property in the countryside and rented a room for my mother. Of course, we invited her come live with us but she wouldn't. Then, this issue of *Jungshindae* came along and she reported. She was able to get her current apartment, a government subsidized apartment. She moved there last November. She didn't discuss reporting with me. She went to her friend first and only after she had reported, did she tell me about it. At first, I was flabbergasted, "How could you do a thing like that? What would you do if my husband found out about it?" "Leave it to me. I know what I am doing. Don't you worry about it," she said. I consoled myself, "Well, if my husband finds out about her, he will just have to understand and accept it. It wasn't her fault. She was a victim of a terrible time and terrible people." [105] I told you about how I overheard something about her past while trying to fall asleep but she would not tell me. Once I asked her directly, "Mom, why did you come south from northern Korea?" She said, "During the war, I was drafted to work as a nurse for wounded soldiers." That's what she said. Because I had known about this, however vaguely, I wasn't terribly shocked to hear about her.

I feel hurt whenever I think of her and all the hardships she had to endure. I do not want her to work. I told her many times to take it easy and be comfortable. We will help whatever she needs but she works all the time. She says, "As long as I can move around, I will be damned if I sit around and stretch my hands for help, even though you are my daughter." That's my mother. Nothing I can do about it.

Now my husband knows about my mother. I told him after a while. He was shocked that his mother-in-law was part of something he thought of merely as unfortunate history. After the initial shock, I could tell that he was full of compassion rather than shame or worry that others might learn about it.

These days my mother acknowledges the heartaches and hardships she inflicted on me and in her own way apologizes. You know all those grandmas, like my mother, have high hopes of being compensated. Most of the time, my mother says, "I don't think about compensation. What happened to me can't be compensated for no matter how much they pay me. Before I blame anyone, anything, I feel sorrowful for a life that includes so much suffering, injustice and sadness." With a deep sigh that could bring down the sky, she would continue, "But if they ever give me some money, I would like to give it to you for your part of the hardship. You were just as much a victim as I was." "Don't you worry about that, mother. I have enough to live on. Just be healthy and live long. That's the only favor you can do for me."

When I think about my mother, my heart wrings with pain. Whatever the cause, she didn't deserve what she had to endure. Now, what consoles me is watching the pleasure she gets from her grandsons. She told me the other day, "Your sons are better than you are. The older one opened the rice jar when he

156

was here. I asked what he was looking for. Do you know what he said, 'Grandma, I am not looking for anything. I am just checking if you have enough rice. I wanted to bring some if you needed it.'" They are devoted to their grandma. They adore her.

My feelings about the Japanese? Quite frankly, I hate them for what they did. More than the compensation, I want to see them offer sincere, official apologies. Otherwise, all these grandmas won't be able to close their eyes on their deathbeds. They are dying fast. Japan must be waiting for all of them to die. At least my mother has me. As stubborn as she is, she knows I am here to help if she needs it but what about the other grandmas? Most of them have no one. They are truly lonely, a frail crowd who live with chestfuls of pain. If Japan wants to join the human race, they must do something about their past sins.

Sometimes I ask my mother to tell me about it. She never goes into detail but says that her life in comparison with others was not so bad; that she had a high ranking officer who was kind to her and wanted to take her to Japan at the war's end but she didn't go. That's as far as she goes but one consistent perspective she wants me to have — there were others who suffered more than she did.

If I had a daughter, I would bring her up not to feel alienated from her own generation and her own world. You know I have two sons. I worry about what I do with them. I have lots of feelings about other people, often full of affection, but my own children, I don't know. My younger son, because he is younger, my feelings for him are different but with my first son I feel constantly disappointed. He does not come up to my expectations. Maybe I expect too much of him. . . I worry about my own feelings and reactions. He is messy, sloppy and not as good at his studies as I would like to see. I know in my head that I should embrace him with love and affection. I know I should be more patient, more tolerant. After all, he is only a boy. But I don't follow my head. I am often judgmental. That frightens me. I am concerned that I lack feelings, maybe love for him.

My husband is more understanding. He assures me that the boy will shape up in his own time. I tell my son how fortunate he is to have so much. I talk about how hard it was for me and urge him to take advantage of his good fortune. I tell them about my childhood. But not the fact that I didn't go beyond elementary school. I can't bring myself to talk about my education, rather lack of it. I know it's irrational but the thing that bugs me the most is my lack of formal education. You have no idea how I wish I could have graduated even from high school, not to mention college. I beam with pride from time to time for what I have achieved, considering what I had to work against. But when it comes to schooling, I don't want to reveal the real story.

157

The teacher in me kept encouraging her to go back to school and she was attentive. On the other hand, it could have been just polite manners. Alas, it was time for me to go. I had to get out of there before her children returned home. As I packed my equipment, she said, "I don't know how I survived my mother's tragic life. What Japan did to my mother did not end with her. You can't imagine how many times it had crushed me into a corner of life and almost killed me. Then, there are my twin brothers. . ." Blowing her nose, she continued, "When my mother registered as a former comfort woman and got her current apartment, part of a government project, I threw out all her old furniture, bought her all new things as if I were marrying a daughter off. She moved in there like a bride." I broke down and cried with her.

Leaving her behind, I took a cab and was on my way to see her mother again. When I rang the bell of her apartment on the 14th floor, there was no response. I sat on the concrete floor and waited. More than an hour passed and as I was just about to give up, she appeared with her eyes still heavy with sleep. "How long have you been here?" she asked. "I had lunch with some friends but they offered me a couple bowls of rice wine. I should not have drunk them but I did. I fell asleep. If my daughter finds out, she is going to have a fit." She was right about her daughter. Smiling I said, "It doesn't matter. I am just glad to see you. May I come in?"

Just like her daughter had told me, her furniture was all new and the place neat. She showed me around and said, "The only thing I don't have is a washing machine. My daughter wanted to buy it for me but I was firm. I won in the end. I said, 'Are you crazy? There's only me, just one person. You can't tell me that I need a machine to wash my own clothes. As long as I am alive with my two little hands moving, I am washing my own things. No machine will wash them for me.'" I asked if she would tell me a little more about herself. "Last night, we talked in the presence of another grandma. So I thought you could tell me a little more." "I have nothing else to tell you." She resisted but I pleaded. "For one, you can start with a special friend you had." I persisted and she gave in.

I received lots of soldiers, but there was this officer, much older than I, who started to like me. He was an army doctor. From my looks now, you could not tell but when I was young, I wasn't bad looking. He thought I was beautiful and paid me special attention. It was because of him that I had a less horrible time than I might have otherwise. He gave me shots, medicine and took care of me. Then, independence came.

You remember what I told you about the cotton quilts I sent my grandma, don't you? Independence was not as important as the cotton quilts I sent to my grandma. I think they gave me some money each month which I saved. I spent all that money to buy the quilts. I remember that shortly after I sent them, someone told me that the war had ended and Korea had become independent. I never did find out if my grandma got them or not. People came to the street with flags and the Chinese drove us out of the house. Any fool would have figured it out.

> *Her story about being searched, leaving China with nothing but her body, opium addicts' going crazy on the ship coming back to Korea, arriving at Pusan, lining up there, receiving some money for ticket home, and staying in southern Korea was pretty much the same as what she had already told me. Then, suddenly she said, "Do you know why I have a hearing problem? Because she repeatedly slapped me." "Who slapped you? Where?" "In China. Would you believe she was a Korean woman?" So she did tell some more stories.*

She was our manager.[106] You know I had venereal disease and down there it was red and swollen. The pain was excruciating but did she care? No . . . she couldn't care less. She just cut there and blood, contaminated with yellow stuff, oozed. That was the treatment and she wanted us to go back receiving the soldiers. The first time it happened, the only thing I felt was pain, such piercing pain.

I do remember a Japanese officer who was kind to me. In the middle of so much brutality, his kindness stood out. I still think of him once in a while. Any small kindness stood out. He wanted to take me to Japan but I didn't want to go with him. I had to see my grandmother's face even if just once. Did I regret it? I had no time for regrets. No time for feelings of any sort. Life was so hard, everyday was pure struggle, down to the basics, what to eat and where to sleep.

Of course, I was happy to hear that Japan had lost the war. It meant I could go home and see my grandmother. "Those fucking bastards lost the war!" I said to myself and felt great. To think of what they did to me, to my life, I still gnash my teeth. Even among the women like us, there are more dead than alive. We have no idea how many died before the war ended. For that matter, after the war, before they could return home.

The government help we receive is not enough. After we pay the rent for this apartment, nothing is left. My daughter is well off and constantly offers me help but I don't want her help. Whenever I can, I work. Government run programs like planting spring onions, that's something I can do with my eyes closed, though it is physically demanding. After a while, my body would not stretch straight. My daughter is disgusted with me. She says, "Mom, you are still setting fires in my chest as if all those years of heartaches and hardships you have given me are not enough." Well, I can't help it. I am fiercely independent. I don't want her help as long as I can move around. This stubborn character of mine, that's part of my fate.

When I think of the times I slaved under the Japanese and the fifty years of life since, the hurt chokes me. It chokes my chest so tight I have to let it out. So I drink to forget, to release the big lump of sorrow, hard as a rock, piled up so long. I didn't drink until I was taken to Manchuria. I started there but drank more when I returned. You have no idea how much. In comparison, what I drink these days, it's nothing. I am tamed these days. Besides, I can't hold liquor any more. Like this afternoon, what I had was nothing, but see my face? It is as red as if I drank all afternoon, only a couple of bowls.

My life when I returned? How can I and where should I start? My daughter's father? He is the one who cheated me. He didn't tell me that he had a wife. After I had lived with him a while, I found out that he had a wife, you know the first wife. I yelled at him, "I could be many things but not a woman who would knowingly set a fire in someone's flower garden. I couldn't hurt another woman!" Alas, I was already pregnant with my daughter. I wanted to get rid of it. I did everything I knew to abort the baby but no such luck. A baby girl was born and I left, taking her with me. Even so, he could have helped his own baby girl but he did nothing, nothing. I had to struggle all alone. Why did I not leave her with him to raise? Are you crazy? She came out of my belly; she was my baby. After a while, I married another man and gave birth to twin sons. But they all died.

> It was clear that she didn't want to talk about her twin sons. I decided to wait. In the meantime, she told the same story about her second husband's death, beaten by the communists, the trials, toils and sufferings she had to go through as a widow with a girl and two boys.

What do I regret most about my daughter? I wish I had sent her to high school. If only she had even a high school education, she could be really something. She could conquer the world. These days I express my regrets to her but she is the one who cuts me off, "Mother, don't say you are sorry. You did what you could. Even if I didn't go beyond elementary school, I was blessed with an understanding husband and see, I have a good life. Don't torture yourself."

You know, human life is resilient. How many times I pinched my baby's legs. They were the only ones dangling on my back I could quickly reach with one hand while the other hand held the big basket containing earthenware. I told her to do me a favor, to die so many times I could not count. But she did-n't die and she is still alive and well. You should see my son-in-law. How he protects her and loves her. Even if I hadn't had that dreadful past and had had a normal marriage, I don't think I could have had that kind of affection like they do. What they have between them is something special, something rare.

She served me yellow melon and we chatted about the vari-ety of work she does to help with her living expenses. I real-ized that she was not about to talk about her twin sons. I ventured, "Could you talk about your twin sons? What hap-pened to them?" She stopped her hand, holding a piece of melon in the mid air and looked at me. I sat still, with the melon pieces already in my mouth unchewed, ignoring my heartbeat thudding. Such a sigh that could bring the sky down.

Well, they both died. It must not have been in their father's fate that he would have sons. After I killed my younger one, I became a heavy drinker. I ordered around people, it didn't matter who they were, whoever there was, I would yell, even to my brother-in-law. "Bring me some more wine. What are you waiting for? Don't you have ears and legs? Move!" People were scared of me. I was not in my right mind. I was out of my mind.

My stomach became a mess, I think it became all rotten. I became all skin and bones. My daughter and her husband came and fetched me to Seoul. The doctor said, "She needs an operation but it is extremely risky at her age." I said, "What's the difference if I die now? I could have died when I was three. We all die someday. What are you waiting for? Please operate on me." The doctor would not operate unless my daughter signed. She was trembling all over. As they carried me off to the operating room, I said, "Please, my good doctor, cut away all the useless mess in my stomach and clean it out thor-oughly while you have it open. You don't want to have to open it again, do you?" I remember laughing and the doctor laughed with me. After a success-ful operation, the doctor told me, "It was your courage, your vibrant spirit that made this operation successful."

Of course, I was worried sick that my son-in-law might find out. But as time passed and as I talked with other grandmas like myself, the anxiety is less and I feel less shame. I didn't go on my own will to do such a terrible thing. All my life I lived with hidden shame, but all these demonstrations and activities that demand justice help me overcome my shame.

My hope for my two grandsons? To grow up to be decent human beings. As simple as that. I want them to be fair human beings who would not inflict injustice on others. What would I do with the money if Japan compensated me? What would I do for my daughter? I think the greatest favor I can do for her is for me to be independent until I die. The money will have to be used for my independence first. I could not stand being a burden to her. You know I would be an impossible old bitch!

Chuckling, she urged me to eat more melon and ate some herself.

Even now when I think of those times, I am not sure if it is real or a dream. What comes back more vividly than anything else is the image of that woman who cut my wound and sent me back to those soldiers. I used to have such good memories. I think she is the one who made my brain go dull . . . her blow was so hard . . . you have no idea. She was evil.

You should have seen what happened to the Chinese. They died like dogs. In the middle of fierce battles, air raids from above and ground battles, fires everywhere, screams and dead bodies . . . even in the midst of all that, the soldiers came. Thinking back, I don't think there was a difference between life and death for those soldiers . . . It was just their reality. If we refused, they would still kick and abuse . . . All those things, they were nightmares for us but for the soldiers, it was their reality, thinking back.

I am still waiting for Korea to be re-unified. I want to go back to my hometown in the north. On the first day of unification, I would be heading north. I would be on my way. I told you that my grandmother raised me. Even while I worked at a factory, I managed to sneak out and learn songs and things from this woman.[107] My grandmother found out; she threw a fit and begged me to marry. But I went off to work in a textile factory; you know that's what they told me when I left grandma. Till this day, when I think that I could not see my grandma once again, I feel as if a huge rock is pressing my chest down. I had other families, too, nephews, nieces and all those. I don't feel much affection for my father. If only he had sent me to school and helped me see the world differently, my life might have been different. I want to go to the north and bow a deep bow in front of my grandma's grave.

I could really sing. When I was young, if I put on some cosmetics, you know, made up myself a little and sing, men around me would pee in their pants. They were crazy about my singing. I could easily have become a singer. I am not good anymore but after a couple of drinks, I sing. I don't care if I sound like a bird or dog. I sing.

"Please sing a song for me." "Are you kidding? You want too much!" "I know but I can't help it. Your daughter bragged about you. She told me that you were a fabulous singer." "Did she say that?" Her eyes twinkled and a smile spread on her lips. I saw a jolly, indomitable grandma! A couple of drinks with her would have been grand!

It's my daughter who can really sing. I can't stand fake modesty. I would

162

say I was good at singing without hesitation. Yes, no doubt that I was good but that was a long time ago, when I was young. Okay, I will try it. Who could stop me from trying?

She began to sing. Slowly, her voice filled the room. "Nak Dong River wind blowing my skirt, I hear news from my man who went to the army . . . " The song itself was not sad but the vibration of her voice blew my heart with grief like a Nak Dong River wind. The phone interrupted her singing and I did not push her to continue. It was more than enough; I could not bear it anymore. "Do you go to church"?

Church? I don't care for church or God. I am so loaded with sin. No sense for begging forgiveness. Not enough time to recite all my sins. What I went through, what was done to me was not human. The only thing I know: I am not afraid of life, I am not afraid of death. I live with a motto, "Don't hurt others; don't be unfair to others." I believe in my own heart and I take care of myself.

Back home in Washington, I thought of this woman of raw courage and her beautiful daughter on and off. When I feel discouraged, this grandma's defiant face, radiant with courage so raw, so sad helps lift my spirits.

I took a moment to call both the mother and daughter when I was back to Seoul in November. Alas, no answer on the mother's phone but the daughter greeted me warmly. We chatted a while; she and her family were fine. Her mother was as usual and as well as she could be. Toward the end of our conversation, she hesitated but said, "I must tell you. After our talk, I thought about what you said, you know, about it not being too late to do something about my education. It made sense. So I enrolled in adult school. I have four classes every morning: Chinese, English, Math and Ethics." I was dumbfounded. It took me a while to respond, "Why, that's wonderful. I am so thrilled for you." "But I must tell you. It has been a struggle. My brain must have been hardened. It is very difficult." "I know but please keep it. Your brain will open itself up and you will be surprised." I promised that I would stay in touch with her.

Postscript

Because her daughter didn't want to reveal her identity, I did not interview this grandma for my film. When I went to a Wednesday demonstration, though, she was there with Grandma X. Her greeting was heart felt. When I asked her about her daughter, she beamed. "She is fine; they are all doing well." I took all my grandmas that day to a small restaurant and treated them to lunch.

Chapter 8

IF ONLY MY FATHER LET ME GO TO SCHOOL . .
.
Yun Doo Ri

Eight Blessings (Matthew 5:3-12)

Blessed are those who mourn,
Blessed are those who mourn,
Blessed are those who mourn,
Blessed are those who mourn,
Blessed are those who mourn,
Blessed are those who mourn,
Blessed are those who mourn,
Blessed are those who mourn.
They shall be ever mournful.

I flew to Ulsan, a harbor city in the south, headquarters of the Hyundai Automobile Corporation. I was accompanied by Yun Chong-Ok, a retired professor from Ewha Women's University and a foremost researcher/activist on comfort women. It was less than a one hour flight from Seoul. At the airport, we grabbed a taxi and asked the driver to find a government subsidized apartment complex. Starved, we found a tiny restaurant, dirty and greasy, tucked away in a basement. We each ordered a noodle dish with soy bean sauce, smothered with chopped onions. I slurped the noo-dles; they tasted amazingly good which, I am sure, had much to do with my empty stomach. We bought a large watermel-on and were on our way to see Grandma Yun.

Prof. Yun had scarcely rung the bell when she was swept into the arms of a woman who quite literally raced out the door to hug her, and I had barely been introduced when a torrent of words gushed toward us. Standing in a narrow

*hallway leading to a small sitting room, she proclaimed,
"The Japanese are human beings, too, aren't they? They
belong to a different country and speak a different language
but they are people made up of the same intestines and organs
as the rest of us, aren't they? If they are, they should just come
out, apologize and offer to compensate us. They should ask for
our forgiveness. But look at what they are doing! They said
they had nothing to do with us women. Only when cornered,
did they say, 'We are sorry.' Now, they are talking about offer-
ing us some money from private funds. I don't want that
money! Come the next day, you never know what they will say
and do. Every time the Japanese respond, I sit by myself and
just hug my body, uncontrollably trembling."*

*Prof. Yun gently pulled her toward the sitting room and
presented the watermelon. Feelings of relief rushed through
my body to see her steady hand taking the melon. "You
should not have brought this. There was no need for you to
bring anything. I am just glad you came." Then, smiling, she
invited me to sit down on a cushion. She put the melon in the
refrigerator and joined us, kneeling on the floor. "No part of
my body is free from aches and pains. But I get up at 4 a.m.
every morning and go to church for dawn prayer. This morning, I hurried back to make sure that I got home before you
arrived. By the way, did you have lunch?" Her voice was
husky and her Korean was definitely southern. To my surprise, I could understand every word she said, thanks to the
Korean War and my refugee life in Pusan (the largest harbor
city in the South) decades ago. "We had to eat first. We were
starved," said Prof. Yun, and tried to make small talk but
Grandma Yun was not interested.*

*"In connection with this issue, I recently learned that
the Park regime (President Park Chung Hee) signed a treaty
with the Japanese government and received some money. Of
course, we were not included in the deal at all. The Park
regime got the money with promises that the Korean government would not request any more compensation. (She
was talking about the 1965 Treaty between Japan and
Korea). No question that Park neglected us but those bastards, the Japanese, are saying that we were included in that
deal. As far as they are concerned, we were paid. That's
what they are saying. Can you imagine?"*

Her eyes were shut and I could almost hear her heart

166

beat. Then, I was brought back to a tiny sitting room as I heard a calm voice carrying each word with emphasis. "I pray every dawn to my Father for the unification of our country. If you are a person full of han (accumulated sorrow and pain), you understand these things." I wondered why she is suddenly talking about unification. As if she had read my mind, she continued, "I pray that a tragedy like mine will not happen again. For that, we need a strong country. For that, this country of ours has to be united. No room for this division. I pray for this country every day." Silence followed, each of us immersed in our thoughts.

Finally, I spoke, no longer able to hold my worries that her words might be lost in my weak memory. I could not risk it. "I have a recorder in this bag. Would you allow me to record our conversation?" She simply nodded. Suddenly, assuming a formal posture, she began to account how she had been captured. I repressed a sigh and remained attentive for a while. Carefully choosing my moment, I asked politely if I could use her bathroom.

When I returned, I said, You know I am dying to know about your childhood, about your parents, sisters and brothers. Do you remember your childhood at all? "How can I not remember?"

My father's family owned land in Ulsan. Both families of my grandfathers were of the nobility and they were both government officials of high rank. Naturally, they were close friends and in a perfect situation to become in-laws. That's how my parents got married; my mother was seventeen and my father twenty. Their first child was a girl and then came a boy, my older brother. There were seven of us, three boys and four girls. I was the fourth. One of two younger brothers died when he was six.

My father lived in this city, right there (she pointed out the window with her stretched arm). You will be surprised how this city has changed. Where the City Hall is now, there used to be a big reservoir. And there were fewer houses. People used that water for farming. My father sold some of this land and moved to Pusan. You see, he built houses. He learned carpentry and architecture, all that. He wanted to try the business, construction business.

But I remember coming back to this city when I was little with my parents for the annual ritual we offered for our ancestors. We had a huge family because my grandmothers, both paternal and maternal, died young and my grandfathers, they both re-married and lots of children were born. I had many uncles and aunts. My father always took care of the annual family rituals for the ancestors. The one thing I remember —I went to my grandfather's grave,

167

holding my father's hand. When I sat there, a gush of wind almost swept me away. At that moment, I thought, "Gee, grandpa must be so cold. This is not a good place for him to rest." As I was coming down the hill, I promised myself that one day I would move my grandfather's grave. Do you know that I actually kept that promise years later?

A rush of nostalgia crossed her face.

In Pusan, my father's business flourished. He had fifty men working for him. He built lots of houses. He became a rich man. We lived in a fabulous house with a large courtyard and a tiled roof. When I was little, I was dying to go to school. I pleaded and begged my father to send me to school. My father would not budge on this issue. He was firm. He told me repeatedly that girls, especially of good families, should not go to public school. There were many scholars in the Yun family but no girls should be exposed to public education. He sent me to my grandfather to learn Chinese characters, you know the basic thousand characters.

She chanted the Chinese characters the way her grandfather made her do, chuckling.

Because I set my heart to going to school, I couldn't be serious. I was often mischievous. I remember one day my grandfather hit my head with his long pipe and scolded me, "You must take this study more seriously. Your mind is not in it. Concentrate." I started crying and protested, "I don't want to learn this stuff. I want to go to school." My uncle had to take me home. Then, I pleaded again to my father to send me to school. He would not give in. "You stick to your Chinese characters!" he roared.

Then, an idea occurred to me. There was a man in his forties who lived in one of the outer rooms of our house. Because I was little, I called him grandpa. One day I asked him if he knew of a family where I could baby-sit and go to school. At first, he simply yelled at me, "What nonsense! Hush up." I was persistent. He finally gave in a little and asked, "Are you serious? Do you really know what you are talking about?" He said he knew a relative of ours who had two sons and that another baby had just been born. Perhaps, I could take care of the baby and go to night school. Did I want to try that, he asked? I gave him a strong nod.

I told my mother that I was leaving home in order to go to school. The house became like a war zone. My mother had heard nothing like that in her life. Her answer was an adamant "no." While my mother was out, I packed a few things and asked the grandpa to take me to that house. He gave in to my persistence. I was eight years old.

I was impressed by the house; it was large and beautiful. I baby sat during the day and at five in the evening, I went to school. The first semester, they started teaching us the Korean alphabet but from the second semester on, they taught us only Japanese. In the meantime, the family moved to Seoul and it was there that I continued going to night school and completed elementary school. The family encouraged me to take the entrance examination to the middle school but, alas, I failed it. I found out that only Japanese students passed. The family consoled me, and told me that I had to try again the following year.

On the 15th day of December according to the lunar calendar, the same year we moved to Seoul, my father appeared on the doorstep of that house. He came to fetch me. Later I learned that during my absence my father almost went crazy. The woman of the house, whom I called "aunt," pleaded with my father. "You have three other daughters. Young Ja (that was my name then) is just like our own daughter. If we committed any crime, we sent her to a night school, but we brought her up just like our own. Please let us keep her." They begged my father for two days but he wouldn't have it. I cried and they cried but there was no use. I had to leave with my father. I got on a train at 9 p.m. and arrived in Pusan at 7 the next morning. It was 1941 and I was fourteen years old. All those years, I was happy. I didn't mind baby sitting. Going to school kept me happy and jovial. Besides, they were really nice to me; they treated me as if I were their own girl.

The place my father took me was not the one I had left. It was a pathetic little room, rented at that. My father, mother, one older sister, a younger brother and a sister — five of them were living in one small room. I stood there, shocked. It was eight o'clock and my father went out, presumably to work, without saying anything. I just stared at my mother and asked why we were living in such a pighole. I demanded to know what had happened to our house. My mother just said we would soon move to our old house.

> *"Well, do you know what happened?" She asked me, her*
> *voice trembling with fury. I made a inaudible sound, no.*

Those bastards, the Japanese, took one look at our house and decided that they could put it to better use. They confiscated our house. My father was unable to get any business. My older brother, after he married, went crazy, I mean insane. My mother's health was in bad shape. She had kidney trouble. My father's money shrank in no time and the family was in a pitiful condition. I gnashed my teeth. The morning after my return, I got up, washed my face with water in the basin in the yard and came in, wiping my face with towel. My mother had brought in a breakfast table for us, my father and myself. I said with a Seoul accent, "Father, please eat breakfast." We both sat down and I had one spoonful of food. Then, I saw my father's hand holding a spoonful of rice hitting the table, not his mouth. He suddenly collapsed and died. He was forty nine. Do you know that my father literally died of bottled up rage. That anger exploded.

Pause, silence hanging heavy in the air, only interrupted by her rough breath.

He must have felt something about his impending death and that's why he was so determined to bring me home. Those Japanese, they took my father's life away. And don't kid yourself, he was not the only Korean who died like that because of those bastards, the Japanese.

She got up and brought a picture of a man. "This is not my father, but he looked like this. My father was a good looking man."

I try not to blame my father. . . My mother once went to a fortune teller to ask about my future. She told my mother, "You should not treat her like a daughter. She was not born to raise a family. It is clear as daylight that she was born to be a great man, maybe a politician wielding power. Send her to school." Perhaps that's why I went berserk wanting to go to school. You see, my parents should have given what was due to me. I was wild with the desire to study; it was almost an uncontrollable urge. They should have sent me to school which I wanted more than anything in the world.

If my father was too stuffy to send me to school, he should have just left me in Seoul. I was happy there, gearing up to take another exam. to enter middle school. Why did my father take me back home, depriving me of my only chance to get an education and throw me into a fate no human should endure? Do you blame me for blaming my father once in a while?

I sometimes wonder whether my mother really bore me. All my sisters were able to get married, have families and enjoy a normal life. Look at me. Most of my life, I kept an empty room with only myself, no love of a man, no children and now I suffer with a body that is sick through and through. No one who could bring me a glass of water. . .

Now she was oblivious of Prof. Yun and myself. Her eyes stared out of the window as if in an intense fight with the fate that should never have been hers.

You know, I constantly ask my Father to give me peace of mind. What does it matter now. I am old. I pray to Him to take me soon. The doctor told me that I have about nine different kinds of ailments. It is as if my body is a battle field.

"Grandma, tell us what you learned at school in Seoul," I asked. Her voice picked up energy at this question.

We learned a lot about the history of Japan. They made us recite some of the important events in Japanese history. I was good at it but I don't remember a thing now.

When her face became calm, Prof. Yun asked if she could suggest a hotel we could book for the night. She almost jumped. "What nonsense! Why are you looking for a hotel? You can sleep here." "But there are two of us. And you need to rest," I said, trying to help out Professor Yun. "No, I won't have it. You are both my guests. Stay here, if it is not too inconvenient." We accepted. Now Prof. Yun suggested that we all go to a nice restaurant, but we ended up ordering food from the same greasy Chinese place. While we ate, she talked about church.

Now, church is my home. I get up at 4 o'clock every morning and walk to church. If my legs and hip hurt too much, I take a taxi. It costs me ten thousand *won* (roughly a dollar and thirty cents). Once I quit church. Why? I could not read the Bible. I told you that in school, they stopped teaching us the Korean alphabet. The very first semester in school, I had a taste of it. After that, the Japanese did not even let us talk in Korean. If you were caught speaking Korean, you were punished. They made us lift up our arms, holding a big bucket full of pebbles just for speaking our own language. No way I could have learned how to read and write Korean. When we became independent, I remember seeing all those signs written in *Han Gul (Korean alphabet)*. I might as well have been blind. I could not read! I was in a fury and then I cried and cried. My brother wanted to know what on earth was the matter. I yelled — I feel stupid and miserable — I can't read my own language. That's what's the matter. He taught me how to read a little. After that, because I was so blindly obsessed to make money, I just forgot studying.

When I joined the church, the first thing I had to do was to read the Bible. I struggled with it when I was alone. But you know we have Friday evening study groups at different homes. We sit around and read the Bible aloud. Everybody has to do it. I struggled as hard as I could. But there was no way that I could read like the others. The humiliation I felt, you cannot imagine! That's not all. when I watched the others in our group, reading, laughing, talking about their families. . . That was the life I was supposed to have, wasn't it? After all, I belong to the human race, don't I? I was suffocated by my growing self-pity. I couldn't stand it. I had to quit!

Even before we put the dirty plates away, she resumed her talk, picking up where she had left off, her father's death, leaving a dirt poor family behind.

So here I was fourteen, going on to be fifteen, with my mother, and a brother and two sisters in one room with daily worries about food. Their sur-

171

vival hung heavily on my shoulders. But you know what? Once I made up my mind to support my family, I wasn't afraid of anything. I feared nothing. At that time, the food was rationed. Every week we received rationed food. The Japanese took away the very best rice grown with Korean farmers' blood and sweat, and gave us beans and barley. And if we did get some rice, it was rice from Taiwan. Did you know that they took our rice to Japan and gave us rice from Taiwan? No matter how carefully handled, the weekly ration lasted barely four days, five days if we added edible plants when we cooked rice.

Of course, I knew that our country was colonized by Japan! What's more, the fact that the Japanese took away all our property never left my chest; it was always there safely guarded. I couldn't worry, though, if Japan was screwing our country or not. My thoughts were concentrated on my family. I had a single desire to feed my family.

"You were still so young. Was there anyone who taught you all that?" asked Prof. Yun.

Of course not. My brain spun around like a well oiled wheel. I was smart. I got a job with a Japanese company manufacturing army uniforms. You might not believe me from my looks now but I was a good looking kid. I was short but I was some runner. When I was in school, I used to beat the hell out of the Japanese kids in all the racing competitions. I was a single minded, hard worker. All I saw was rice for my family. Soon they made me a section leader and I supervised quite a few people. I was also a leader in air raid drills. Most important, I was in charge of handing out rolls of thread for sewing, brown thread for army uniforms. And that gave me a chance to get some extra rice for my family. How? Thread was a precious commodity in Korea at that time. I stole some, but I could not just take them because they had to be accounted for. I had to submit the spindle with the number on it, each time when all the thread was used up. Well, I figured out how I could just take the thread; you had to press both sides of the spool and pull the rolled thread out. It wasn't a big deal at all, actually quite easy. Then, of course, I submitted the spindle with the number.

She chuckled, which was contagious. Prof. Yun and I giggled together.

I hid the stolen thread with my maternal grandmother and, when I had enough, exchanged it for rice. We had a day off on the first Sunday of every month, just once a month. Even then, we could not take the whole day off. Half of it, we had to do the air raid drills. I told you I was a leader for that, too, didn't I? After the drills were over at noon, I went to my grandmother who had already exchanged the thread with rice.

You have no idea how hard I worked. No one could go home until the

172

daily work was finished. For me, because I was a section leader, even after I finished my own work, I had to wait until all the others had finished. Almost every day, I could not leave my work until after 9 o'clock at night. Every night, in the dark, I had to pass by the place called "foreigners' hill." It was a spooky place. There was this Japanese guy who had his mind set on me. He tried to rape me three times. The third time, he nearly succeeded but I was rescued by Korean men who repaired sewing machines. After that, there was no way I could work there. I had to quit that job. Had I stayed in that factory, perhaps I could have remained a normal person.

Then, I got another job at a glove manufacturing factory. One night in September, I think, the third month after I had that job, I think it was September, I decided to walk home on a main street. You see, I used to go home through back streets, avoiding Japanese policemen as much as I could. I had heard that the Japanese were taking women away. That night, it was very dark and I felt too scared to walk through the dark back streets. In the morning, on my way to work, I had seen a corpse under a small bridge. All day at work, I couldn't get rid of the image of that dead body. I didn't want to walk back home the same way. I was passing a police station when I heard a voice calling me. I stopped and looked back. A policeman was calling me. I stood motionless and asked in Japanese what he wanted. He insisted that I come near him. I did not budge. "If you have something to tell me, I can hear. Please say it." He suddenly ran toward me, grabbed me, and took me to the station. Inside, without a word, he opened the door to a room where the night guards slept and threw me in. There were seven girls there,[108] sitting with their faces hidden between their knees. I felt my heart go down like a heavy stone falling down a slope. "They got me!" With that thought, my mind lost its function; it went out of my body. I only felt the sky falling down on me, thinking of my mom with her kidney ailment, waiting for me.

After a while, gathering my senses, I started pounding on the door as hard as I could. The door was locked and there was no response. I kicked and yelled as loud as I could. Desperate, I grabbed my lunch box and hit the glass window with it. At the sound of glass shattering, did they come! I yelled, "What crime have we committed? Why are you locking us up, a few innocent women? If you have anything to say, say it! What right do you have to rule over Koreans and lock up innocent people?" Now, the other seven joined and a war was on. "Shut up," one of them said to us. "This is our country. We are free to shout. What right do you have to lock us up like this. I was merely going home from a long day's work. I am starved. None of us has eaten. You could bring us some food!" I used every dirty Japanese word I could think of. Nothing worked. "You fucking bastards, we are thirsty. Bring us some water." Water was the only thing they brought.

About eleven at night, we were taken out of that room and ordered to get into a truck. I protested and fought. I was short but strong. I kicked and bit anybody who came near me. One of them tried to hit me. I kicked his balls hard. He put one hand on them and jumped around and around, with only one foot on the ground. He was in excruciating pain. You should have seen his face; it was a sight! Another slapped me hard and said, "Look what you did to him, you bitch!" I hit him back and yelled, "You have no right to come to our country and detain us!" I grabbed his neck and tried to bounce him with my head. I wouldn't get in the truck. Then, suddenly I saw a pistol in front of me, "Get in," he said. I just wanted to die right there and then. "If I die, who is going to feed my mother and brothers and sister?" That thought made me climb into the truck. We were taken to another location and locked in a barracks. About one o'clock in the morning, we were ordered out. They always moved us around during the night.

She paused, closing her eyes. Her face was contorted, darkness hovering over it.

You know, I had two older sisters. Both of them got married and led normal lives, enjoying everything a woman is entitled to—a loving husband, children and all that. I was the fourth child but because the older ones all went their own way, because my father died, I was stuck with my mother and younger ones when I was only fourteen, going on fifteen. That's why I was also subjected to that horrendous thing. I can't help but blame my parents till now . . .

"No, you mustn't! What's the use of all that prayer . . . You pray three to four hours every morning. . . " Prof. Yun sounded upset. Grandma Yun dismissed her.

You listen to me. Yes, I pray. Do you know what I pray for? I ask God the Father to take my life away, to end my life. Then, to bring me back to this world, not as a man but as a woman. I want to live a life of a normal woman who can get married, be loved, have children of my own. That's what I pray. If only my father had left me in Seoul. . .

Her eyes were dry but her voice was wet with grief. She blew her nose.

I don't know about the others but for me marriage was unthinkable. You know, I was only fifteen when that thing happened for the first time. After that, my uterus must have been torn. I could hardly walk; the pain was excruciating. During my menstruation, I told them that I could not do it. They gave me wad of cotton and told me to put it inside the uterus and to continue receiving the soldiers. After a while, the cotton ball was found way inside the uterus. Many times it went so deep inside that the doctor had to take it out. I can't tell you how painful it was. When the pain was unbearable, I had to see the doctor and every time I was given a shot. At the time, I had no idea what it was. It was only when I stopped getting those shots, I found out that I was a junkie.

I thought to myself. I endured what was unendurable, what was inhuman but how can I die as a junkie. I was born a human being. At least I have to die a human being. As long as I have my father's family name and my mother's flesh, I can't die a junkie. I ran away to Seoul. I rented a room the size of a hole (a Korean expression for an extremely small room), bought two big logs, nailed them on the door inside and put a cross on them. Then, I lay down on the quilt and the battle started. In a little while, I couldn't tell which was which, my head and wall. They were bumped against each other so many times . . .

I don't know how many days passed by. The landlord couple felt that something was wrong since they had not seen me for days. They came and knocked at the door. No response. They knocked louder. No, nothing. They broke the door open and found me stretched out like a corpse with a wooden cross nearby. They felt my pulse and found the slightest sign of life. They saved my life and I got rid of my drug addiction. They took care of me for days. I was too weak to move around. I am still grateful to them.[109]

> *I saw a gleam of sweat on her forehead. I stood up, wet a towel and handed it to her. As she wiped the sweat, I could feel a great lump of pain passing through her chest. Prof. Yun and I both waited in silence. She lit a cigarette and sucked in, long and hard.*

I know it isn't good for me to smoke. But whenever I think about it and talk about it, fire blazes inside of my body and I can't extinguish it. The only thing that helps me is smoking.

Pause.

Do you know that even while they did that thing like animals, they were often discriminating. They wanted good looking ones. I wasn't bad looking. Actually, I had a reputation as a pretty girl. So I had more soldiers who crawled on top of me. What an honor! Is this a comedy or what? Later even the thought of men sent chills through my spine. How could I even think of marriage?

I thought about becoming a nun when I was little, off and on. Whenever I saw nuns with black outfits and white collars, they looked so pure . . . Now, look at me. After birth, maybe the single most precious moment in a woman's life is her wedding day. But look at me. Take a good look at me. Tears flow in my chest. As long as I am alive, this sadness will be always with me like a knot tied around my chest. My favorite hymn is the wedding of the spirit. Maybe, I will get married in heaven in front of my Father. Or, if I could be reborn, I would like to come back as a female again. Then, I would do all the

175

things I could have done — go to school to my heart's content, experience what love is, get married, have kids and live like a normal human being.

When I returned home after the war, nowhere could my mother be found. I asked a woman next door, "Where is my Mom?" Startled to see me, she nearly jumped out of her skin. "Oh, my, Young Ja,[110] you are alive, are you alive? Where have you been? Where did you go? Your mother sells parsley at a market place." I ran in the direction my neighbor's finger pointed and found my mother at a corner of the vegetable section of the market. Her face was small, especially under a soiled white scarf on her head. She looked as if she would fall down at the slightest touch. In front of her were some bunches of parsley in a round, steel pan. Seeing her like that, I couldn't see anything — nothing in front of me, no sky, no earth. I could not move my feet. I stood there, tongue tied and my feet were stuck to the ground. Tears flew down my cheeks endlessly.

I don't know how long I stood there, watching my mother. Finally, I walked up to her and whispered, "Mama." She didn't respond. She looked like a woman in a trance. "Mama," this time a little louder. Still no response. Suddenly, I almost yelled, "Mama!" "What? Who?" shaken, my mother just looked up at me, like a dispirited body. Without saying a word, she touched me, her grasp becoming strong. An eternity passed. "Oh, my God! You are alive. I thought you were dead," with those words, tears just poured out of her eyes down her cheeks.

"What are you doing, Mom?" I said. "I am selling parsley." "What for? why are your selling that?" "To survive. I realized that I didn't have the strength to end this miserable life. To feed the young ones." "Can you make money selling these?" "Barely enough to buy some barley." Suddenly struck by uncontrollable fury, I was like a tree caught in a hurricane. I was overcome with the rage to kill all Japanese. What did they do to us? To my parents? Why did they ruin us like this? "Why do you want to stay alive that much?" Yelling at my mother, I kicked the pan over and stomped on the parsley. My mother clung to me, shouting. "What are you doing? We have nothing to feed the young ones at home. We will all die, if I don't sell these. Nothing to eat for supper tonight." "Then, let's die. What's the use of living? The life, this miserable life — there is nothing to save it for."

I dragged my mother with me. She kept looking back at the ruined parsley. "What are we going to do tonight? What are we going to eat for supper? Where have you been? She poured out endless questions. "Death will end everything. That will be better than living like this. What does it matter if we eat one more time?" I shouted. "Where have you been?" "I went away to have good time."

Back in our little rented room, I saw my brother and sister. "What kind of world are they going to grow up in? We are now independent but just like our

176

family, nothing is left in our country. The Japanese took everything away from us." I kept thinking. "I will be right back," I said to my mother and left.

When I was doing that dreadful thing, sometimes navy officers came. One of them, a Korean born in Japan, always chose me. When he could not come in, he would stand by my window and look up. Every time he was paid, he gave me some money. I never spent any; I saved it. So I had some money with me. I bought lye, three lumps, enough to kill all of us. They didn't cost much. I still had money left. On the way home, I thought, "Even if I am going to kill them, I want to feed them a bowl of rice . . .

Her voice broke down and the small room containing the three of us felt heavy with silent sorrow and fury. Then, she continued mixing her words with sobs.

I bought some rice and mackerel. My mother and I cooked rice and mackerel with bean soup base. I wanted them to have one decent meal before we died. At the sight of real rice, the young ones' eyeballs rolled. The kids ate and ate until I feared that their stomachs might explode. My mother kept asking me where I got the money. "Didn't I tell you that I went away to earn money? Mom, please, don't worry about anything. Don't you see I am back; I am here. Just try to eat some rice." "How could I eat? Food would not go down my throat." She put some rice in water and put a couple spoonfuls in her mouth. Despite my mother's urging, I, too, found it impossible to swallow any food.

Around eleven o'clock at night, the little ones went to sleep with full stomachs. I crushed the lye, and wrapped it in a candy paper made of sweet rice. There were ten of those, looking like candies. I sat and watched the two little ones sleep. Their faces looked so content and innocent. "I am soiled through and through. Mother is already old and has nothing to look forward to but hardship. So the two of us do not have enough a reason to stay alive but what about those kids? What did they do to deserve death?" Those sleeping faces of my brother and sister, with their mouths open, happy with full stomachs . . . My throat closed in on me, overcome with feelings beyond anything I had known, not sorrow, not pain . . .

She covered her face, her shoulder shaking with sobs.

I put the ten "candies" in front of my mother and said, "Mama, go to sleep. We will throw these out. From now on, don't you worry about anything. I am back. I will take care of the family. There is plenty of cooked rice left over from tonight. Eat that tomorrow with the kids. I will not let you starve to death, I swear." Lying on a corner of a dirty quilt in the deepening night, I racked my brain. No thought came but I knew that morning would come. I was eighteen years old.

The next morning, I wandered out to the street and walked without destination. I passed a tiny restaurant, with a sign, "Help wanted." I opened the door and was greeted by a kind looking woman. "What can I do for you? Why are you here?" she said. "I saw the sign. I thought I could work for you." She inspected me from top to bottom. I looked small. "How old are you?" "I am eighteen. What would be the job?" I asked. "Serving food to customers. Where do you live?" "Not far from here. I have a younger brother and a sister and a mother to feed. I have to work." I heard her saying to herself, "She is not tall but looks pretty and smart." Then, she told me I could try out with her.

I asked her how much I would be paid. She said, one hundred *won* a month. It was a lot of money at that time. I could not believe it. "I have a favor to ask of you. Could you advance me fifty *won* now? You can take that from my first pay. I have to feed my mother and younger ones right now. We have nothing. If you can't trust me, please come with me to where we live. You can see for yourself. I have no place to run away." She was quiet for a moment. Then, she handed me fifty *won* from her apron pocket. With that money in my fist, I felt tremendous energy surging and could see the sky, future and everything around me. I must have bowed to her more than a dozen times. "Are you sure that you don't want to come with me?" She shook her head with a smile.

On my way home, I bought rice, some wood for cooking and ran. My mother was in the yard. Surprised, her butt fell flat on the ground, her face turning gray. "Where on earth did you get money to buy those?" "Oh, no . . ." She covered her mouth with her hands. "Mom, I didn't steal. I swear. I got a job at a restaurant." "What kind of a job? Do they serve liquor?" "What do you care if they sell rice or liquor? What's the difference? Are you really in a position to worry about those, considering all the things we have gone through . . ." My mother just looked at me. Then, I told her the truth, the dreadful truth. My mother fainted. I put cold water over her. After about an hour, she became conscious.

I gently took my mother's hands in mine and told her, "I got a job, a good one, at a nice place. I will be serving sober people, not drunkards. I got an advance, half of my monthly pay." I put thirty *won* in her palm. "Now you don't have to worry about starving. You can send Hee Chun (my brother) to school. I will be eating at my job and come home at night just to sleep. If you don't believe me, you can come with me and check it out yourself." My mother was already up on her feet and was ahead of me. We walked to the restaurant. My mother, she was quite a woman. She was an upright person. You know, she comes from a good family. When she married my father, she brought her own maid. She wanted to know for sure . . .

After confirming my story from the owner, my mother sat and pumped out tears. Her voice trembling, she thanked the owner, "How can I thank you enough. Please take good care of her. I will send her back tomorrow." At night, the two of us, a daughter and mother sat together and I told her some of the things. We hugged each other and either one or the other tried to stop the other's long, wrenching sobs. Finally, my mother held my hand and said, "I am glad you came back alive despite your awful fate." We watched dawn break without a blink of sleep. I washed my face.

Her words fell apart again as she described her swollen eye lids from crying all night.

My mother made some rice porridge and forced me to swallow a couple spoonful before I left home for work at 7:30. I worked, worked hard. I even felt joy in my heart, working. A lot of customers told me to keep the change. I would say, "You forgot to take your change and they would say, 'You keep it.'" They often commented, "What a alert, smart girl she is." I made a money bag with a piece of cotton I found at home and wore it with a string tied around inside of my skirt. I put all the change in it. From my regular pay, I didn't give everything to my mother. I gave her enough for food and things. The rest, I saved. I had a single objective. I wanted to save money and start my own business. Some money, I put in a large bag; the rest I buried underground in a secret place.

I observed and absorbed every thing my boss did. My eyes and hands missed nothing. I learned to cook, with every detail of what goes into cooking, ingredients, where to buy. etc. After twenty months, I had enough money saved to rent a small place of my own, to open a business. I was twenty years old.

One morning, on my day off, I asked my mother to go somewhere with me. She said, "Where?" "You will find out soon enough." My mother and I got on a street car and got off at Young Do. I showed her a small house in the business section. "What's that?" my bewildered mother asked. "I want to rent this place to open my own business." "Where did you get money?" Immediately, a dark cloud hovered on her face, obviously worried that I had done something bad or illegal. "Mom, I did not steal the money. I did not do anything bad with men or with anybody else. Remember, I am your daughter. I saved." I explained to her in detail how I had saved. We went in together and she watched me sign a contract.

Then, I got up an hour earlier every morning and did all kinds of things to prepare for my own restaurant— bought plates, pots and pans—before I went to work. One day, about ten days before I planned to leave, I told my boss that I was leaving in order to open my own restaurant; she wasn't surprised, just sad. "Young Ja, how was it possible for your mother to bring a child like you to this world? She is a lucky woman to have a daughter like you. I am thankful for all you have done. If you have any questions about cooking or anything else, you know where to find me." She even spent a few days helping me open the place. What a woman!

Customers literally flocked in. It felt like everyone in the neighborhood came to my place to eat. My business thrived and money came in fast, and I was almost too busy to count it. It was a confusing time. After independence in 1945, all sorts of things brought social chaos. Lots of women lived as if they were floating around, one day wanting to learn western dance, the next day organizing *kei* (a system whereby people put money into an account with different individuals taking the total amount each month). I knew a woman who ran a cabaret and played lots of *kei*. She was cheated by many and her finances were in a state of collapse. She was desperate. One day she came to see me. "Please lend me money. You can have my cabaret as collateral."

In the end, she could not pay back the money and I got her cabaret. This was a huge jump from running a small restaurant. But at that time, I didn't think the sky was high enough. I was determined to make money and with that determination, my cabaret flourished, with dancing girls and all. Would you believe that I even had *Kiesang,* not just one but quite a few, to serve the customers. Money came in hand over fist. After a while, the paper money didn't feel like money.

Then, one day, a friend of mine told me that there was lots of money in smuggling, importing from and exporting to Japan illegally. That's how I got into the smuggling business. At first, I started on a small scale. I simply gave money to people who went to Japan and we shared the profits. It was just side work while I was running my cabaret.

Do you know that people's greed is endless? I became like that. Greed is like a chain. One greed produces another and it just goes on. When I decided to buy my own ship, I was twenty six. I smuggled cosmetics, nylon, whatever. It was the 1950's, and at that time nylon was a novelty . . . It was two way smuggling — import and export. I heard that, for some reason, the Japanese bought bullet casings like crazy. I went around military compounds and bought them by the truckful and sent them to Japan. Money flowed, in fact, overflowed. It was during the Rhee Syngman regime. The smuggling made money like crazy. Whichever way I turned, there was money. I bought a house for my mom. I hired a manager for my cabaret and planned to launch into smuggling full force.

I went to Japan only twice as far as Osaka. Other times I sent my captain. I did the smuggling with the same captain for five years. One time, in Pusan, security around the harbor became tighter and I smelled danger. I told the captain of my ship not to come into Pusan harbor. I gave him specific orders to go into Gu Jae Do. I had told this guy that my husband was a big businessman and was terribly busy. I had invented a husband in order to protect myself. Clearly, the captain did not believe me after a while, because no husband ever appeared. He thought it would be easy to go against a mere woman and take the money himself. After all, it was an illegal business to start with.

He pulled the ship into Young Do in Pusan.

I was tipped off by a crew member and was taken to the ship in a boat. Alas, custom officers spotted our ship. I ordered the crew to throw all our goods into the sea. The more we had in the ship, the heavier the punishment. Customs people fired warning shots. Had it not been for one of my crew who pushed me down to sit, I could have been hit by one of those bullets. I jumped into the sea with my stylish clothes on. My body was swept by rough waves. It was useless to try to swim. Piece by piece I discarded my clothes. Soon only my underwear clung to my body, and I was a helpless captive of the rough waves. All the energy seeped out of my body and I must have lost consciousness.

I opened my eyes, and found myself on a rock by a beach near a village for lepers. Three of my crew members rescued me. "What happened to the crew?" I asked them as soon my brain started to function a little. They told me that all of my eighteen member crew except for those three had been arrested. I went to see a police chief who was on my payroll, so to speak. I must have looked pitiful. "What happened?" he asked with his eyes rolling. "Didn't you see the fifteen men arrested?" "I didn't know they were your crew." I made a deal with him, an enormous bribe, half of which was to be handed over then and the other half due after the release of my crew. It didn't work out, though. There was a new man in his department. He was offended that I had gone over his head. He refused my money and reported my offer to a superior of my chief.

I barely escaped the police who raided my house that night. I hid myself in a relative's house but the police found me in no time. No matter where I ran, the police were able to trace me. In desperation, I thought of someone, actually a former judge. He married a woman of his family's choice. They had one child but even after that, he could not develop any feeling for his wife. So he left home, came to Pusan and fell in love with a prostitute whom he took to Seoul. This woman, though, engaged in lots of business ventures and soon debt collectors swarmed around his house. He felt betrayed by this woman whom he loved. He sold everything he had, paid all of her debts and came to Pusan. He was to leave Korea for Japan on my ship but missed it. He was on the brink of going insane. When he had no place to go, no one whom he could rely on, I welcomed him at my house and consoled him. "No reason to mope around. Actually, the fact that you missed the ship was a curse turned into blessing. Why would you want to leave Korea for Japan? Gather the bits and pieces of your life and look for a meaning for yourself. Make something out of your life. It's not too late." I helped him until he could get on his feet, went to Seoul and opened a restaurant. He sent me his address in Seoul with a note, "Please feel free to come here anytime, especially if and when you need help." My disaster happened late in 1959. After trying everything I could, I went to him. That was January 1960.

It was after I went to Seoul that Park Chung Hee took over the government, you know, the famous May 16th *coup d'etat*. Actually, the *coup d'etat* happened while I was in jail for violating the curfew. I heard gun shots in jail. I asked a prison guard to release me, which he did. When I got out, the street was so quiet. The government had changed and I felt free to go about. I rented a small room for myself and got involved in smuggling again, only on a smaller scale. Most of the money I had saved was blown away. I had to start all over again. I went to Inchon and bought the smuggled goods wholesale from ships and sold them in the black market for three, four times the price I paid. However, this kind of illegal dealing does not last long. I was caught again and was supposed to serve a ten month prison sentence. The night before the judge was to announce the final decision, my father appeared in my dream. He brought a horse driven cart and urged me to leave the place. The next day when I appeared in front of the judge, he let me go with a stern warning.

All this time, I've never thought it possible for me to get married. Are you kidding? Of course, I had men chasing me. And there were plenty of them who wanted to take advantage of me. After all, they must have thought, I was only a woman but they were men. You should have heard me curse. No one could match my mouth. I would say, "If you don't behave, I am going to take your eyeballs out and play marbles with them!" "You, fucking bastard, if your prick is too hard, pluck it out, bury it somewhere or put some sesame oil on it and put it in your mom's hole!"

> *I exploded, laughing. I've never heard such expressions . . .*
> *Prof. Yun covered her face with her hands. She groaned with*
> *embarrassment and asked me, "how come you can laugh*
> *about such obscene words?" "Look, Prof. Yun, an occasion-*
> *al curse would not hurt—it is therapeutic and it is a con-*
> *densed form of expression, a short-cut way of making a*
> *strong point. Sometimes, you just have to cut out words and*
> *get to the point in one single word or a short phrase." I kept*
> *laughing and Grandma Yun chuckled.*

Anyway, it was impossible for me to feel deeply for any of them. If anything, I just enjoyed momentary pleasures. I learned all kinds of dancing — our traditional dance and, of course, western social dances of all varieties. I could really dance but, you know, I had no time to enjoy. But Christmas and New Years — we went wild. We danced and drank. Sometimes, we roamed around Seoul, bar hopping. I also enjoyed a card game. You know "Go, Stop," don't you? I played that for money. Those were wild times. Fleeting pleasures and obsession with money, those were my companions for life. Just when you thought you were catching the pleasure, it's gone — fleeting. No matter what

I did, how much money I had, what filled my life in the end was emptiness. Contradiction — emptiness filling my life. Do you know that feeling? It is worse than sadness. It is worse than anything.

Time froze in silence.

You know what? Are the Japanese human beings? Are they people like the rest? I wonder sometimes. Look at me. They took my life away. They took away my virginity, made it impossible for me to get married, dried up my emotions . . . Of course, I wanted to get married. Do you know what it's like to hug loneliness inside of you while you are surrounded by people, laughter? People talk about compensation, pension, etc. For me, the money is a secondary matter. Actually, it is a non-issue. What am I going to do with it? Take it to my grave? It is a matter of principle, conscience. Japan has to admit their guilt, I mean, really confess. As for our government. . . they say, we will take care of you. I don't want our government's money. I want Japan to compensate us legally.

You asked me if I was aware of Korea being a Japanese colony. When I was about seven, I went to a market place with money my mother had given me. I could buy a basket of pop corn with it. Then, I saw uniformed soldiers who were not Koreans. I thought to myself — who are they? Why are they in our country? I wanted to know about everything. That's why I wanted to go to school. At school, I only learned Japanese history but I could gather bits and pieces from people. I learned that Japan took away our country and that we became servants to Japan.

So even when I was a little school girl, my feelings toward the Japanese were not good. In fact, I detested them. So I often rebelled against Japanese teachers. They beat me if I did not obey. Once a female teacher hit me hard for talking. I asked, "Why are you hitting me?" She hit me harder saying that I had lousy manners. I was so mad that I bit her hand. She bled and a small piece of flesh came off *(Her words were mixed with chuckles)*. She took me to a teacher's room that day and I was punished all day. Yeah, I figured out what Japan did to us from the time I was little. You can't imagine how gutsy I was. Even now, I often wonder how I could be that way.

Her laughter was hearty. She was happy recollecting her childhood.

It is a miracle that I am still alive. You have no idea how many times I was on the brink of death. Did I tell you about my operation? They told me that I had a great, big lump in my ovary. Of course, the trouble started at the comfort house when I had to put a cotton ball inside and receive those animals. The doctors told me that it had to be taken out. It was in 1976 in Seoul. I checked into the hospital by myself. At that time, I was pretty much out of touch with my siblings.

What about the younger ones I took care of? My younger sister, she married a soldier and lived in Kang Won province but died young giving birth. And the brother, he also died when he was about fifty. He had liver trouble. Those two, they would have gladly died for me, but more than anything else, they were more afraid of me.

Before I was rolled into operating room, I was told to put my signature seal on a piece of paper. As I put the red seal on that paper, I cried. I thought to myself, "This is it. If my life is to end like this, why was it necessary to go through so much — so much dirt, so much pain, so much suffering." I remembered seeing a needle in a doctor's hand. When I regained consciousness, it was 9:30 at night. I learned that they had operated on me from 10 in the morning until 5 p.m. In the recovery room, a nurse noticed my fingers moving around 9:30. Even the doctors had given up on me — they didn't think I would make it. My ovary and uterus, everything was taken out. After that, I had to be hospitalized four more times. Even now, my body is a one big mess. If I didn't have my own money, I would have been dead long ago. You know, life is a resilient thing.

> *Professor Yun slept in the bedroom and I in the sitting room with Grandma Yun. I was emotionally drained and wanted to sleep but her groans kept me awake. She turned her body every which way, uttering, "O, Father, take me to thee." Everything in her body seemed to hurt. In the darkness of the night, I prayed for peace for her soul and comfort for her body, however momentarily. At dawn, she slipped out of the room, on her way to pray to her Father.*
>
> *In the morning, she fed us the breakfast of my childhood — steaming rice, bean sprouts soup, home made kimchi, and fish. We talked about church, neighbors and food. I knew that I had to ask her to tell me more about her "experience," the surface of which she scratched and left. "You don't have to if you'd rather not. Yesterday, though, you did not tell me what happened after you were taken to a big barracks in Young Do," I observed with care.*

You are right. Oh, I don't mind talking about it. Whether I talk about it or not, it does not leave me alone anyway. Well, where was I? (*I quickly reminded her*) Oh, yes, we were at Young Do. All of us were ordered onto a ship. When the ship pulled in somewhere, we were taken to another huge barn. We found more girls there. There were fifty two of us. I learned from one of them there that we were in Japan, Nagoya. We were kept for two days in that barn.

Then, three Japanese officers with long swords came and ordered us out.

I did not get up. "Who are you to order me around? I don't have to obey you," I said. He rushed to me, lifting his leg to kick me. I crawled swiftly, my body flat on the ground, and pulled one foot toward me. He fell. Quickly on his feet, he grabbed me full force. I yelled in Japanese, "What have we done? You wicked Japanese, what right do you have to drag us Koreans to Japan and beat us?" He yanked me and I bit his face. The other girls all came forward, screaming, yelling and biting. The war was on. The three officers withdrew.

After a while with bandages on their faces, they returned and ordered us to line up. I just sat there, wild with rage and fury. "I will either walk out of here or die," I said to myself as I put my face between my knees. All the other girls lined up. They made three lines. One line was sent to Manchuria and the second to the Philippines, I later learned. My line, which I was forced to join, got on a ship again. When our ship pulled into port, it looked familiar. We were back in Young Do.[111]

Once again, we were locked in a barn-like barracks. The next day, the girls were called out one by one. And those who left did not come back. Finally, there were only three of us in the barn. We were taken to a large, two story house and ordered to take a bath in a round tub with lukewarm water. Then, they gave us a white top and a black skirt. Our own clothes were taken away. I didn't know then, but later I learned that it was what they called, No. 1 Comfort Station, a former inn.

I was ordered to go upstairs and enter one of the rooms. Well, I thought, maybe, I was to serve food or something. When I entered, an officer was sitting alone. "Stupid bastard," I remember thinking, "if you want to eat, you should go to a restaurant or something. Don't just sit there by yourself in the middle of an empty room." He told me to come and sit. I said "no," and asked, "What do you need?" "I don't need anything," he said. "Then, why did you call me?" "I just want you to have a good time with me." "I never saw you in my life. How could I have a good time with you." "Well, as you can see, I am in the military. I have no one to talk with." "I am a Korean. I have nothing to say to you. If you want to talk with someone, why don't you bring Japanese people?" I said. But he demanded that I sit. As soon as I sat, he stood up and pulled me toward him. Frightened and furious, I grabbed him by his throat and would not let him go. He pushed me away and slapped me hard. I fell but got up quickly and pounded him with my fists. Soon, we were kicking and hitting anywhere we could reach. Suddenly, his foot came around my leg and made me fall down.

> She looked at me and commented, "You know, so many women cry rape these days. I don't believe half of them. You would be surprised how much you can resist. If you really don't want to, you will have the strength to resist, the strength you never dreamed you had."

When I fell flat, he got on top of me and tried to pull my underpants off. Underneath, I wriggled around and put my leg in place and then kicked his chest as hard as I could. He flew, hitting the wall on the other side. I'd almost gotten out of the room when his hand snagged me and pulled me flat again but I still wouldn't give in, this time using my teeth. I bit him anywhere, everywhere I could get my teeth. I was ready to die at that point. He yelled and a man came in, grabbed me by the throat and pulled me out of the room. Outside, he stood me up and struck me over and over gain. In pain and fury, I drew whatever strength I had left and kicked his thing between his legs. Now he rolled around in excruciating pain. "What right do you have to strike me like this? My mother brought me up without ever laying a hand on me." I was left alone for two days with my body full of wounds.

When my cuts and bruises had healed slightly, they put me back into the same room. Another officer was waiting for me. They must have warned him about me. He did not wait and did not give me a moment even to think of protesting. He swiftly knocked me down, and started pushing his thing inside of me. It happened all so fast. I found myself bleeding. I wasn't even sure where the blood was coming from. I only felt pain. Something in my body was torn apart. I put my teeth into his cheek. Now we were both bleeding, he from his face and I, somewhere below . . . I was fifteen.

My bottom, vagina and uterus, everything felt like they were torn in shreds. They hurt but the soldiers kept coming in one after another. After each, I washed down there using water with some kind of disinfectant. The sting was so bad that sometimes I crawled and other times I jumped around. I crawled so much that my knees became like worn out clothes, and they bled.

> She pulled her pants up and showed me the scars on her knees. "See these, they are from crawling and bleeding. You can't imagine the pain." My tape ran out. Here she was, still shaking, feeling the unshakable pain of her tragic past but all I could do was to rummage through my big shoulder bag looking for a new tape.

After a while, I stopped protesting. I had no energy, no desire, no nothing. Much of the time, I was like a machine with a human shell. No feelings. I just wanted to die. I was simply there and they were on top of me endlessly. Sometimes, I wondered if they would do it on top of a dead body.

One day, something happened that woke me up from the deep sleep of despair. Someone came in, another faceless someone but I did not feel anything on top. Instead, I heard awkward Korean. "I am a Korean. My father is a Korean living in Japan. He taught me Korean," the voice said. I lifted my limp body and sat. "Tell me how you came here," he asked. He did not touch me. Only his eyes touched me with compassion. I told him how I ended up there and begged him to help me escape or better still, to take me with him. He said it was too tricky and dangerous for him to attempt such a thing but he would figure out how to help me. In the meantime, I should be patient and hold on . . . He gave me 10 *yen*. At that time, that was a huge sum.[112]

With my hopes renewed, I plotted escape. I told two of my friends about the plan, make the Japanese guards drunk and then run. One of the cooks was a Korean. I gave her Japanese money and told her to buy five bottles of wine. One evening around six, when it was reasonably quiet, the three of us went downstairs and found two guards. I started talking to them and we sang some Japanese songs. "Come, let's have a good time." Soon they were drinking wine and we with them but we only pretended . . . we threw most of our wine under the table in a bowl. When their eyes became heavy with sleep, we stood up and ran out of the house.

Outside, we could hardly walk, as if our feet did not belong to us. If we had used our brains, we should have walked through dark back streets but with our minds racing to go away, and not thinking fast, we waited for a streetcar. Five of them found us and we were dragged back to the house like luggage. They made us lie flat on the ground and struck us with their gun stocks. Blood streamed out of my friends' mouths. When the sixth strike was coming down on me, I grabbed the gun with all my strength. Then, I must have passed out. When I woke up, I was dripping wet. They must have poured water over me. They brought a bowl of hot water for me to drink. I kicked the bowl and said, "You drink it and live long." They put me in my room. That night, they didn't send anybody in.

Come the next day, it was the same. Nothing stopped them from coming. They started to come around ten in the morning. Between three and four o'clock in the afternoon was the most crowded time. Usually, officers came at night. Many of them spent the night. They would leave around five in the morning. So little time to be alone. I was lucky if I could spend one night a week alone.

My vagina felt like it was rotting, and my waist, back, everything hurt. I felt a big clot on my lower back developed from wounds, from the gun stock. I touched it and pain went through my body like electricity, oozing from flesh starting to rot. Every time when they got on top of me and banged like animals, my back was crushed and the pain was so sharp . . . "Please stop. I am in pain." "Don't you worry, I will do all the work." My body was a small battle field—on top, soldiers attacked, and my back and everything else that touched the mattress screamed with intense pain, gradually turning into rotting, blue flesh. Some times, their thing felt like a knife piercing through and other times, I felt nothing — I was just there between life and death, hugging my pain. Soon, my whole body burned with fever. Rotting flesh on my back and fever. Still, they came.

When one of them was rushing to grab me, I clutched his thigh with both of my hands and begged, "Please look at me. No, not at my face but down there and my back." I broke into wrenching sobs. He put his pants back on, knelt beside me and said, "Please forgive me." "There is no need for that but you've got to help. Get some medical help for me." The next day, I was taken to a hospital. The doctor found the clots on my lower back badly infected and he had to cut them out. Even then, they did not treat me daily. They did not wait until the cuts were healed. You can still see the scars. I still have difficulty moving the bottom half of my body.

> She turned around, lowered her pants and showed me the scar. I saw the spot where they cut out the large chunk of flesh.

Whenever I had a chance, I listened to the radio. One day, I caught the Emperor's voice surrendering. I gathered all my nerves to my ears. I thought I was going to faint but before I knew it, I was on my feet, kicking open the door of my room. I ran downstairs like a mad woman. I found two guards with rifles. They must not have heard the news. I took one of the rifles and hit them on the head over and over again like a mad woman. Then, I ran into the street and threw stones at every Japanese passing by.

The Japanese can be so inhuman, so cruel. It is difficult to understand how they can be so inhuman. Let me tell you something. Nearly all the houses in the neighborhood of the comfort house were occupied by Japanese. One of the families had an insane daughter. One evening when they were gathering their things to go back to Japan after the defeat, her parents fed the girl, put a quilt in one of their straw suitcases, and told the girl to lie down there. They closed the suitcase, tied a large stone to it, and threw it into the sea. Then, the rest of the family went back to Japan.

One of my friends became pregnant in the Comfort Station. On top of that, she had venereal disease. She was treated but nothing seemed to work. The disease got worse by the day. Her bottom was a mess and her stomach looked like a balloon. She was in the eighth month of pregnancy. The soldiers stayed away from her. One day, on my way to the toilet, I saw two soldiers taking her away. I thought she was being taken to have a baby. I followed them quietly. They took her to the barn where we had been locked up. I stood by the window and looked in.

There was a wooden bed there. They tied her to that bed, both her arms and legs. Then, those soldiers put on gloves. One of them took out his sword and cut her stomach. I saw her intestines dropping out of her open stomach. I fainted. I was found and beaten until what felt like the end of the world.

If I tell these stories, people say, "how awful," "how cruel," but do you have any idea what it does to you, to witness such an unimaginable thing? "To tolerate such an intolerable?" If I had an atomic bomb, I would drop it on the Japanese. If the Japanese repent their sins and ask for forgiveness, that's one thing. But they behave as if we were still their playthings. One day, they say they had nothing to do with it and the next day, when there is no way out, they say, well, we are sorry. When my body aches, pain travelling from the top of my head to the bottom of my feet, I kneel in front of my Father and pray. Pray that I could forgive them. Other times, I am obsessed by the thought of Japan vanishing from the face of this earth. Do you know what I pray for? I ask my Father to send two earthquakes to Japan. I pray, "Dear Father, after you wipe away the land of Japan, please start over, start a new history worthy of human children, your children."

You know, most of those men in the Japanese Diet are of the war generation. Inside, they can still see what they did. For them to deny the past, for me it's unthinkable. It is easier for me to live with denial from the younger generation. They were not there; they don't know any better. My body burns with killer rage, with a desire for revenge so intense that no word can describe . . . Their crimes should not go unpunished. I wish half of the former comfort women were like me, obsessed with the thought of revenge. If we all wished Japan's downfall, it will happen. Japan's behavior, half of it reflects how they still think of our country. They look down on our country. I don't care for compensation, for money.

> *Quietly, I asked if she ever thought about doing something,*
> *maybe telling the Korean government. Her response was so*
> *fast, half of my words stayed inside of my mouth.*

Of course, I did. My mother died when I was twenty seven. She died because of me. I was her cross day and night. Dying, she said, "You were born in the wrong time. I wasn't a good mother to you. I could not see you get married. Now I am leaving you with a heavy burden for the family. I can't close my eyes." I closed her eyes.

After my mother's death, my older sister was the only one with whom I could try to discuss what was on my mind. "Do you think I should write a letter to President Rhee Syngman about what happened to us, you know, the women like me?" I brought it up with her. Her kids, my nephews and nieces, were all college educated. They said those kind of letters would never get through to the President. Someone working way down in the system will read it and throw it away. "No advantage in advertising your past," they said. At that time, the media did not work as it does today.

My sister just dropped the issue and went on with her living. Do you understand the loneliness, the "aloneness" you feel after you have done so much for your family? My older sisters did not even try to understand me. They didn't mind taking my money to send their kids to school but the bottom line was — they were ashamed of me.

189

She took a newspaper picture of Grandma Kim Hak Soon
and asked me if I knew her.

I saw her on television but still I was hesitant about reporting about myself. You know, when I first moved back here, my health was deteriorating by day. And no money to get medical help. I was reluctant but I had no choice—I decided to register for the government program for the poor. But this official asked me all kinds of questions. One day he said, "I thought you had a son. Could he not help you?" He meant my nephew, my older brother's son. "You got it all wrong," I said, "He is my nephew. I have no son. How can a woman who never married have a son? Do you think I am a virgin Mary or something?" "How come you did not marry?" "You want to know why I didn't marry? I'll tell you. I could not marry because I had the misfortune of being born in this country." "What do you mean?" "How can you be a government official when you don't know a thing about anything? You should know something about your own country, some basics." "What the hell are you talking about? Why don't you cut the nonsense?" I was provoked to a fury. "Do you know anything about *Wianbu*?" "What's that? I don't have the slightest idea." "You, mother fucking son of a bitch," curses streamed out of my mouth. "I don't want to talk with you any more. Let me talk with your supervisor. No need to waste my hard earned energy on you." I stood up. He grabbed the end of my skirt and begged. "Grandma, please tell me. I want to learn." "Did you hear about virgins being taken during the Japanese colonial period?" "I heard something about that." "That's what I am talking about." "You mean . . . "He was silent for a while. He apologized profusely and did all the paper work for me to be enrolled in the government program for the poor.

It was after that, that all kinds of people, not just Kim Hak Soon but also lawyers and activists, urged us on television to report: "Please report if you were a former military comfort woman. If you know anyone, also report, your neighbor, relative, mother, sister . . . " The wife of this government official dialed the phone and reported about me as she watched the television. I was furious. All kinds of media came. I could not lift up my face and walk straight.

Do I feel shame? You bet. Not a single day passes by without feeling the shame of my past. People like you tell us that we should not feel shame; that it wasn't our fault. That is easier said than done. Whether it was my fault or not, I went through a shameful experience and no amount of theorizing can erase that. But it is quite another thing for other people. They have no right to shame us, to make us feel shame. It is hard enough to deal with the shame that comes from within. Because I reported, now quite a few know about my past. I hear whispers, even at church. Those whispers make my chest roar like great big waves.

You want to know my feelings about men. Well, I don't have any. The

190

Japanese took my feelings away, made me barren, not just my body but also my mind. When I was young and rich, lots of men were after me. To me, they were not male; they were just people. Exasperated, many of them told me, "Your skirt is deceptive. You are not a woman. You should not wear it."

How did I feel about the navy officer who was born in Japan of a Korean father? Around the time our country was about to become independent, his ship came to Pusan from Japan. When he heard the Emperor surrendering, he simply left the ship. He did not go back to Japan. He stayed at a friend's house. One day, I bumped into his friend and learned that Kuramoto (that was his name) was staying with him. I went to see him. His face was very thin. He did not bring himself to ask me to marry him then, but he did ask if we could live together. I couldn't.

Why? How could I? There was no room in my heart to do anything but earn money. I had to take care of my family. I said to him, "Please understand. I can't think of anything else but earning money. All those empty stomachs at home — there is no one else to fill them but me. Besides, it is not good for you to live with me. I know you want to marry me but I know I can't. Of all the people, you should know that the Japanese made it impossible for me to marry. I can't be happy and I can't make you happy. I know I sound cruel but the sooner you forget me, the better. Please, please find a nice woman. Do it for me. You deserve better."

Of course, I had feelings for him, but I don't know if it was love. With the brutal loss of my virginity and my torn uterus, I think what people call "love" vanished from my life. When I was leading that dreadful existence, he would come and sit with me. We didn't even talk that much. He played a harmonica. He played it so beautifully and I would sing along. He never had intercourse with me but he did say every time — "Let's get married when this war is over." "Perish the thought," I used to say, "How can I marry you or anybody else? Look at me. Look at this body, so defiled. If we were married, do you think all this would be erased? You will remember, yes, you will remember. It simply won't work." He would hold my hand and say, "Don't say no now." He always gave me whatever money he had. He had such a tender heart and he was handsome too.

What happened to him? He died of tuberculosis. About three years after I visited Kuramoto, his friend came to see me. "You must come with me. His days are numbered." He told me that what started as a "heart" ache for me turned into a serious sickness, tuberculosis. I could not go. How could I watch him die with my own eyes? "Please give me one of your undershirts. That's what he wanted me to bring, if I could not bring you." I did not go to his funeral, either. It was impossible. Remorse and guilt choked my throat. I tried to think that it was his fate, an unfortunate fate just like mine. He was so good and he had to die for a worthless thing like me. I know what he felt was "love." "Real love."

I don't know what love is. But when my rotting body was thrown around and abused and physical pain is knife piercing sharp, it was not possible to hold feelings that you might call love. Of course, I had deep feelings for him. I think he understood that. I told you we never engaged in the sexual act, not even once. Whatever love is, I know he did love me.

Pause.

I often thought I should have given him what he wanted. I should have married him. But what's the use of regret, anyhow? Many of the things we did or didn't do in the past, we did because that was the only way we could see then. Later when I did shaman rituals to drive away the devil, I always did one for his soul too. I wanted his soul to rest in peace.

"Shaman rituals?" my voice went a pitch high. "You didn't tell me anything about that," Prof. Yun chimed in.

That's not the only thing I didn't tell you. If you really mean to write about anything about my experience, you should come live with me at least a month. I not only did shaman rituals, I was a shaman for a while. Surprised? There is no end in my story. There is no way that you can take back my life in that little recorder. I have stories to tell until I die and even beyond my grave. My life is an endless story pressing my chest down like a heavy stone.

She brought us chilled barley tea. As tea went down my throat, I breathed deeply, desperate to exorcise my guilt. It wasn't my fault that I escaped this woman's fate but . . . As a good Christian kid, I held the sacred teaching about original sin at a simmering point just to feel the guilt, careful not to reach a boiling point to commit an actual sin. I dare not commit actual sins but I should be Christian enough to share the guilt. Later when I pondered more about it, my head cried "ridiculous." "Why should people feel guilty for a sin they did not commit? Why should the sin of Adam and Eve make me feel guilty?" However, her fate should be my burden, our burden, as well. She carried the burden of humanity and I should not be free of that. After all I am a fellow human being, fellow woman, a Korean woman at that.

She was right. Her story was endless. A shaman turned into a Christian, praying for salvation, release, peace. What would finally release her from the torture she carries to church at 4 o'clock every morning?

My mother started going to temple when my younger brother was sick.

Once I accompanied her to the mountain where she went to pray to a god of the mountain for my sister, for her to get pregnant. It was autumn. I sat by a beautiful stream and lifted pebbles, looking for small fish. A sudden chill invaded me, turning my whole body so cold, and my spirit seemed to leave my body. After that day, I started losing weight, hardly any flesh in my body but bones and my face turned yellow.

I had business in Young Do. I was twenty three. One morning when I woke up, I found myself devoid of any desire — I did not want to go outside, no appetite, no nothing. I locked my door, closed my eyes and sat. A month must have passed like that. Naturally, my mother was going bonkers. Finally, she dragged me out, took me to a large temple, paid lots of money, and had them perform shaman rituals (*gut*).

When I returned home, I felt that my spirit had returned and I was able to swallow some food. The next morning, our maid told me that someone was waiting for me at the front door. I stood in the dining hall and felt my spirit leaving. I stood there, feeling my body shake. I saw a woman with a dying baby in her arms. She begged me, "Please cure my baby." "What can I do?" As I said this to the woman, I heard a voice. "You are not the one who will do the trick. I will. Just do as I tell you." It was something that took over my body, ordering me. "Just take the baby and put him in front of the temple."

As I went to the temple, driven by a force inside of me, I started speaking in tongues. I could not stop talking. The baby's breath came back and he was cured. I have no idea how people found out but they came, asking for help. I was twenty three, engaged in a thriving business. I did not want to do that sort of thing. But this force, this spirit, did not leave me alone. I told people's futures, cured their diseases. When I did those, I felt no pain but as soon as I became myself, the pain returned.

I was haunted by this force, this spirit until I was sixty three. It was a constant struggle. Then, someone told me that I could get rid of the devil if I believed in the Christian God. That's how I went to church. I didn't know anything — I didn't know to whom to pray. I just knelt and said with my eyes closed, "Please get rid of this thing for me." That was March, 1990. One morning, as I lost myself in prayer inside the church, I felt such a bright ray of sun hitting my chest. My body was drenched with light and I heard a voice, "You are made well." Since then, it has been my Father who has instructed me from time to time to help people, people in need. Sometimes, I can make insane people well with the power of my prayer.

What about myself? I am not well totally, but I am better than before now that I go to church. I have my Father to cling to. He doesn't free me totally but at least He is someone I can cling to. Also, He is someone to whom I can pray for the welfare of our country, to help make our country strong so that it will never be stepped on by any other power like Japan, so that no misfortune like mine would fall upon my fellow country people, other human beings. I am not always sure He listens to me all the time but at least He is someone I can talk to.

I feel I could have been somebody instead of nobody. I don't want to, but I can't help blaming my father who did not grant my wish to study. My childhood dream to study to my heart's content . . . It was crushed. Then, whenever I think about how I lost my virginity . . . how I was defiled . . .That was going against my destiny.

> *"But what about your God, the Father? Isn't he omnipotent and omniscient? Don't you think it is He who is finally responsible? And if He is a loving God, why did He throw you into such a miserable lot?"*

Part of me says that He was testing me. He threw me into the most unbearable situation to test my strength and to see if I could come to him in spite of everything. You are right, maybe I shouldn't blame my father but when the pain is so terrible that I could not bear it any more, I blame him. I don't mean it either. What I really feel for both of them, my mother and father, is compassion. When my pain becomes unbearable, I find myself blaming my father. I know he meant well. Sometimes, I groan calling out, "Lord," "Lord," which changes into "Mom," "Mom" without my knowing.

Sometimes I blame God for my life, for my birth. It would have been better if I had not been born at all. However, I do believe that he had a purpose for me, for bringing me into this world. Whatever it was that He had in mind, it was all shattered. If only I had been left in one piece, with only God's purpose on my shoulders, I believe I could have been somebody who could have had our country in my palm and ruled.   Before I believed in my Father, I used to have nightmares — Japanese soldiers would come to me with their long swords drawn. Then I would struggle to take those knives and kill them . . . Now I am at least free from those dreams but after my "dawn prayer," back in this room, often what I feel is not peace. I feel so alone. I feel as if I either fell from the sky or sprouted from the depths of the earth.

Postcript

We drove to Ulsan to film Grandma Yun Doo Ri in 1997. It was a Saturday morning when we arrived at the government subsidized apartment complex where Grandma Yun Doo Ri lived. Reluctant as she was, she had given me a permission to come, but when we arrived, she was in a foul mood. "Why did you have to come on Saturday? I told you that I am usually frantic on Saturdays with all the things I have to do for the Church. It would have been so much better if you had come on Wednesday like I told you." "Grandma, I am sorry for imposing on you but I thought you understood my difficulties as well. Largely because of financial restraints, I cannot spend too many days in Korea. Because Ulsan is so far away from Seoul, it gives me added difficulties. Please forgive me for the inconvenience. I beg of you. I will need only a couple of hours of your time." I was practically on my knees, pleading. I knew that she had the right to be disgruntled—it is true that I had pushed pretty hard for Saturday in order to schedule this interview with other activities in the area. Angry as she was, she told the crew to bring the stuff up and unpack.

Michael Lim, an assistant camera/production co-ordinator, moved around silently setting things up. Grandma Yun, one look at Michael, turned her head toward me and said, pointing to Michael, "Who's he? He looks Japanese. If he is, I don't want him here. Tell him to get out and stay out." "Grandma, he is not Japanese. His parents are both Korean. He was born in America. He is a Korean-American." "You are pulling my leg. I am sure he is Japanese. He looks like one."

Then, Jon, my sound man, walked in. "There, he is a Korean. I can tell." Jon, not knowing what was going on, stood looking more bewildered than usual. "What's wrong with him? Why is he standing like that? Can't he say 'hello' or something instead of standing like a borrowed barley sack?" I could no longer hold down laughter, not even my guilt and fear of Grandma Yun. Bursting into laughter, I said, "Grandma, he does not speak a word of Korean. He was born in Hawaii and never learned Korean." "How stupid can he get? If he came out of the belly of a Korean woman, he should speak Korean!" Then, glaring at Jon, "Look here, what's wrong with you? How come you can't speak Korean. You certainly look like one. You should live up to your looks." I translated this into English to Jon. He immediately assumed a Buddha-like expression on his face, standing on two feet parted wider than usual. Grandma Yun was not done with him. "Are you married?" she asked him, refusing to believe that he could not understand her. "He is a bachelor," I answered. "What's wrong with him? He has a nice enough face. Is he a cripple or something? Why is he *not married?" By that time, Jon had already turned around, put on ear phones and was testing sounds in the room. I saw a Buddha-like smile on his face but no words came from his mouth.*

By this time, Willie had taken over the camera work, since Charles had to leave Korea for a film he had postponed for me. Willie, with his large eyes dancing, went to Grandma Yun, greeted her with a smile, and gently sat her close to the kitchen. Not a word was exchanged between Grandma Yun and Willie, but the tight muscles around her lips had disappeared and she even looked tamed. Willie the charmer. When we were on the street, people stopped and stared at Willie but for the grandmas, Willie's ebony skin warmed their hearts.

With Willie's camera rolling, she recollected her painful past. Once started, I didn't have to ask questions. She told her experience pretty much the way I remembered from my previous interview. When she relayed her story about how she found her mother at a market place upon returning home, she cried again just like the first time. I didn't bother wiping my tears either.

Once film ran out in the middle of her story about the ferocious protest against a Japanese officer. Grandma Yun said to me, "If you think I have a temper now, you should have seen me when I was young. I feared nothing." I understood it to be her way of saying, "I was kind of rough to you, huh?" That was good enough for me. Needless to say, she ended up giving us a lot longer than two hours and as we drove off from her apartment complex, I felt a tight knot in my stomach finally relaxing.

EPILOGUE

Seven years have passed since I met Grandma Hwang in Washington.

During that time, we have seen the long silence being broken bit by bit, finally catching attention at the United Nations. Japanese sexual slavery was defined officially as "crimes against humanity, slavery, and war crimes."

Even in the United States which did little to render justice regarding Asian atrocities committed by Japan, these grandmas received some attention. The California State Assembly approved on August 23, 1999 a resolution by Assemblyman Mike Honda (D-San Jose), "aimed at healing the lingering wounds of World War II by urging Japan to apologize for its wartime atrocities and offer individual compensation to American veterans, former sex slaves and other victims."[113] The United States Congressman William O. Lipinski had also introduced legislation, House Concurrent Resolution 126, in August 1997 "urging the Japanese government to extend a formal apology for its aggression in World War II and pay reparations to American Prisoners and other victims of Japanese war crimes." Tucked under "other" victims were comfort women. The HCR 126 died in Spring, 1999 but still it is a long way from the Tokyo Tribunal.

Prior to the current economic crisis, the South Korean government, boasting economic progress, began its six billion dollar program to demolish the former Japanese headquarters that the Japanese military had constructed inside a Korean palace. It represented a symbolic cleansing of the Japanese occupation. At the same time, the government's help for the former comfort women who registered with the government was barely enough to cover their daily subsistence. In 1998 South Korea paid about $22,000 each to the registered women, after the visiting South Korean President, Kim Dae Jung received in Japan the "remorseful repentance and heartfelt apology" in a written statement,[114] from Prime Minister Obuchi Keizo.

Even in China, some progress is evident. According to the *New York Times* (June 7, 1996), China expressed strong indignation "over assertions by Japanese lawmakers that Japan did not force women in its military run brothels to become prostitutes during World War II." Further, President Jiang Zemin of China visited Japan on November 29, 1998, the first ever by a Chinese head of state, and asked for a proper written apology for Japan's wartime crimes, not the usual oral statements of "remorse." Japan refused but still the China's demand for apology is a sign of progress.

We have come a long way but we have far to go. Japan has not changed an iota in its position about the legal liability about the comfort women and the Korean government is unwilling to push for official action, i.e., individual compensation from the Japanese government on legal grounds. President Kim Dae Jung, pleased with the apology and eager to move forward on a future oriented relationship with Japan, decided that the $22,000 compensation by the Korean government was enough. If it is a long way from the 1965 Treaty between Japan and the Republic of Korea, it is far short of respecting fundamental human rights issues.

We do not have to go back far to find fundamental human rights of women being violated in gruesome rapes, often in the name of justice. We remember Rwanda—how during the 1994 genocide Tutsi women were subjected to sexual violence on a massive scale by members of the Hutu militia, by soldiers of the Rwandan Armed Forces and by other civilians. Thousands of women were individually raped and gang raped, many after witnessing the torture and killings of their loved ones. Actually, rape is an essential part in almost every modern conflict. Raping soldiers are rampant from Somalia to the Balkans, from Rwanda to Columbia.

In light of the continuing saga of rape, this unending crime, it is even more important that we not bury history; that we not bury the issues of human rights under the economic/political or any other expediency. We must review afresh how Japan and the Allied Powers wrote off past rivalries and overlooked fundamental issues of human rights, especially those of Asian women, their hands joined for political considerations and expediency.

These grandmas were assigned to oblivion by Japan, by world powers, by their own country and, on occasion, by their own families. In short, they were enslaved, violated, abandoned and forgotten by their fellow human beings. We dare not let the long silence finally broken be settled by economic and political manipulation; nothing less than the basic human rights and dignity of these grandmas should be recovered and honored. Time is running out, however. These grandmas are going to the land of no return one by one. Of the over 200,000 girls and women forced for sexual slavery, only about 25 percent are said to have survived. We have no idea how many died after the war's end en route to their homelands. In South Korea, since Grandma Kim Hak Soon gave public testimony in August 1991, 190 former comfort women have come forward. Of them, forty have passed away.

During a production trip in Korea in April 1997, I spent my last day at the bedside of Grandma Chung Soo Jae, who was hospitalized in Choong Ang Hospital. She was one of three grandmas brought back by the commitment, money, sweat and time of one Korean man, Kim Won Dong, an elder of a Holiness Church in Seoul. She had lived in China for 53 years, counting the days until she could step on the soil of her motherland, like the grandmas in Wuhan and countless others. According to her doctor, her remaining days were numbered. Yet, she enunciated clearly in Chinese to me, "Please tell the doctor to make me well." She wanted to live a bit longer to join the movement to right the long-delayed wrong committed against her and countless others. She passed away on November 21, 1997.

198

When I brought the crew with me to talk with Grandma Kim Hak Soon in April 1997, she coughed constantly and was short of breath. I offered to come back but she said, "Stay. I am rarely free of this kind of ailment. This pain is *han* (long sorrow and suffering turned inward). From the time when I was little, what the Japanese did to me, to my family—that's what made knots in my chest. The knots are my *han*—how can it be untied? You can't untie it. Then, all the time I have been fighting in the open since 1991, this knot of *han* has become even tighter. It is completely blocked now so I can hardly breathe." She told me again on camera between coughs that blocked her breath what she had said earlier when I visited her for my book. "The apology should be proper. No more apologies in words. I don't want that kind of apology. They are the kind of people who like official treaties with documents and appropriate signatures. They are like that. Even if it takes rifles and swords, that's what they do. So how come they do it differently when dealing with Koreans, with us? The Japanese Emperor must write to our President, admitting their guilt properly." Her breathing stopped on December 16, 1997, choked by the knotted *han*. What she told me on camera became her last wish, stronger than any legal will.

Prime Minister Obuchi Keizo's written apology to President Kim Dae Jung for its occupation of Korea and President Kim's $22,000 is far short of Grandma Kim's wish as long as Japan denies that what they did to these grandmas were "crimes against humanity." Admitting its legal guilt is the least Japan should and can do, and Korea, together with the world community, must press Japan for this. What was inflicted on these grandmas was far beyond moral, intellectual and legal wrongs. It was a violation of human spirits, both individual and collective. What happened to these grandmas is not just unspeakable atrocities but loss of lives by the waterfalls, in mountains where the spirits roam, by azalea blossoms where maiden love sprouts and in the hometown where life on earth was claimed with a cry. It was a willful interruption in the natural flow of life that comes with birth and returns to earth in death with all the joys and sadness in between. It is the common grief of humanity. It is our grief.

We should honor Grandma Kim Hak Soon's wish.

YUN DONG JU (1917 - 1945)

More than a half century ago, the poet Yun Dong Ju died in a Japanese prison but his poems are as alive as the stars in the sky.

He was born on December 30, 1917, the oldest of the four children, in the town of Myongdong, Kando (Jiandao in Chinese and an area of the Tuman River basin along the border between Korea and Manchuria). After attending both primary and middle school there, he went to Yonhui College (now Yonsei University) in Seoul and was graduated in 1941. The following year he went to Japan first enrolling in Rikkyo University, then transferred to Doshisha University in Kyoto, where he studied English Literature. In July 1943, just before he planned to return to Korea, the Japanese police arrested him for participating in activities for Korean independence. He fell seriously ill in Fukuoka prison and wrote his father. Alas, the telegram from the prison announcing his death preceded the letter. Thus ended his brief sojourn on earth (February 28, 1945) in a country that had colonized his motherland. He was buried in Kando, the land where so many Koreans had migrated, some driven by poverty and others to fight for the independence of their country.

He began to publish children's poems in 1937 and many of his poems were written during his undergraduate years at Yonhui. Only after Korean independence was a collection of his poems entitled, *Sky, Wind, Stars and Poetry,* published posthumously by his younger brother, Yun Il Chu and his friend, Chong Pyong Uk (1948).

His poems sing for two worlds, human and natural, interweaving suffering, loneliness, love and shame with the sky, wind, stars, flowers, and brooks. From the seeming contrast between the natural and the spiritual emerges a vivid picture of the spiritual world. He was a poet who felt born of and stood in the depth of the dark night, floating in infinity with nothing to hold his feet and head. His personal anguish was at once the anguish of his people whose country was lost. This loneliness and sadness were also his shame. He found a unique world of his own in the star studded night. For in the night sky, even with the sorrow of death, he could also look for rebirth, his inner being stretching into the vast space.

He would have understood and mourned the suffering, loneliness, and shame of these women and would have sung for their courage, tenderness and longing for purity. He would have looked for their stars at night.

ACKNOWLEDGMENTS

Innumerable people helped me. Kang Soon Im, who in 1992 started printing testimonies of former comfort women in her garage helped my research with her own collection of materials together with her unsparing support that continues till this day. Her daughter Gi Hyun Ahn, then a law student at Georgetown University, did research in general but more particularly on legal aspects. Jayne Park, an attorney, conducted invaluable additional research on legal matters and on the topics ranging from Korean Shamanism to the Stockholm Syndrome. Michael Lim, a physics major at the University of Chicago who turned to filmmaking, played an incredible range of roles, from serious research to rescuing me from computer jams of the most elementay nature. Additionally, Yoon Ah Lee, James Lochart, Joy Kim, Ilyon Woo, John Kim and Keun Gwan Lee helped me with information gathering at different stages of this project. My brother-in-law, Kook Mann Cha, helped with Japanese translations, and Joobong Kim, a Korea Area Specialist at the Library of Congress, assisted me with bibliography and fact checking. Many members of the United Methodist Church of Greater Washington, including Dju H. Park and Lee Dong Woo, extended support.

In Korea Yun Chong-Ok, a pioneer researcher and activist, helped me, starting with the introduction to the Korean Council for the Women Drafted for the Military Sexual Slavery by Japan, to accompanying me to Ulsan to meet Grandma Yun and feeding me scrumptious Korean meals, not to mention invaluable pointers and information, including her own research. Yamashita Youngae shared her research and opened doors to other scholars.

In Japan, nothing would have been possible had it not been for the generous assistance of Yang Ching Ja, a Korean woman born in Japan and a devoted writer/activist on the topic. She introduced me to former Japanese soldiers, offered her house to meet with them and translated Japanese into Korean for me. Yun Myung Sook, a Korean student pursuing graduate studies in a Japanese University also helped me with the translations. Attorney Takagi Ken'ichi, the chief counsel representing the former comfort women and other victims of the war, arranged a meeting with Yoshida Seiji, former chief of the National Service Labor Resruitment in Shimonoseki.

My trip to Beijing to attend the Fourth Women's Conference in August 1995 would not have been possible, had it not been for Rev. Kim Young Ho, the energetic leader of the New York Coalition of Korean Comfort Women who included me in the group travel he headed. The trip would have never been the same without Lori Tsang, a friend and lawyer/filmmaker/poet, who went with me and videotaped the conference participants as well as former comfort women from South Korea, China, the Phillipines, and elsewhere.

Kang Soon Im, Lee Hi Kyung, Yoo Soon Mi and Han Young Sook transcribed countless hours of my talks with the women. Many read the manuscript.

Norma Field, Professor of Japanese Literature and the Chair of the Department of East Asian Languages and Civilizations at the University of Chicago, and Joan D. Hedrick, author of the Pulitzer Prize winning *Harriet Beecher Stowe: A Life*, Professor of History and Director of Women's Studies at Trinity College, read the first rough draft and provided me with insightful comments. Michael Allen, then professor at the University of California, Berkeley, and currently teaching at the University of Auckland in New Zealand, read a chapter on Korean history and Japanese colonialism and sent me back to a few more books and sources. Dr. Warren Tsuneishi, a Japanese historian and David Boling, a trial attorney at the US Department of Justice, commented on the sections of their expertise. Elaine Charnov, Carole Huxley, Sue and Don Kaul, Olivia Kim and Virginia Kassel all read a chapter or two and gave me eye-opening responses. Charles Burnett, my mentor, and partner in filmmaking and above all, a friend, read all of the women's stories and, moved by their incredible power, encouraged me to make a film. My sister, Dai Gook, my niece Mi Hee Kim and her husband David Bath, and my father-in-law, Donald L. Gibson also read the stories. My best friend, Miae M. Han, read the entire manuscript and told me in no uncertain terms that I needed to dig deeper even if it would take the rest of my life. Most recently, Lawrence H. Fuchs, Meyer and Walter Jaffe Professor of American Civilization and Politics at the Brandeis University, read the entire manuscript and sent me five page comments, many of which made my face red. To all these people I am deeply grateful and those whom I fail to thank, I ask for forgiveness in advance but none is responsible for any mistakes and/or shortcomings of this book. I am, alone, responsible.

Three people gave me some financial help. Anna Rhee who believed in this project was instrumental in getting me funds from the General Board and Women's Division of the United Methodist Church. Marcus Cohn, a former member of the National Council of the National Endowment for the Humanities, sent me a check. My sister, Dai Gook, once asked me if I ever thought about engaging in the Christian ministry with my Ph.D in religion. I told her that whatever religious faith and knowledge I had, I was using in my films and in this book. She sent me a check with a scribble, "Please use this money for your book. This is part of my tithe." I am deeply grateful for those checks which gave me far more than the actual amounts, the much needed spiritual uplift.

Inshil Sohn Moon, a graceful woman of compassion and dignity who understands the pain of these grandmas, born and reared in the family of Rev. Sohn Jung Do, a much respected Korean independence fighter, gave me beautiful calligraphy on the cover design.

Many publishers turned the manuscript down, for "marketing" concerns, usually followed by the question, "Hasn't there been a work already on the topic?" I am profoundly grateful to Robert Neymeyer, my publisher, who believes that this topic deserves more than a book or two and that the American public will buy this book even though it does not seem to have direct bearing on their current lives. To help prove Bob's conviction is right, Grace Kim gives countless hours, a true labor of love, to spread the word about this book.

I was fortunate to be born of parents who taught me to respect human dignity and rights. My maternal grandmother whose sorrow of losing her husband at a young age became our gain. She lived with her only daughter, my mother, and showed me how to be a strong woman holding onto values and principles that mattered. If I am one tenth of what she showed me, and if I can embody just a glimpse of my mother's grace and gentleness, I should be grateful. Finally, I count my blessings everyday, breathing and working in the steadfast love, support and help of my husband and friend, Don. This book was unthinkable without the help he gave me, editing, reading and commenting countless times, always with a genuine smile on his face, never any sign of boredom or weariness. My father who was originally disappointed that Don was not a Korean, bless his soul, but when he passed, he loved his Iowa farm boy, son-in-law. "Don, you are a good man," the highest compliment from my father. Everyday I am grateful to Don who teaches me about compassion, kindness and the importance of principles, not by words but by deeds.

NOTES

1. Daws, Gaven. *Prisoners of the Japanese* (New York: William Morrow and Company, Inc., 1994), pp. 17-18.

2. Dower, John W. *War Without Mercy* (New York: Pantheon Books, 1986), p.11.

3. Rigoberto Tiglao, "Memory and Apathy," *Far Eastern Economic Review* (August 24, 1995), p. 38.

4. *Ibid.*, p.37.

5. More about this in Chapter Five.

6. In his mid-fifties, Mr. Fujioka leads the group of neo-conservatives in Japan that opposes the "gutless" behavior of fellow Japanese who regret the country's "misconduct" during the Asia/Pacific War.

7. Koreans use the expression *aigo* for sad as well as joyful occasions. So Grandma Hwang says *aigo* to express her joy to see me. Then, at the funerals, Koreans wail with repeated *aigo*.

8. What is the connection between poverty and asshole splitting? One might ask. I did. Poor people in Korea were frequently forced to eat tree roots and barks. Often, they boiled pine barks and ate them. The ingredients apparently cause the most severe constipation imaginable.

9. When I interviewed her for my film in 1997, she told me that she was about to become a fourth grader when the draft notice came.

10. I cannot shake my nagging doubts about Mr. and Mrs. Choi. It is difficult to believe that they were totally unaware of the fate that awaited her, especially Mr. Choi. There was no way he could have been so blind if indeed he was such a successful businessman as she described. I said nothing to her since she seems to have such affection for them.

11. For my film interview, she told me that it was the neighborhood official who exchanged rolls of paper with a Japanese military policeman, not a Japanese soldier.

12. I heard her speak in Japan in July 1995, actually not long after I visited her in Korea. I went to Tokyo and there she was testifying at the seminar held by the International Commission of the Jurists (ICJ). Her words came down like a thunder, "I am tired of you, especially your words. They mean nothing to me because you don't say what you mean. You have one mouth but your mouth always plays tricks; it utters two conflicting words at the same time. That's the talent you should get rid of, the sooner, the better." I found her different in Japan than in the United States. The feelings she conveyed were fury, mixed with pity and a little disgust.

13. "606" is an arsenic-based drug which was frequently used to treat syphilis, but so toxic that it was also used to abort babies.

14. Japanese scholars at the Center for Research and Documentation on Japan's War and Responsibility wrote in 1994, "It is a historical fact that the 'protectorate treaty' was imposed on Korea by military coercion; the representation of the subsequent 'Annexation of Korea' was an agreement entered into in 'equality and free will' is fiction." *The First Report on the Issue of Japan's Military "Comfort Women,"* March 31, 1994, p. 25. Further, a letter by Emperor Kojong was published in the *Dae Han Daily Newspaper* on February 1, 1906 in which the Emperor stated that he had not consented to the treaty and appealed for the joint protection of the powers. Lee, Ki-baik, *A New History of Korea,* trans. by Wagner, Edward W. with Edward J. Shultz, (Cambridge, Mass: Harvard University Press, 1984), p. 311.

15. Nahm, Andrew C. *Korea: Tradition and Transformation*, (New Jersey: Hollym International Corporation, 1988), p. 534.

16. As quoted in Nahm, Andrew C. *Ibid.*, p.536.

17. The Governor-General, the highest body of authority in the colonized Korea, in royal edict 319, "On the Establishment of the Government-General of Korea," his powers are stipulated: "control of the armed forces and all matters of Korea within the extent of the trust of the Emperor." *Chosun Ch'ongdokpu Kwanbo (The Bulletin of the Government General of Korea),* Vol. I, (Seoul: Asea Munwhasa, 1984-1988), p. 15.

18. See Duus, Peter, *The Abacus and the Sword,* (Berkeley, Los Angeles, London: The University of California Press, 1995) pp. 399-406. Alas, Duus quotes and describes how contemporary travel and other accounts portray Koreans as requiring the "firm hand of the Japanese to lift them out of their poverty, filth, and lassitude."

19. Duus, *Ibid.*, p. 303. He states that "the policy of 'concentrating migration in Manchuria and Korea' also provided a graceful way to justify its acceptance of the humiliating American demand that Japan curb emigration."

20. Hong Sang Jin, "Korean Forced Laborers," *War, Victimization and Japan* (International Public Hearing) (Osaka-shi: Toho Shuppan, Inc., 1993), pp. 99-100.

21. Chung Chin-sung, "An Overview of the Colonial and Socio-economic Background of Japanese Military Sex Slavery in Korea," *Muae: A Journal of Transcultural Production* No. 1, Walter Lew, ed., (New York: Kaya Production, 1995), p. 207.

22. *The First Report on the Issue of Japan's Military Comfort Women,* Center for Research and Documentation of Japan's War Responsibility (Osaka, Japan, 1993), p. 2.

23. Yoshimi Yoshiaki, *Documents on Military Comfort Women,* (Seoul: Seo Mun Dang, 1993), p. 216.

24. *Ibid.*, Document No. 46, p. 205.

25. *According to the Jinchu nissi* (field journal) of the 1st Company of the 42nd Independent Automobile Battalion for the month of July 1942, the 25th Army Headquarters in Singapore announced the creation of military comfort houses for "discipline, prevention of espionage, and detrimental disease." Yoshimi (Seoul: 1993), p. 354.

26. Grandma Yun Doo Ri (Chapter 8) served in a comfort house in Pusan, Korea. And according to the Associated Press of Seoul (August 23, 1999), North Koreans announced the discovery of a comfort station in Chung Jin, Ham Kyung province.

27. Yoshimi Yoshiaki explains that recruitment was limited in mainland Japan because Japan had signed the "International Arrangement and Conventions for the Suppression of Traffic in Women and Children," in 1904, 1910 and 1921. That prohibited Japan from recruiting women who were not prostitutes and women under the age of twenty one. "However," he writes, "the international conventions contained a special clause that allowed a member nation to exclude its colonies from application of the conventions." At the time of the conventions, Japan had announced that it would exclude Korea and Taiwan. Thus, in those two colonies, Japan endured no restrictions. "Historical Understandings on the 'Military Comfort Women' Issue," *War Victimization and Japan: International Public Hearing Report,* (Osaka-shi, Japan: Toho Shuppan, Inc., 1993), p. 83.

28. Australian National Archives Documents, Yoshimi (Tokyo: Otsuki Shoten, 1992), pp. 565-580.

29. About 190 women have registered with the Ministry of Health and Social Affairs in South Korea as former comfort women.

30. The most often used expressions by the women for those who bought and sold were literally "those who conducted business or those who bought and sold." In many cases, those who initially bought these women remained as managers of the military and privately run comfort houses and in other cases not. Further, some Japanese scholars use the term "purveyor" for those who acted on behalf of the military to bring these women. The

close English synonym would be "pimp." I use the word, trader to convey the literal sense of the women's expression, interchangeable with manager.

31. *The First Report on Comfort Women,* p. 50.

32. She now lives in an apartment of a government subsidized building like many other former comfort women. She is careful to maintain an air of dignity and authority. As soon as I sat down, she handed me a name card. "Many of these grandmas are not equipped to handle problems. So I organized a group, consisting about ten former comfort women. I co-ordinate and organize our concerns and much of the time I represent them," she announced with pride. At the end of our talk, she arranged a meeting with another grand-mother in the same complex. That was Grandma Bae Jok Gan.

33. I met Grandma Kang Soon Ae at the International Commission of Jurists seminar on "Sexual Slavery and Slavery-like Practices in World War II," held in July 1995 in Tokyo. I had phoned her countless times in Seoul. Imagine my excitement when I bumped into her in Japan! She was with other grandmas to testify at the seminar. All of them were dressed in white Korean costumes. A woman of small bones, her thin body wrapped in the white Korean costume, with her head high, she stood at the podium and started talking. Soon, though, her voice became chapped, words trembling with emotion, then her entire body shook in sobs beyond her control. I saw her again the next day when the same grandmas went to a Japanese labor union to testify. Outside in the hall, I was able to sit down with her and told her how I tried to reach her in Seoul. Her bony hands wrapping mine, words streamed out unmindful of the noise in the hallway. My recorder picked up most of her story. Because it was a hallway talk with limited time, I was unable to go into details of her life. I later learned that she is a practicing shaman.

34. I met her at the group Home called "Sharing Home" in Seoul. She was the first one who volunteered to talk with me. Because she talked all the time, her housemates called her "loud mouth."

35. The rose of Sharon is the national flower of Korea.

36. When I visited her for the first time, she lived on the outskirts of Seoul in an apart-ment building and was very sick; she could not walk. I offered to come back but she insist-ed that I stay and talked to me from her bed. As I was leaving, she crawled to the next room and took out two persian blue cushions on which she had embroidered white camellia flowers. "As you can see, I am still embroidering to make a living!" I have those cushions in our family room. When I went back to Korea in 1997, she had moved into the Sharing Home. Her health had been recovered.

37. I had heard from a researcher in Korea that according to family registration papers, her father was not a well-to-do landowner but a candy peddler. Ever since, I have been look-ing for a chance to confront Grandma Chung with this. In August 1999, I invited Grandma Chung to give testimony for a screening of **Silence Broken** at Flushing, New York in con-junction with the celebration of the 54th Korean Independence. After the event, I brought her to our home. In the privacy of our kitchen, I cautiously asked her. Her expression was calm, hardly any sign of emotion other than a hint of smile on her lips. "That's not true," she said. "You don't seem to be upset. How can you be so calm?" I prodded. "No reason to be upset. It's not worth my emotion." Pause. "You know, even if I tell only the truth for all the remaining days of my life, I can't find enough time. Why should I add lies?"

38. In 1997, for my on-camera interview, she relayed the same story with little change. but her age when she left home—it was fifteen the first time and then fourteen the second time. My guess is she understood the different ways of counting one's age between Koreans and Americans. In Korea, one automatically becomes a year old at birth. So she told me her age the American way.

206

39. On the kitchen counters, there were usually two big holes where pots are put, one for the rice and the other for soup, and the wood burned underneath for cooking.

40. For the documentary, she told me she was seventeen.

41. When I interviewed him (1995), he talked about how some accuse him of making up stories. In 1997, the majority—both liberals and conservatives— discredited his stories. Professor Fujioka, for instance, cited him a lot to substantiate his points that much of assertions about comfort women are exaggerated, if not false. My researcher in Japan, Yang Ching Ja, also advised me against interviewing him on camera. In my view, there's no real way of verifying the truth or falsity of his stories but much of the content checks out with what we know through other sources. So if he made up the stories, he did his research.

42. For example, in the "Comfort House Rules" issued on November 22, 1942 to Iloilo Provost Guard Unit in Visaya branch of the Philippines, it is stated: "Supervision and guidance of comfort houses are under the control of military administration; Medical doctors of the garrison, who take leadership in hygiene, should conduct examinations for service girls from the 15:00 hour every Tuesday; Comfort Houses are to be used only by military personnel wearing a military uniform and by military workers." For the complete regulations, see Yoshimi Yoshiaki, ed., *Jugun Ianfu Shiryo Shu* (Documents on Military Comfort Women, Tokyo: Otsuki Shoten, 1992), pp. 324-326.

43. A quiet woman who speaks slowly with a heavy southern accent, lives with a junior high school boy, Hyung Chul, her nephew's son. Hyung Chul's mother died when he was a baby and his father practically abandoned him. Grandma Moon took him in and brought him up. I made a few attempts to meet Hyung Chul, one day waiting for him late at night. He was never at home, even on Saturday. Like many other students at his age, he was forever in school or in extracurricular lessons. "He is a good boy. He is devoted to his studies. He swears that he will take care of me," Grandma Moon told me.

44. In the "Comfort House Rules," it is specified, "Comfort women are allowed to take a walk only between 8 a.m.and 10 a.m.everyday. Those who need to leave the complex during non-specified hours must obtain permission from the chief of the Iloilo Station, Visaya Branch of the Military Administrations in the Philippines. Also, the area of walking is specified in the attached table." Yoshimi, *ibid.*, p. 324.

45. A tall, erect woman with a distinct laugh, she lives in the Sharing Home. She had worked on the American military base and learned some English. She was eager to try it out on me.

46. I went back to interview Mr. Hirabayashi on video camera in October 1996. He told me that he had been wrong about the *Mama-san*. He learned that she was Japanese, not Korean.

47. "Rules for Authorized Restaurants and Houses of Prostitution in Manila," issued in February 1943 by Lieutenant Colonel Onishi. Under Part Four-Hygiene: 23. "Hostesses will ordinarily be examined by an army physician once a week at a designated place. Hostesses who are not geisha will be examined twice a month. Other employees will be given a physical examination once a month. Expenses incident to these examinations will be taken care of by the managers. It may also be necessary at times to examine such other employees as maids." 25. "Persons failing the physical examinations or receiving unfavorable diagnosis will be forbidden to entertain guests while under treatment." Allied Translator and Interpreter Section, Research Report, No. 120, November 15, 1945, United States National Archives, p. 10.

48. 606 was an arsenic-based drug. It was used in treating syphillis and also to induce miscarriages.

49. If you meet Grandma Kim Sun Duk, you will understand why the Japanese general was crazy about her. Small boned, with soft curves and her face oval, she exudes beauty even now at the age of 76.

50. Grandma Kim was born in a poor family which had no land to till. They burned the fields and grew some potatoes and vegetables (fire-fields). "We were always hungry. I remember picking mushrooms but we could not eat them. The Japanese took them away from us. I don't recall a time when I wasn't hungry growing up but things got worse after my father died when I was fifteen." She showed me some of her paintings many of which deal with the recollections of her childhood. A rural village girl picking mushrooms, for one. The images of her paintings are powerfully evocative and appealing with a childlike simplicity. Some of these grandmas' paintings have been exhibited in Japan and Korea.

51. Grandma Kim Hak Soon presented the first public testimony about her experience as a comfort woman in August 1991, a crucial event that gave impetus to the movement to bring justice to the comfort women. I went to see her in 1995 in Seoul. She was dressed simply, a white polyester blouse and black pants. An air of beauty and dignity was unmistakable. Just looking at her, I felt the strength of this grandma who told the world what Japan had done to hundreds and thousands of women.

52. After that song, with my recorder packed away, we lingered and talked some more. "I did go back to Korea and saw my sister. I was too ashamed to tell her about my life in China but I could tell she knew. She said she had looked for me all over. She is the only blood relation I knew in Korea but I don't have feelings for her. Why? She thinks of nothing else but 'money.' I can't deal with that. So I am totally alone in this universe. What I want most in the world? A friend. A friend who loves me from the depth of his/her heart." As we parted, she invited me to come to her house and spend a few days. "When you come, bring your husband." "But my husband is an American." "American?" she yelled, raising her eyebrows. "But he is a good man," I said, meekly. "O.K. As long as he is a good man, bring him with you. But I don't cook. You have to feed him." "I will cook for all three of us. I am a moody cook. If you are nice to me, I will feed you good food." "That's a deal." I listen to her song once in a while and wonder when I can make that journey.

I didn't make that journey with my husband but I did go to her house with my film crew in 1997 and she sang the same song by the sea which our camera caught. I open the film with her singing "Life in a Strange Land."

53. This is how she pronounced it in Korean. I don't know exactly where it is in China.

54. Most of the times, she used the Korean word, kal, which literally means sword but I gathered that sometimes she meant bayonet, not sword.

55. The initiation process for a shaman starts with *sinbyong* whereby spirits and gods enter into her body and she becomes sick. *Sinbyong* can only be cured when a shaman conducts an exorcism through a formal initiation ritual called *naerim-gut*. During *naerim-gut*, an experienced mudang invites the gods to complete their descent and allow the initiate to dance and sing as a *mudang* (shaman).

56. Now it's about $125 (1998).

57. "*Chung*" is neither love nor affection. It is more feeling than intellect but is neither. There is no English equivalent for this word. It is a special feeling, close to the heart, that can be accumulated over time, over the thick and thin, or it can be developed during a short period of time, even instantly. For instance, Grandma Bae said of me a number of times, "You were a stranger when you came through that door but I felt *chung*. That's why I waited for you to come back. I was afraid you might not. To me, you are a kind of person who evokes *chung* right away. Maybe we had a special relationship in our previous lives. Who knows?"

58. Rubber shoes were traditional footwear for women. On one's wedding day, no matter how poor, one was expected to wear at least a new pair of rubber shoes.

59. I visited her once again in November 1995. For some reason, without being asked,

she rambled about how Japanese killed Chinese people. "I can still hear the drums. That sound of drums whenever they brought Chinese and lined them in the field to kill, I can still hear it. When the wind blew, the smell of the blood travelled. Would you believe that they practiced killing with swords on the living bodies of the Chinese? The most horrible of all was to see those people who just wouldn't die after being struck by a sword three times, four times. . . ." I drank her barley tea, admired her flowers on the balcony and caught up with other grandmas, who is doing what. . .She told me a great deal about the sick grandma of whom she had spoken of before. "She is not getting better. . . The way things are, I don't think Japan is going to compensate us in our life time. Maybe, they are waiting for us to die." I didn't say, "Yet, you still like the Japanese." I didn't even feel tempted to say it. I just felt towering sorrow. I could not stay there long. Again, we parted outside on the street.

60. A former Japanese soldier whom I interviewed in 1995 told me, "Many believe that soldiers were willing to die for their Emperor but that was not always true. I for one did not want to fight, let alone die for the Emperor."

61. Takagi, Ken'ichi, *A Review on the War Compensation in Japan*, trans. by Choi Yong Gi, (Seoul: Hanul, 1995), p. 25.

62. Yoshimi Yoshiaki, "Historical Understandings on the 'Military Comfort Women' Issue," *War Victimization and Japan, International Public Hearing Report*, (Osaka-shi: Toho Shuppan, Inc., 1993), p. 87.

63. Sanger, David E., "History Scholar in Japan Exposes a Brutal Chapter, " *The New York Times International,* January 27, 1992.

64. Despite the protests in Japan and abroad, Japanese sex tours continue. According to the report prepared by the Japan Federation of Bar Associations for the Fourth World Conference on Women, "Japanese men travel to Thailand, the Philippines and other Asian countries and engage in group prostitution activities," which apparently extend to child prostitution. "For example," the report states, "in the Philippines a case was reported in 1991 in which two Japanese men confined a number of children of both sexes and sexually abused them." *Report on the National Report for the Fourth World Conference on Women,* Japan Federation of Bar Associations, February 1995, p. 75.

65. Kim Hak Soon was not the first who became known as a former comfort woman; she became famous as the first public witness. It was Bae Bong Gi, a Korean comfort woman who died in Okinawa in 1991. In 1972 when the United States returned the island to Japan, Grandma Bae who had been taken there as a Japanese citizen was declared an illegal resident. In the process of investigating her case, it was discovered how she had ended up in Okinawa. In a way, she traded her secret identity for special permission to continue to reside in Okinawa. For a detailed account of her tragic life, see Kawada Humiko, *Balkan Gi Wa Jip* (Red-Tiled House), trans. by Han Woo Jung, (Seoul: Economic Daily, 1992).

66. I attended a few of these demonstrations with the former comfort women whom I interviewed. For those grandmas, Wednesday is like a Sabbath, set aside for something sacred. In rain or shine, cold or hot, sickness or health, they assemble at noon in front of the Japanese Embassy in Seoul every Wednesday. Some of them have to transfer buses twice or three times to get there but they still come and demand justice from the Japanese joined by other concerned people, often some from abroad.

67. "Japan Apologizes on Korea Sex Issue," *The New York Times International,* January 18, 1992.

68. Since then, several public hearings and conferences have been convened: the United Nations World Conference on Human Rights (Vienna, June 1993); the International Commission of Jurists Seminar on Sexual Slavery and Slavery-Like Practices in World

War II (Tokyo, July 1995); and the NGO Forum on Women, at the Fourth World Conference on Women (Beijing, August 1995).

69. As quoted in E/CN.4/1996/137, p. 4.

70. The often used word, *hansei,* in apologies is translated as "contritition" or "remorse." However, a more exact meaning is "reflection."

71. Theo van Boven, Professor of International Law at the University of Limburg, Maastricht, the Netherlands, and former Special Rapporteur of the U.N. Commission on Human Rights, Sub-Commission on the Prevention of Discrimination and the Protection of Minorities, was assigned to conduct a study about the comfort women. The result was a report entitled, "Study Concerning the Right to Restitution, Compensation and Rehabilitation for Victims of Gross Violations of Human Rights and Fundamental Freedom." This was submitted in 1993 with the recommendation that the women have the right to restitution, compensation and rehabilitation, accompanied by a set of proposed basic principles and guidelines (UN doc. E/CN.4/Sub.2/1993/8). This was adopted as a resolution of the Fiftieth UN Human Rights Commission in March 1994. The report that the Japanese government submitted in response to this is UN doc. E/CN.4/Sub.2/1994/7Add.1.

72. For detailed historical information and legal arguments, see Dolgopol, Ustinia and Paranjape, Snehal, *Report of a Mission*, International Commission of Jurists, (Geneva: Switzerland, 1994).

73. Japan ratified this treaty in 1911 and it became effective in 1912.

74. IMTFE Charter, Appendix C, Ginn, John L., *Sugamo Prison, Tokyo: An Account of the Trial and Sentencing of Japanese War Criminals in 1948, by a U.S. Participant,* (Jefferson, NC: NaFarland & Co., Inc., Publishers), 1992, p. 261.

75. The trial judgment was pronounced in November 1948. Two of the accused had died during the trial and one was declared insane.

76. The jurisdiction of the Tokyo Tribunal was divided into three categories: Class A, B, and C. "Crimes Against Peace," Class A, were defined as "the planning, preparation, initiation or waging of a declared or undeclared war of aggression, or a war in violation of international law, treaties, agreements or assurances, or a war in violation of international law, treaties, agreements or assurances, or a participation in a common plan or conspiracy for the accomplishment of any of the foregoing." Class B consisted of "Conventional War Crimes," i.e., violation of the laws or customs of law. Class C consisted of "Crimes Against Humanity" and codified the same provision in Article 5 of its Charter as that of the Nuremberg Military Tribunal which reads, "murder, extermination, enslavement, deportation, and other inhumane acts committed before or during the war, or persecutions on political or racial grounds in execution of or in connection with any crime within the jurisdiction of the Tribunal, whether or not in violation of the domestic law of the country where perpetrated." Article 5 of IMTFE Charter, Ginn, John L., *op.cit,* p.262.

77. The Allied Translator and Interpreter Section, the Supreme Commander of the Allied Powers, in November 1945, issued a report entitled "Amenities in the Japanese Armed Forces." (Research Report, No. 120, National Archives of the United States) From this report, we learn about the booklet, "Rules for Authorized Restaurants and Houses of Prostitution in Manila," issued in February 1943 by Lieutenant Colonel Onishi.

78. The details of my interview with Mr. Hirabayashi are in the Chapter 3, Slaves of Sex. His experience is also documented in *Burma: The Untold Story by Won-loy Chan,* (Novato, CA.:Presidio Press, 1986), pp.93-98.

79. Kristof, Nicholas D. "Japan Confronts Gruesome War Atrocity," *New York Times*. Ishii Shiro, head of Unit 731, lived peacefully until his death from throat cancer in 1959. Dr. Kitano Masaji became head of Green Cross, Japan's largest blood-processing facility. The

knowledge he had obtained by performing many experimental operations was useful in his post-war career. Many others involved in this work rose to such positions as Governor of Tokyo, president of the Japan Medical Association and head of the Japan Olympic Committee. According to James MacKay, author of *Betrayal in High Places,* the cases of the comfort women and cannibalism were also included in this "bargain" package.

80. Takagi Ken'ichi, *Junfu Bosang ui Nonri* (A Review on the War Compensation in Japan), trans. by Choi Yong Ki, (Seoul: Hanul, 1995), p. 118.

81. Gavan, *op. cit.*, p. 104.

82. United Nations Treaty Series, Vol. 136, No. 1832, p. 46.

83. The Japanese use this argument only when it benefits them. If indeed Korea was not autonomous before the San Francisco Treaty, Japan had the responsibility to treat Koreans as its citizens. They didn't. For instance, the Korean forced laborers on Sakhalin island were completely abandoned by Japan when the Russians took over the island in 1945 and the Japanese were repatriated. The Koreans were left there to live an exiled life of toil and suffering under the Soviets. For first-hand information from the surviving laborers, see the documentary *A Forgotten People: the Sakhalin Koreans* by Dai Sil Kim-Gibson (1995).

84. This way of thinking has never stopped. As recently as November 1995, prior to hosting President Clinton and other world leaders at the Asia-Pacific Economic Cooperation Forum, Eto Takami, head of the Management and Coordination Agency, remarked that Japan did good things for Korea. Kevin Sullivan writes in his report, "Remark Costs Tokyo Aide His Job," in the *Washington Post*, November 14, 1995, that his remarks included "an assertion that Korea benefitted from Japan's 35-year occupation because Japan built schools, railroads and ports."

85. UN doc. E/CN.4/Sub.2/1994/7Add.1.

86. UN doc. E/CN.4/1996/137, p. 9.

87. E/CN.4/Sub.2/1998/13

88. UN doc. E/CN.4/Sub.2/1994/7Add.1.

89. *Ibid.*

90. *Ibid.*

91. To date, the fund has failed to raise much money. See Kristof, Nicholas D., "Japan Fund for War's 'Comfort Woman' Is in Crisis," *New York Times International,* May 13, 1996. "The fund has raised only a fraction of the money that is necessary."

92. Remember asshole splitting poverty from Grandma Hwang? Pine barks and constipation?

93. According to her account, she had to stay at Rabaul longer than she was supposed to because of the shipwreck. It is unclear, however, how long she stayed before the shipwreck and afterwards. At some point in her story, she mentions that she was at Rabaul for seven years, which makes me wonder. She told me clearly when she returned home, December 1944. I was not able to obtain the year of her departure from Korea but according to the Korean oral history book, *Forcibly Drafted Korean Military Comfort Women,* she could not have gone to Rabaul before 1942 since the Japanese occupied Rabaul in January of that year. Perhaps, she does not remember precisely. . . Whatever the length of her stay in Rabaul, I am certain about her going and the shipwreck that delayed her stay and the date of her return.

94. Koreans, especially in the rural villages, drink rice wine in big bowls, much like a soup bowl.

95. Here she clearly says "seven" years. To me, it does not add up.

96. I call her Grandma X to protect the other grandma's identity.

97. I was unable to obtain the name of that front, somewhere in Manchuria.

98. She took a great deal of pain to remember exactly how much but couldn't.

99. I assume she needed to do this for practical as well as emotional reasons. In order to register, she needed a family (sponsor).

100. I am not sure if sex was included in "things."

101. She skipped lots of details at first. So I had no idea who this man was and how she hooked up with him. I asked her about him when I talked with her for the second time.

102. According to her mother's account, her husband died because of the beatings by the communists. The sickness and the beating could be related; he became sick after the incident. And this is the man whom her mother had referred to me as "the man she was hooked up with." Her mother also told me that this man was her daughter's father. To me, this could mean only one thing; her mother didn't want to talk about the real father during our first visit.

103. I didn't know then but later learned that her lack of formal education in comparison with her husband has always been a sore point in her heart.

104. A fairly big city not so far away from her home. Now the city houses the National Archive for Korean Independence.

105. Her mother had told me otherwise; that she discussed reporting with her daughter.

106. It is not clear whether this woman was a manager or a nurse.

107. It was a fleeting statement but clearly she did not wish to dwell on her learning songs from "this woman." I can only guess. She had a real talent in singing. She wanted to be a singer but there was no way she could get proper training. She tried to go to *Kiesang* training school. Pyong Yang was famous for training refined artisans to entertain men. Her grandma was dead opposed to that.

108. In 1997, she told me "four" girls, not seven. Strange. Usually the numbers increase . . .

109. She did this many years after she returned home from the comfort house. I never had a chance to ask her what she did all those years when she worked at a restaurant, saving every penny, etc. Later, when she was earning money hand over fist, I can easily see that she could accommodate this need but in the beginning . . . I had so many lingering questions. I wanted to pay her a return visit, possibly by myself. When I went back to Korea in 1995 in the late fall, I tried to reach her numerous times but I could not even talk on the phone. I should have just gone and waited in front of her apartment door. When I finally saw her again for my film interview in 1997, I tried to clarify these questions but it was impossible to obtain detailed information in the midst of filming.

110. I didn't have a chance to clarify it but she had three names: people used to call her Young Ja when she was young, then there was a Japanese name and the current one, Doo Ri.

111. This is significant information. This indicates that there were comfort houses even in Korea.

112. The same navy officer whom she talked about when she bought lye, rice and fish. . .

113. *The Los Angeles Times,* August 24, 1999.

114. Kristof, Nicholas D, "Burying the Past: War Guilt Haunts Japan," *The New York Times,* November 30, 1998.